Childm

A Handbook for the Diploma in Home-based Childcare

4TH Edition

Christine Hobart
Jill Frankel

Series Editor: Miranda Walker

Nelso

First edition published 1999 by Stanley Thornes Publishers (Ltd)
Second edition published 2003 by Nelson Thornes Ltd
Third edition published 2006 by Nelson Thornes Ltd

This edition published 2009 by:
Nelson Thornes Ltd
Delta Place
27 Bath Road
CHELTENHAM
GL53 7TH
United Kingdom

09 10 11 12 13 / 10 9 8 7 6 5 4 3 2 1

A catalogue record for this book is available from the British Library

ISBN 978 1 4085 0493 2

Cover photograph © BananaStock/jupiterimages.com
Illustrations by Jane Bottomley
Page make-up by Northern Phototypesetting, Bolton

Printed and bound in Spain by GraphyCems

Contents

About the authors

Christine Hobart and Jill Frankel come from a background of health visiting and nursery education. They worked together in Camden before meeting again at City and Islington College. They have worked together for many years, training students to work with young children and have written 12 books encompassing all areas of the childcare curriculum. Christine is an external examiner for CACHE.

Miranda Walker has worked with children from birth to 16 years in a range of settings, including her own day nursery and out-of-school clubs. She has inspected nursery provision for Ofsted, and worked at East Devon College as an Early Years and Playwork lecturer and NVQ assessor and internal verifier. She is a regular contributor to industry magazines and an established author.

Acknowledgements

The authors and publishers are grateful to the National Childminding Association (NCMA) for its help and co-operation in producing this book, and acknowledge NCMA as the source and inspiration of parts of the text.

The Children's development and learning information on pages 106–7 and the Preparing for self-assessment article (Appendix C) are reproduced by kind permission of NCMA.

The table 'Sequence of language development' (Appendix B) on pages 295–8 from Beaver M. et al., *Babies and Young Children, Book 1* (2nd Edition), 1999, is reproduced by kind permission of Nelson Thornes Ltd.

Our thanks to Carol Banyard for advice and help on writing policies.

'The extent of violence involving children' on page 212 is taken from *Children and Violence: Report of the Commission on Children and Violence* convened by the Gulbenkian Foundation, and reproduced by kind permission of the Calouste Gulbenkian Foundation.

The procedure for investigating a case of possible child abuse on page 221 is adapted from *Child Protection: A Guide for Midwives* by Jenny Fraser, published by Books for Midwives, 174A Ashley Road, Hale, Cheshire, WA15 9SF.

The table 'What places children "at risk" of child abuse?' on page 225 is reproduced from *Child Abuse and Neglect: An Introduction*, Work Book One, *Making Sense of Child Abuse*, by kind permission of the Open University.

The authors and publishers have made every effort to trace the owners of copyright material. Should copyright have been unwittingly infringed in this book, the owners should contact the publishers who will make corrections at the reprint.

The authors and the publishers are grateful to the following for permission to reproduce photographs and other copyright material in this book.

Alison Lapper sculpture by Marc Quinn/Justin Kase/Alamy: 183; BananaStock E (NT): cover, 100; Helen Broadfield: 195, 250; Corbis © Grace/zefa: 177; Corbis © LWA-Dann Tardiff: 181; Corbis © Royalty-Free: 90, 115; Digital Stock 3 (NT): 113; John Foxx (NT): 163; NCMA: 21, 31, 36, 128; Scott T Baxter/Photodisc 45 (NT): 157; Jules Frazier/Photodisc 45 (NT): 201; Ryan McVay/Photodisc 76 (NT): 7; Martin Sookias (NT): 3, 54, 57, 71, 92, 97, 105 (both), 116, 118, 121, 133, 136, 138, 147, 151, 179, 180, 234, 236, 275, 283.

We would also like to thank the following for photographs in the book: the authors, Christine Hobart and Jill Frankel, Anna and Sarah, Matt and Emily Bromley, Max and Ted Phillips, Tony Thould, Nick and Kirsty Tyler; Claire Hammett (Childminder 1), Javene Campbell, Marcus and Melissa Drennen, Kacey Martin, Leah and Ethan Norman; Rachel Greaves (Childminder 2), Shannon and Lucas Atkinson, Tessa, Warren, George and Michael Greaves.

Crown copyright (c) material is reproduced under Class Licence No. CO1 W 0000195 with the permission of the Controller of HMSO and the Queen's Printer for Scotland.

Every effort has been made to acknowledge copyright. The publishers apologise to anyone whose rights have been inadvertently overlooked, and will be happy to rectify errors or omissions.

Introduction

This book is written for people who are thinking of entering the childminding profession, for experienced childminders who are updating their skills and for all home-based childcarers such as childminders and nannies.

The government's childcare strategy has had an impact on the childminding profession. The National Standards for Childminding make clear what is required from home-based childcarers and they will be expected to have documentation in place to show they are meeting those standards. This book aims to prepare people who wish to register or become approved as home-based childcarers, addressing each standard in turn and encouraging the reader to prepare for questions that may be asked during registration and inspection.

Some home-based childcarers may wish to commit themselves to training courses such as the five units of the CACHE Level 3 Diploma in Home-based Childcare (DHC) or to gaining a Level 3 National Vocational Qualification (NVQ) in Children's Care, Learning and Development. The activities introduced throughout the book could be used by individuals, members of childminding groups or study groups. They could also contribute to written evidence for a National Vocational Qualification portfolio, allowing an assessor to evaluate understanding and knowledge. The table on the following pages shows the links between this book, the National Standards and the Diploma in Home-based Childcare.

The National Childminding Association (NCMA), which was established in 1977, has 50,000 members. The Association promotes good childcare practice and offers information and support to home-based childcarers, including childminders, nannies and parents. NCMA has a strong commitment to training and the need to take a professional approach to childcare.

Since the vast majority of home-based childcarers are female, we have referred to the childminder as 'she' throughout the book.

DIPLOMA IN HOME-BASED CHILDCARE

Chapter	Unit 1	Unit 2	Unit 3	Unit 4	Unit 5
1 Childminding as a career	Establishing a safe and healthy childcare environment in the home-based setting Inclusion and anti-bias practice	Promoting children's rights	The reflective practitioner Policy writing Inter-agency working and other professionals	Confidentiality, data protection and the law	
2 Relationships with parents	Introducing children and their families to your childcare service Starting a home-based childcare service Inclusion and anti-bias practice			The childcare practitioner and the community Families and cultures Promoting positive relationships with parents and the importance of valuing the child's primary carer	

3 The needs of children	Establishing routines for home-based childcare Introducing children and their families to your childcare service Inclusion and anti-bias practice	Children's development and well-being		
4 Children's development and learning	Providing play and other activities for children in the home-based setting Inclusion and anti-bias practice	Children's development and well-being		Prepare, implement and evaluate plans for home-based groups of children of different ages and abilities

Chapter	DIPLOMA IN HOME-BASED CHILDCARE				
	Unit 1	Unit 2	Unit 3	Unit 4	Unit 5
5 Understanding children's behaviour	Managing children's behaviour in the home-based setting Inclusion and anti-bias practice				Observation and assessment of children's development in the home-based setting Meeting individual learning needs in the home-based setting
6 Caring for babies and toddlers	Establishing routines for home-based childcare Providing play and other activities for children in the home-based setting Inclusion and anti-bias practice	Children's development and well-being		Promoting positive relationships with parents and the importance of valuing the child's primary carer	

Chapter				
7 Caring for the school-age child	Establishing routines for home-based childcare Inclusion and anti-bias practice	Children's development and well-being		Prepare, implement and evaluate plans for home-based groups of children of different ages and abilities
8 The safe environment	Establishing a safe and healthy childcare environment in the home-based setting Inclusion and anti-bias practice			
9 Disabled children	Inclusion and anti-bias practice	Working with disabled children and their families		Observation and assessment of children's development in the home-based setting Meeting individual learning needs in the home-based setting

Chapter	DIPLOMA IN HOME-BASED CHILDCARE				
	Unit 1	Unit 2	Unit 3	Unit 4	Unit 5
10 The sick child	Establishing a safe and healthy environment in the home-based setting Inclusion and anti-bias practice	Children's development and well-being			
11 Child protection	Inclusion and anti-bias practice Child protection in the home-based setting	Promoting children's rights	Inter-agency working and other professionals Child protection	Confidentiality, data protection and the law	
12 Communication skills	Inclusion and anti-bias practice	Children's development and well-being	Assertiveness and valuing yourself Inter-agency working and other professionals Policy writing	Communication	

Good Practice in Childminding

13 Observing and assessing children	Providing play and other activities for children in the home-based setting Inclusion and anti-bias practice		Observation and assessment of children in the home-based setting Meeting individual learning needs in the home-based setting
14 The business side of childminding	Inclusion and anti-bias practice Starting a home-based childcare service	Marketing and managing your childcare service	Contract and complaints
15 A return to learning		The reflective practitioner Continuing professional development	

1 *Childminding as a career*

This chapter includes:

- Advantages and disadvantages of childminding
- What makes a skilled home-based childcarer?
- Registration
- Inspection
- Preparing yourself and your family for childminding
- Support systems
- Training
- Professionalism
- Anti-bias practice
- Policies and permissions

Learning objectives

Unit 1
- Establishing a safe and healthy childcare environment in a home-based setting
- Inclusion and anti-bias practice

Unit 2
- Promoting children's rights in your community

Unit 3
- The reflective practitioner
- Policy writing
- Inter-agency working and other professionals

Unit 4
- Confidentiality, data protection and the law

There are several reasons why you might choose to care for children in a home-based setting. You might have given up a career while you stay at home to look after your own young children, and need to earn some money. You might have a childcare and education qualification that you wish to use at home. You might 'like children', and miss the constant company of your own children now they have started school. You might be looking after your grandchild with great enjoyment, and feel that a companion for her would be a good idea. You might prefer working in your own home and being self-employed. For whatever reason, you have decided to make childminding your career.

As an experienced home-based childcarer you might, in the future, become involved in community projects, such as offering support to teenage parents, respite care to mothers with post-natal depression, or various 'SureStart' projects.

Childminding is the largest form of daycare provision outside the home for under-fives. There are approximately 75,000 registered home-based childcarers in the UK. They provide the equivalent of more than 150,000 full-time places for under-fives, although the actual number of children cared for is higher, as many attend on a part-time basis. Home-based childcarers also provide care for a substantial number of school-age children outside school hours and during school holidays.

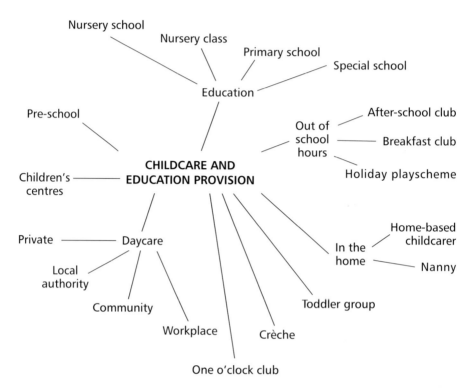

Advantages and disadvantages of childminding

The advantages are:

- it is a useful way of earning money while remaining at home and of gaining experience with children of various needs and ages
- it is a satisfying career, providing personal fulfilment
- it is a flexible job, where you can set your own hours and organise your own work. It gives you independence
- it provides companionship for your own children, and satisfies your wish to play a role in children's development
- it offers possible access to some training programmes and can lead to training for a professional qualification
- through the National Childminding Association (NCMA), it provides help and support through local groups
- there is support from local childminding network co-ordinators.

The possible disadvantages are:

- low pay and long hours
- interference with your family's social life
- wear and tear on your home and furniture
- some families find it difficult or are unwilling to pay, and it can be embarrassing to chase defaulters
- a sense of isolation and a lack of adult company
- needing to buy a number of expensive items of safety equipment
- having to deal with difficult parents without immediate support.

Activity

What would you consider would be the greatest advantage and disadvantage for you in becoming a home-based childcarer?

Parents who work often choose home-based childcarers to care for their children because, apart from the flexibility of the hours, they prefer their children to:

- be in a domestic setting
- be cared for by one carer consistently
- have the opportunity to play with a small group of children
- receive individual attention.

What makes a skilled home-based childcarer?

Before starting the process of registration and training, you should consider the nature of the job. Childminding involves:

- working in partnership with parents, recognising that they have the main role in their children's upbringing
- being prepared to understand and accommodate various child-rearing practices, always putting the welfare of the child first
- educating children, supporting and stimulating their learning and development by offering a wide range of activities and play opportunities
- ensuring equality of opportunity, recognising each child as an individual and giving children opportunities to develop their full potential
- commitment to children and their families, preparing to offer stability over a period of time

1 chapter

- anti-discriminatory practice, presenting a positive role model and helping children to develop positive attitudes towards others from a variety of cultures, backgrounds and religions, and towards disabled people
- adopting safe and hygienic practices
- playing a part in protecting children from abuse and neglect
- developing a professional approach, and the ability to work in partnership with other professional workers
- being open to scrutiny, personally and in your home.

You need to ask yourself whether you have the qualities required for a caring and demanding profession. While it is not totally necessary to have previous experience of working with children, it is sensible to have some knowledge of different age groups and some experience of how children behave in groups of two or three. You will need to be able to tolerate a high level of noise, enjoy messy activities, and be patient, firm and consistent. You should be open-minded and responsive to other child-rearing practices.

You need to be in good physical and mental health. Looking after children is a strenuous physical job as well as an intellectually stimulating one. Young children are prone to many minor illnesses, and you will need to build up resistance to coughs and colds very quickly. Recurrent back problems or eczema are examples of chronic medical conditions for which you may wish to seek medical advice before pursuing a career in childminding. Someone with a neurotic or depressed personality will not be able to offer children a happy, stable environment.

Men and women who represent the ethnic groups within the local community have much to offer as home-based childcarers. Men are generally under-represented in early years work.

If you have outside interests and hobbies, such as a love of music, enjoyment of reading, skill at various crafts, an understanding of art, or an interest in nature and animals, you will be able to share these experiences with the children. This will widen their horizons and aid their learning and development.

As well as caring for the children, you will find yourself working closely with the parents, social services staff and, perhaps, other professional people. Confidence in yourself is the key, whether you have a quiet, calm manner or a lively, impetuous nature. A sense of humour is especially important when working with children and with other people.

Registration

Under national legislation, it is illegal to care for other people's children under the age of eight in your own home for more than two hours a day unless you are registered as a childminder or a close (blood) relative of the child.

There are also local regulations for each of the four nations of the UK: England, Wales, Scotland and Northern Ireland. We will look more closely at the registration process that applies to England. You can find out more about the processes in the other home countries by visiting the following websites:

- For Scotland, visit www.carecommission.com
- For Wales, visit www.csiw.wales.gov.uk
- For Northern Ireland, you can find the contact details of your local Health and Social Care Authority by visiting www.nicma.org/06/documents/EY%20Phone.pdf

All daycare providers in England caring for children under the age of eight years are registered and inspected by the Early Years Directorate within the Office for Standards in Education (Ofsted). In the document 'Guide to registration on the Early Years Register: childminder', Ofsted defines a childminder as:

A person who is registered to look after one or more children to whom they are not related on domestic premises for reward. Childminders work with no more than two other childminders or assistants. They:
- care for children on domestic premises that are not the home of one of the children, or
- care for children from more than two families wholly or mainly in the home of one of the children

and:
- must register to care for children under the age of eight
- can choose to register to care for older children.

Childminders care for at least one individual child for a total of more than two hours in any day. This is not necessarily a continuous period of time. For example if you provide care for the **same** child aged under eight for an hour before and an hour and a half after school then registration is due; however, if you provide care for one child aged under eight for an hour before school and provide care for a **different** child aged under eight for an hour and a half after school then registration is not required.

Childcare Register

This is a register of providers who are registered by Ofsted to care for children from birth to 17 years. The register has two parts:

- **The voluntary part**
  Providers who are not eligible for compulsory registration may choose to register here. These are mainly people looking after children aged eight and over, or providing care in the child's home (including nannies).
- **The compulsory part**
  Providers must register if they care for one or more children following their fifth birthdays until they reach their eighth birthdays.

More information about registration on the Childcare Register is available online at www.ofsted.gov.uk. You can also contact your local family information service (www.familyinformationservices.org.uk/contactcis/england/index.htm).

In addition, all registered childcare providers caring for children under five years must deliver the Early Years Foundation Stage (EYFS), which is a curriculum framework. Further details about the curriculum can be found on pages 81–6. Providers will be registered and inspected against the requirements of the EYFS by Ofsted.

In the 'Guide to registration on the Early Years Register: childminder', Ofsted explains that it registers early years childminders on the Early Years Register to:

- protect children
- ensure that childminders meet the requirements of the Early Years Register
- ensure that childminders provide good outcomes for children that keep children healthy and safe and ensure that they enjoy and achieve, make a positive contribution and develop skills for the future
- promote high quality in the provision of care and learning and development
- provide reassurance to parents.

(To read the guide in full, visit www.ofsted.gov.uk, enter 'childminding' in the search box and then follow the link.)

The Early Years Foundation Stage welfare requirements

Settings to which the EYFS applies must also meet the Early Years Foundation Stage welfare requirements. These fall into the following five categories:

Safeguarding and promoting children's welfare

- The provider must take necessary steps to safeguard and promote the welfare of children.
- The provider must promote the good health of the children, take necessary steps to prevent the spread of infection, and take appropriate action when they are ill.
- Children's behaviour must be managed effectively and in a manner appropriate for their stage of development and particular individual needs.

Suitable people

- Providers must ensure that adults looking after children, or having unsupervised access to them, are suitable to do so.
- Adults looking after children must have appropriate qualifications, training, skills and knowledge.
- Staffing arrangements must be organised to ensure safety and to meet the needs of the children.

Suitable premises, environment and equipment

- Outdoor and indoor spaces, furniture, equipment and toys must be safe and suitable for their purpose.

Organisation

- Providers must plan and organise their systems to ensure that every child receives an enjoyable and challenging learning and development experience that is tailored to meet their individual needs.

Documentation

- Providers must maintain records, policies and procedures required for the safe and efficient management of the settings and to meet the needs of the children.

During registration and during subsequent inspections, an Ofsted inspector will evaluate how you meet the welfare requirements. The home-based childcarer will be expected to demonstrate the safety and suitability of the domestic premises, inside and outside. Among other factors this will include:

- access to outside play space and safety factors
- safety with regard to electric fires, sockets, gas fires, open fires and radiators
- safety with regard to windows
- safety with regard to floor coverings
- safety with regard to glass
- safety in the kitchen and stairways
- the use of safety equipment, such as stair gates and cooker guards
- cooking facilities
- arrangements for the care and control of pets
- the cleanliness of the premises.

Staff/child ratio

One childminder can care for:

- up to six children under eight years
- of these six, usually no more than three children can be under five years
- of the three under five years, usually no more than one child can be under a year.

These figures include the childminder's own children. Exceptions can be made for multiple births and siblings. Childcarers who demonstrate that they can meet and reconcile the varying needs of all the children they care for may be able to care for two babies under one year.

Any care provided for children aged 8–14 should not adversely affect the care of the children under eight years.

The size and suitability of the premises will also be a factor in determining the number of children allowed. Two or more home-based childcarers may be jointly registered and work together in the same premises if the premises are suitable. Planning permission for change of use of premises may be needed for more than six children under eight years.

A home-based childcarer may work with an assistant. The assistant must be registered as such by Ofsted. Working with an assistant does not allow you to increase the number of children minded. The assistant must not be in sole charge of a child except in an emergency.

In some families, the partner of the prospective home-based childcarer may also apply for registration. This will provide emergency cover only (unless the partner is a registered homebased childcarer in his or her own right) and some additional assistance, but will not affect the number of children minded. If you plan to work with three or more people, you will need to find out about being a 'childcarer on domestic premises'. The NCMA can offer advice on this (www.ncma.org.uk). They can also offer advice on childminding networks – these are local groups of registered childminders who are supported by an employed network co-ordinator, whose job is to manage the network.

Making an application

All persons applying to Ofsted to find out about childminding registration details will be asked to attend pre-registration briefing sessions. All aspects of childminding will be discussed at the briefings, and all the relevant forms will be handed out in an Ofsted application pack to those who wish to proceed. There will also be handouts to take away and read, including the EYFS Framework, which will have been introduced during the briefing.

Once you return the completed application pack, Ofsted will advise you on how to apply for a Criminal Records Bureau Disclosure (often called a 'CRB check'). Everyone aged 16 or over living in your home must apply. Ofsted will also follow up information you have supplied in your application. This includes checking your references and carrying out a medical record check (you will have completed a health declaration which includes a section for your GP to complete). Ofsted will also be in touch to arrange for an Inspector to visit your home.

The purpose of the registration visit is to check the suitability of the applicant to care for children by conducting a suitable person interview, and to check that the home environment is child-friendly and safe.

There may be visits from the fire prevention officer and the environmental health officer. The process of registration can be quite lengthy, particularly if alterations to the premises have to be carried out. You will be reminded that until you are registered you are not able to care for children legally.

Next, applicants are required to attend an introductory childminding course in preparation for their new role, and to take a first-aid course. The childminding course is likely to be the Introduction to Childcare Practice (Home-based), which is the first Unit in the Diploma in Home-based Childcare. You can read more about qualifications in Chapter 15.

After the courses a registration fee must be paid, and a registration certificate can be issued. At this point, you can welcome your first child.

The following chart appears in Ofsted's 'Guide to registration on the Early Years Register: childminder'.

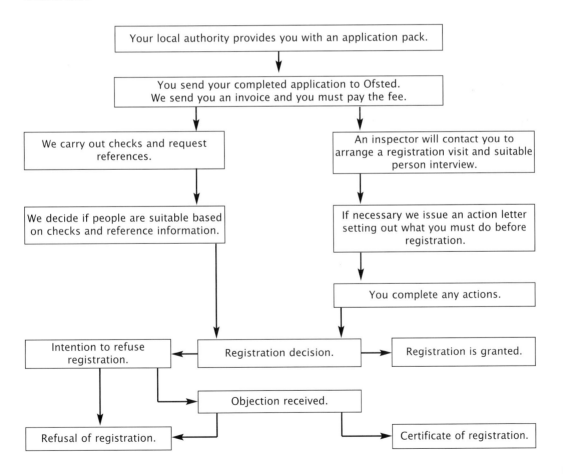

Requirements of registration

At the conclusion of the registration process you should be clear about:

- how you will meet the welfare requirements
- how you will deliver the EYFS
- the number and ages of the children for whom you are registered
- what records you are required to keep concerning the children and the families
- safety procedures
- holding public liability insurance (available from the NCMA)
- your requirement to attend training sessions
- your commitment to equal opportunities
- the time when you will be required to renew your registration
- ongoing inspections.

Inspection

Along with their registration certificate, new childminders receive a copy of the Ofsted booklet, 'Are you ready for your inspection?' This is a guide to preparing for an Ofsted inspection. Childminders are inspected soon after registration, usually within seven months, (provided they are actively caring for children) so the quality of the care and children's learning can be assessed. The first quality ratings will then be given. After this initial inspection, childminders are inspected at least once every three years. An earlier inspection will be carried out if a childminder moves home, if Ofsted receives a complaint about the provision, or if the provision is found to have significant areas of weakness at the previous inspection.

Ofsted has produced a self-evaluation form (SEF) which childminders complete as part of their inspection preparation. It asks you to consider and grade:

- your strengths
- areas for improvement, and how you could work on them
- facts that the Ofsted inspector will need to know about the care and learning you provide for children.

When an inspection is due, the Ofsted inspector will call the childminder a few days in advance to ask if there are any days on which the childminder is unavailable, but an appointment will not be made. This is because the purpose of the visit is to assess the provision when normal day-to-day activities and routines are taking place. You will be asked to submit the SEF. The inspector will read it before the inspection and discuss it with you during their visit.

During the inspection

Childminders on Ofsted's Early Years Register will be inspected against the Early Years Foundation Stage. An inspector will consider the will consider the Every Child Matters (ECM) outcomes and concentrate on how well the service performs against the National Minimum

Standards associated with each of these outcomes. The four key judgments to be made are concerned with:

- how effectively the needs of children are met during the EYFS
- how effectively children are supported to learn and develop during the EYFS
- how effectively children's welfare is promoted
- how effectively the provision is managed and led.

During the visit, the inspector will:

- observe what the children and the childminder are doing together
- talk to the childminder, the children and possibly parents
- discuss the SEF, including the grades the childminder gave themselves
- look at records, particularly those that relate to how children's needs are met. This will include looking at policies, procedures and records such as assessments, registers, accident records and medication logs
- check the premises for safety, security and suitability
- make notes as they work, generally using a laptop computer.

In the 'Guide to registration on the Early Years Register: childminder' Ofsted tells us that, 'Particular attention will be paid to safeguards for children and staff knowledge of good practice. This is done to check the provision of care and also to determine to what extent needs are being met.'

Childminding inspections are expected to take about two hours, although the inspector will take a bit longer if the EYFS applies, or if providers are working in a childminding network.

The inspector will have planned some discussion time towards the end of the visit. During this time they will give feedback to the childminder. They will give their judgement for each ECM outcome and explain any improvements that need to be made. If anything needs urgent attention, this will be discussed. The overall outcome of the inspection will also be given.

The outcome

The following overall grades may be given:

- Outstanding – only awarded in exceptional circumstances to settings which provide excellent outcomes for children in all areas of the inspection. The provision is of exceptionally high quality. Providers who are judged as outstanding will receive a certificate and will be able to use a special logo on stationery and signage.
- Good – given to strong settings. The provision effectively promotes the outcomes for children.
- Satisfactory – given to settings which are sound but have scope for improvement. The outcomes for children are acceptable.
- Inadequate – given to weak settings which are not good enough. The outcomes for children are unacceptable. One or more of the EYFS requirements have not been met.

After the inspection Ofsted publishes a report on its findings. This evaluates the quality of the provision for the people who use the service. Childminders generally receive a report in the post 15 working days from the end of the inspection. The report will be published on the Ofsted website within a further five working days. All providers are required by law to give parents and everyone else who asks for one a copy of their inspection report.

For childminders who achieve a good or satisfactory grade, the areas in which they could improve will be highlighted in writing. At the next inspection the inspector will consider if the improvements have been made. If provision has been graded as inadequate, the childminder will generally receive a Notice to Improve, outlining the action that must be taken. The childminder is required to inform Ofsted when they have implemented the improvements, and a visit may be made to assess the action taken. Another inspection will take place within six to twelve months. However, if provision judged as inadequate requires immediate attention, Ofsted may serve a Compliance Notice exercising legal powers to insist on urgent changes. If improvements are not made or if children are not being looked after properly, Ofsted can take action to suspend or cancel the childminder's registration, closing down the provision.

Preparing yourself and your family for childminding

It is often difficult to balance work, one's own needs and those of the family. With childminding, this is even more difficult, as you will have a sense of obligation to the children and their families which might, on occasion, mean that you put the needs of your own family second.

Possible effects on you

You will be:

- working very hard
- working longer hours
- taking on a professional role
- making relationships with people outside the family
- changing your routines
- finding it difficult to make time for yourself, such as having your hair cut, going to the dentist or meeting friends, and having less time for recreational activities and hobbies
- feeling stress from time to time
- managing a business
- having to assimilate new knowledge and understanding of children's needs and development
- feeling anxious about keeping another person's child safe
- having to balance the needs of your family with the needs of the children you mind.

Possible effects on your partner

Your partner may be:

- aware of other children in the house
- putting up with changes in the family routine
- involved with making the home environment safe
- expected to play a part in meeting the needs of children
- expected by you to register to provide you with emergency cover
- expected to do more chores around the house
- expected to submit to the registration checks
- expected to interact socially with the parents of the children you look after
- expected to give up smoking in the house, or in front of the children
- expected to be up and dressed before the children arrive
- disturbed when trying to sleep, if he or she works shifts.

Possible effects on your children

They may:

- have to share you with other children
- have to share their home and possibly their toys
- find it is more difficult for you to attend school events
- have to be tidier and keep their own treasured possessions stored away
- be expected to do some of the household chores
- have the opportunity to make lasting friendships
- have the opportunity to be caring towards younger children
- have the opportunity to enjoy the company of older children
- have the opportunity to learn about other cultures
- have more play equipment
- be restricted as to choice of pet.

Possible effects on the home

There may be:

- more wear and tear on the furniture and equipment
- extra space taken up by safety and play equipment and for storing nappies
- extra storage needed for catering for larger numbers
- additional cleaning
- a large investment in safety, which might include new safety glass in doors, bars or locks on windows, locks on some doors and cupboards, and fitting safety gates
- a need to make the garden safe and secure.

When considering becoming a home-based childcarer, you should talk it through with your partner, your older children and other members of the extended family who may be in frequent

chapter

1

contact with you. Childminding will make many changes in the life of everyone in your family, and it would be very difficult to carry out this demanding career successfully without the support and encouragement of everyone concerned.

Many home-based childcarers in England and Wales receive a 'start-up' grant, to cover the cost of setting up a childminding business. These grants are given through the Early Years Development and Childcare Partnerships (EYDCP). Some partnerships will provide free or subsidised training for home-based childcarers.

Activity

Identify any particular difficulties you or anyone in your family will encounter, as a result of you becoming a home-based childcarer.

Support systems

We all need support and advice, particularly when we start a new job. Many minders decide to choose childminding because they have had their own children looked after in family daycare. Many of these relationships turn into friendships, and most experienced home-based childcarers would be pleased to support new people in the field.

Your local Children's Information Service (CIS) will provide support and information on getting started and all essential training. Local authorities continue to provide an advisory and development role with early years teams and advisers.

Seeking help and advice is not a sign of weakness, but shows maturity and an awareness of the difficulties of the job. Many home-based childcarers will be able to call on family and friends to sustain and encourage them and they will be a source of strength in times of uncertainty. All discussions and conversations must observe the rules of confidentiality.

Professional support

The National Childminding Association of England and Wales (NCMA)

NCMA acts as a support network to promote quality and to improve the status and conditions for home-based childcarers, the children and their parents. It is a public voice for home-based childcare, lobbying political parties and using the media to promote childminding. NCMA also liaises with various government departments. It produces information for members, provides free legal advice, and offers training, insurance, publications and business materials to help home-based childcarers run their businesses effectively. It has established childminding networks and quality assurance schemes that make a major contribution to best childminding practice.

NCMA realises that childminding can be an isolated job and encourages home-based childcarers to set up their own groups, which offer the opportunity to:

- meet other home-based childcarers with similar experiences
- discuss problems, issues and concerns
- borrow equipment and use the toy library
- participate in vacancy co-ordination schemes

- provide emergency back-up
- attend drop-in sessions or more formal meetings with speakers
- attend outings and social occasions
- participate in in-service training.

Most childminding groups are affiliated to NCMA and are able to take advantage of the benefits this brings to their members.

Other professionals
Other people who support home-based childcarers include:

- Early years advisory teachers
- Ofsted inspectors
- NCMA Children Come First network co-ordinators (see page 17)
- Children's Information Service
- SureStart and local authority early years advisers or development workers
- NCMA officers or network co-ordinators
- NCMA county/borough committees
- health visitors (either your own, or those of the families you look after)
- infant and primary school teachers.

If you are discussing a child with other professional people, it is important not to pass on confidential information without gaining the permission of the parents first. By contributing support and help to other people, you are more likely to receive support yourself.

Training

'I hear: I forget. I see: I remember. I do: I understand.'

(Chinese proverb)

Prior to registration, Ofsted requires childminders to attend pre-registration briefing sessions and a recognised paediatric first-aid course. Once registered, childminders are required to complete an 'Introductory Childminding Training' course. Unit 1 of the CACHE Level 3 Diploma in Home-based Childcare (DHC) fulfils this criteria.

Home-based childcarers can now prepare for a nationally recognised qualification by taking the DHC. This consists of five units:

1 Introduction to childcare practice
2 Childcare and child development (0–16) in the home-based setting
3 The childcare practitioner in the home-based setting
4 Working in partnership with parents in the home-based setting
5 Meeting children's individual learning needs in the home-based setting.

Home-based childcarers will benefit from training by:

- valuing the skills of home-based childcare
- developing knowledge, skills and professional attitudes
- developing good childminding practice
- gaining greater self-esteem and self-confidence

- learning by participating in discussion and from the experience of others
- reflecting on their practice
- learning through observation how to assess children's needs in an objective fashion
- being able to offer support to other home-based childcarers
- gaining a qualification.

NVQs

Home-based childcarers may choose to follow the DHC with the National Vocational Qualification (NVQ) **Level 3 in Children's Care Learning and Development**. A Level 3 qualification is thought appropriate for home-based childcarers, as they are independent practitioners who are not supervised in their practice. You can also progress on to a **Level 4**.

Foundation degrees are Level 5 on the QCA National Qualification Framework. They are offered by colleges and universities, but they are designed for people who are working within the field they are studying. There are no set entry requirements – your prior experience and on-the-job training will be considered alongside any formal qualifications should you apply. There are several suitable foundation degrees for childminders to choose from.

Those with **Early Years Professional (EYP) status** (Level 6) are role models for colleagues working with children aged 0-5 years. They seek to improve the quality of practice within the workforce by supporting, leading and bringing about change. To gain EYP status you must meet graduate level standards.

As childcare professionals childminders can progress all the way to Level 6 if they have a thirst for learning.

Professionalism

Caring for other people's children is skilled work which depends upon a sound foundation of knowledge about children and their families. Looking after other people's children is not the same as caring for your own. It is quite difficult to balance the needs of your own children and partner with any employment that you might take up outside the house. It is much more difficult if you are self-employed and caring for children in your home alongside your own children. It requires a professional approach to make it work.

Becoming a professional is a gradual process, and encompasses knowledge, skills, behaviour and attitudes. The concept of professionalism includes:

- working in a skilful, expert and well-organised way, reflecting on one's own practice and seeking to improve performance
- being paid for work done
- working in a detached, objective way, that keeps personal emotions and opinions separate from judgements and behaviour related to work
- working in a way which demonstrates adherence to certain principles of conduct
- being committed to work, to providing a service as agreed, but not permitting oneself to be exploited

- expecting to take up opportunities for training and other ways of developing practice and keeping up to date, including maintaining contacts with colleagues.

Childminding groups and networks

NCMA has worked to support registered home-based childcarers for over 25 years through the development of local groups and associations. Today, over 1000 groups and networks offer a range of support to local home-based childcarers, holding drop-in sessions providing information to parents about childminding vacancies, and running toy libraries and equipment loan schemes.

In addition, there are 180 approved NCMA Children Come First networks. These are approved formal groups of registered home-based childcarers who are assessed, recruited and monitored by a network co-ordinator. Co-ordinators ensure that the home-based childcarers receive training to develop their skills, and provide a link between parent and home-based childcarer; most operate a toy library and equipment loan scheme. Home-based childcarers in the network can become accredited providers of early education for three- and four-year-olds. For a network to be approved by NCMA, all home-based childcarers in the network must be practising according to the NCMA Children Come First Quality Standards. See the NCMA Children Come First website, www.ncmaccf.org.uk, for more details.

Meeting regularly with other home-based childcarers and hearing their views and opinions will help you to reflect on your practice and will prevent feelings of isolation.

Knowledge

During your preparation or induction, ongoing training and perhaps through undertaking the Diploma in Home-based Childcare, you will be gaining knowledge. Using your library, reading books, NCMA publications and relevant journals, and learning through theory and observation about the all-round development of children will make you sensitive to their needs and so enable you to develop good standards of practice.

Such knowledge plays an important part in preventative work, for example identifying children who are in need of protection or need to be referred to the health services. As you grow in knowledge, you will be better able to understand children in your care and to interpret records and observations, so that you spot problems quickly and ensure that the child receives the necessary help and support.

You will never come to the end of what you can learn about looking after children. A good indicator of a professional home-based childcarer is the willingness to update knowledge and understanding regularly by attending courses and reading professional journals. The professional home-based childcarer will always be ready to question and challenge in a thoughtful and constructive manner.

Behaviour

A professional home-based childcarer will display motivation, enthusiasm and commitment at all times, showing a positive attitude towards the work. You will become aware of your role and responsibilities, and reach a good understanding of what you can and cannot do in your childminding setting. You will take time to review and evaluate your practice, reflecting regularly about your provision and identifying strengths and weaknesses.

Reliability and commitment

Being reliable means:

- always making sure that you and your household are ready to welcome the children you look after at their expected time of arrival
- keeping to the contract you have with the parents, and putting the children's needs before your own
- giving the parents good notice if there should be a time you are unable to look after the children
- collecting school-age children in good time from school, and younger children from pre-school.

The well-being and safety of the children in your care has to be your main concern. Be cautious about taking on too many responsibilities, or commitments where you feel you may not have the necessary knowledge, time or experience to carry them out successfully.

Being committed means:

- offering a professional service over a period of time
- negotiating contracts with parents, that are kept to
- being organised and businesslike, maintaining well-kept records and accounts.

Communication

You will be using three methods of communication, writing, speaking and body language. You will need to keep written records and make written observations. From time to time you may have to write to the parents and outside agencies. If you are not confident about expressing yourself in the written word, seek support from other home-based childcarers and NCMA.

The clarity of your speech, and the ways in which you talk to children, parents and other professional people, will show them that you are a caring, knowledgeable and sensitive person. You should be able to state your views and ideas clearly and concisely.

Your body language should convey that you are interested and motivated. Shrugging your shoulders and turning away is no substitute for expressing your point of view over a disagreement calmly and clearly. Share your knowledge, opinions and observations in a positive way with parents, while valuing their knowledge and expertise and being aware of variation between different cultural groups.

Janet Gonzalez-Mena points out in her book *Multicultural Issues in Child Care* (1993) that there are cultural differences in the use of five types of communication: smiling, eye contact, and sensitivity to personal space, touch and time.

Confidentiality

You will become aware of information concerning the children and their families. Some of the information that you receive, either written or oral, is strictly confidential and you will learn, as a professional person, which information should be kept to yourself. You might hear this information either directly from the parents, other professional workers, or from the children. You should never share it with your family, friends or other home-based childcarers. Even on training courses, your tutors will not expect you to reveal the identities of the child or family in class discussion or when writing assignments.

You will make it clear that you will not take part in gossiping about the children and their families with other parents, whatever pressure you are put under. Be careful what you say in front of your own children or other members of the family.

As a professional person, you will be expected to share information with professional colleagues if this is in the best interest of the child. For example, the child might have special health needs and the parents will give you permission to discuss the child with the doctor or health visitor. Particular care should be taken in childminding groups. The issue of confidentiality should be discussed and the groups should have an agreed policy.

There may be times when you might have to pass on information in the interests of protecting children from abuse without gaining the permission of the parents. The welfare of the child or children must always be your first concern in these matters.

Any records or documents you have concerning the children should be kept in a locked secure cupboard or box to which only you have the key.

CASE STUDY

Aisha looks after six-year-old Peter as well as three other children. Peter's mother, Selina, tells Aisha that she is about to leave her husband, as he has lost his job and has started drinking excessively. He is violent towards her and she fears for Peter.

The other parents know something is wrong in Selina's life, as she is monopolising Aisha's time when the children are being collected. One of the mothers starts asking awkward questions.

1 How should Aisha respond?
2 Should she encourage Selina to discuss her problems with the other parents?
3 Should Aisha get in touch with social services?

Attachment

The children will develop a close relationship with you and, while you must meet their emotional needs, you must always keep in mind that the parents are the primary caregivers. Love and affection are not finite emotions, and children are capable of relating lovingly to many adults. However close an attachment is formed, you must always bear in mind that your relationship is temporary, and that of the parents is permanent.

Attitudes

As a professional home-based childcarer, you will show awareness of and sympathise with the needs of children and their parents, regardless of racial origins, class, cultural background, religion, disability, gender or age. You will never display favouritism or special treatment towards some children in preference to others, but always show respect and interest in the customs, values and beliefs of all the children. This will help you to provide them with positive images of themselves and each other.

Anti-bias practice

A home-based childcarer with a professional attitude needs to recognise that no member of society should be discriminated against because of his or her race, gender, class, culture, age, religion, disability, family background or sexual orientation. This is especially important for you, working with young children, since you are in a good position to influence their developing attitudes. All children will be damaged by prejudice and by bias. Those who are subjected to discrimination are made to feel ashamed and inferior and their self-esteem is damaged. Research has shown very clearly that young children do notice differences in gender and skin tone. We should show by example and by talking honestly and accurately to children that these differences should arouse interest and enjoyment.

Activity

You are an experienced home-based childcarer caring for an African-Caribbean child. Your aunt, of whom you are very fond, drops in unexpectedly. She sits the child on her knee and starts singing a nursery rhyme that contains derogatory references to black people.
1 What is your immediate response?
2 What range of emotions might you feel?
3 How might you discuss this issue with your aunt?
4 Should you discuss it with the child and her parents?

Children need to feel confident about themselves and be sure that they are valued. If children are not cared for with a commitment to equal opportunities, they may develop negative feelings about themselves that would lead to lack of self-esteem and inhibit their development. We are all products of our environment and heredity. The way we have been treated by our families and by society will have a bearing on how we see others. In spite of legislation against racial, gender and disability discrimination, many people still experience negative and hurtful attitudes.

You may, as a home-based childcarer, care for children from various cultural backgrounds and racial groups, with many views of the world and possibly speaking several languages. The society in which we live is multi-racial and multi-cultural, and both home-based childcarers and children need to acknowledge and learn about racial and cultural groups other than their own in a positive way. When children go to school, or out into the wider world, they will come into contact with various racial and cultural groups, and they need to develop their interpersonal skills and ability to form relationships with a wide range of people. If people from one particular segment of society are allowed or encouraged to feel superior because of their racial origins and cultural background, the all-round development of their children will be impaired.

Gender

Any play opportunities that you offer the children in your care should be available to both boys and girls. You might find that some parents still expect to see girls engaged in doll play while the boys are encouraged to use the construction toys. If this happens, opportunities are being limited, and the young children are learning stereotypical expectations of gender roles. Attitudes are learnt very young in the home and from the media but you can challenge stereotypes. A stereotype is a generalisation of expected behaviour from a certain group, for example, expecting a football fan to be a lager-swilling, abusive male.

Stereotypes may be positive or negative. Either type might be damaging to children because, if we label them and have certain expectations of them, we might deprive them of the opportunity to develop other skills or interests. We all have fixed ideas about certain groups. For example, if you join your local NCMA group and prepare to attend your first meeting, you will make certain assumptions about the people you may meet there and what will happen in the group. This can be helpful and aid your settling into the group.

Activity

Think of a group that you recently joined or an occasion that you attended.
1 What assumptions did you make prior to the event?
2 Did the people you met behave in the way you expected?

The pressure later on in life for children to conform to certain behaviour is very strong, and it is most important that the children experience equal opportunities in their play at the youngest age. Denying girls the opportunity to ride bicycles may inhibit the development of their spatial awareness and delay mathematical ability. Not allowing boys to play with dolls may hold back their emotional expression and make them fearful of appearing caring when they grow up. Boys should be allowed to cry if they are hurt and not told to be 'brave little soldiers'. You will be seen as a role model by the children and must try to offer and participate in all activities. If you play football in the garden, the girls should be encouraged to join in. All play materials, including books, should show men and women in a variety of different roles, such as female firefighters and male nurses.

It sometimes appears that boys monopolise the attention of adults, with rough and noisy play demanding adult attention. You need to be aware of this, and make sure that you value the contribution of both boys and girls. Watch your use of language with the children; making sure that you sometimes comment on how caring the behaviour of one of the boys has been towards a younger child or how well a girl has constructed a Lego building.

Racial origin

Britain is a multi-racial society and the children you care for may reflect this racial diversity. Even if this is not so, children need to have a good understanding of other racial groups and cultures. Your own attitude to cultures other than your own will influence the children and their families.

Racism manifests itself in various ways:

- racism supports the idea of one superior race or culture
- racism prevents people fulfilling their own potential because of their racial origin
- racism creates a hostile atmosphere for people of different ethnic groups where learning cannot take place.

As a home-based childcarer you can play a key role in confronting and challenging racism. You may hear a child, or even a parent, make a racist remark or 'joke', or insult another individual. As a professional, you should challenge such remarks, making it quite clear that they are unacceptable to you and certainly should not be repeated in front of the children in your care. It is difficult to confront racism at first, whether from children or adults, and it may be helpful to discuss strategies for dealing with this issue with your training group or local childminding group.

Activity

Jonathan, aged five, who is African-Caribbean, asks a group of children at a childminding group meeting, who are playing with blocks, if he can join in. Sarah, aged four, says, 'No', and makes a derogatory racist remark. You overhear this remark.

1 What do you do immediately?
2 How do you help Jonathan deal with his hurt feelings?

Children need to have a good understanding of racial and cultural groups other than their own, and this should be reflected in your home. Books should have positive images of black adults in positions of authority and of black children in active roles in the story. Your dressing-up box should contain clothes from a variety of cultures, and you should offer the children food from a variety of cultures such as pasta, pizza, rice, lentils, sweet potatoes, tropical fruits and much more.

Religion

You may be caring for children who come from families with beliefs different from your own. Respect, tolerance, acceptance and willingness to learn from others are essential, so that you can develop awareness and sensitivity to the needs of children in your care. Knowledge of various religions, customs and festivals is important to those working with young children. You will need to discuss, with the parents, details concerning beliefs, diet, dress and festivals. All religions have many facets. Do not make assumptions that a particular family keeps strictly to orthodox practices; they may adopt a more relaxed approach to the faith.

Disability

If the children you care for have the opportunity to mix with disabled children, ensure that your remarks about disability are positive, informative and correct, and that the language you use is acceptable and preferred by disabled people. The children will see the disabled child as a child like them and, with your support, will understand that all children should be treated fairly and included in all activities.

CASE STUDY

Cherie, an experienced home-based childcarer, has been approached by Natalie, requesting her to mind her son Jason, aged three, who is unable to walk unaided. At their first meeting, it is obvious that Natalie is apprehensive and tense about leaving Jason in someone else's care.

1 How can Cherie help Natalie manage this separation from Jason?
2 How can Cherie demonstrate that she understands Jason's needs?

Anti-discriminatory practice

Since the Children Act 1989, anti-discriminatory practice is required by law in all places where children are cared for. The child's religious, racial, cultural and linguistic background must be taken into account. This practice should be active in promoting positive images and reinforcing the self-esteem of all the children. Your home should show all children in a positive way, in pictures, dressing-up clothes, books, jigsaws and the toys that you provide. Challenging bias and prejudice where it is encountered is a major responsibility for all home-based childcarers. (The Children Act 2004 has not replaced the Children Act of 1989, and it amends very little. The purpose of the 2004 Act was to lay out the integration of services to support the outcomes of the legislation *Every Child Matters*, which is outlined on pages 43–4.)

1 Present positive images of all cultures, racial groups, gender, religion and disability in your home in your choice of books, your selection of equipment, and in any dressing-up clothes you may provide.

2 Present yourself as a good role model.

3 Acknowledge what you do not know, and be prepared to ask for help and advice.

4 Confront all discriminatory remarks, whether from children or from adults and whether directed against yourself or others.

5 Answer children's questions honestly, with explanations appropriate to the child's age.

6 Make sure you pronounce and spell all the children's names correctly, so as not to give offence, and that you understand the naming systems of many cultures and religions.

7 Make sure you know and pronounce correctly the names of the garments the children wear.

8 Understand the varying skin- and hair-care needs of all the children.

9 Encourage children to have positive feelings about their skin tone, hair texture and facial features.

10 Make sure you provide a varied diet that will appeal to all the children in your care, and which will introduce them to a variety of interesting foods, while obeying the dietary laws of their religion.

11 Challenge stereotypes. You and the children may be watching a television programme that shows girls as passive and in an inferior role to boys. You will need to discuss this, pointing out that females often show more leadership and can be just as assertive as males.

12 Prevent children from developing stereotypes. There may be a programme on the television, showing starving black children in Africa being given food by white adults. You will need to point out that this is because of climatic and economic conditions, and has nothing to do with the skin tone of the children.

13 Involve all children in all activities. You may need to adjust the environment or provide special equipment if you are looking after a disabled child, so as to make sure that he or she can take part.

14 Encourage all children to be assertive and to stand up for themselves.

15 If modest dress is a requirement of the religion, be sensitive to the parents' wishes and do not insist that the children get undressed for any physical activity.

16 Show that you respect the child's home language by learning a few rhymes and words in this language, and keep a few books in the house if you can obtain them.

SELF-APPRAISAL

Areas to consider	Strong	Satisfactory	Weak
Business organisation			
Relationship with parents			
Always ready for children's arrival			
Commitment to equal opportunities			
Observation skills			
Awareness of health and safety issues			
Provision of equipment			
Good range of activities available			
Enjoyment of reading with children			
Enjoy company of children			
Knowledge of support groups			
Interest in training			
Keeping up to date with care and education issues			
Find it easy to provide a range of nutritious meals			
Professional attitude and approach			
Able to balance the needs of all the children			
Manage time well			
Liaison with other professional workers			
Able to balance needs of family and employment			

chapter 1

Completing the 'Self-appraisal' table on page 25, honestly and by yourself, might help you to appreciate your strengths and indicate areas that you might try to improve.

NCMA produces a workbook for home-based childcarers linked to the Quality Standards; using the workbook would encourage you to reflect upon your practice and identify improvements that might be made.

Policies and permissions

Written policies exist to protect children, home-based childcarers and parents. They make sure that everyone understands the rules and the underpinning ethos of the home. This ensures that everyone is working together in the best interest of the children.

When providing environments for children you must comply with the laws and regulations relevant to your home country. All of the laws and regulations referred to here apply in England. However, health and safety legislation is fairly universal. You can find out more about the specifics for your home country online:

- Scotland: www.scotland.gov.uk
- Wales: www.wales.gov.uk
- Northern Ireland: www.deni.gov.uk
- England: www.direct.gov.uk

Every Child Matters

Every Child Matters is the government agenda that sets out five major outcomes for all children:

- being healthy
- staying safe
- enjoying and achieving
- making a positive contribution
- economic well-being.

You can read about how the Early Years Foundation Stage aims to meet the *Every Child Matters* outcomes on pages 81–6.

The Early Years Foundation Stage welfare requirements

Childminders to whom the Early Years Foundation Stage applies must meet the EYFS welfare requirements in addition to the learning and development requirements. The welfare requirements fall into the following five categories:

Safeguarding and promoting children's welfare

- The provider must take necessary steps to safeguard and promote the welfare of children.
- The provider must promote the good health of the children, take necessary steps to prevent the spread of infection, and take appropriate action when they are ill.
- Children's behaviour must be managed effectively and in a manner appropriate for their stage of development and particular individual needs.

Suitable people

- Providers must ensure that adults looking after children, or having unsupervised access to them, are suitable to do so.
- Adults looking after children must have appropriate qualifications, training, skills and knowledge.
- Staffing arrangements must be organised to ensure safety and to meet the needs of the children.

Suitable premises, environment and equipment

- Outdoor and indoor spaces, furniture, equipment and toys must be safe and suitable for their purpose.

Organisation

- Providers must plan and organise their systems to ensure that every child receives an enjoyable and challenging learning and development experience that is tailored to meet their individual needs.

Documentation

- Providers must maintain records, policies and procedures required for the safe and efficient management of the settings and to meet the needs of the children.

Policies that childminders should have in place to meet the requirements of the EYFS include:

- Accident and emergency – including evacuation procedures, first-aid, use of an accident book and procedures if a child is lost. Written risk assessments are also required.
- Arrivals and departures – including registration and collection procedures, and procedures followed if a child is not collected as arranged.
- Behaviour – including how inappropriate behaviour is handled.
- Child protection – including procedures if child abuse is suspected.
- Complaints – including the procedure for parents wishing to complain to Ofsted.
- Confidentiality – including how information is stored with regard to the Data Protection Acts.

- Equal opportunities – including how an inclusive service is offered.
- Food and drink – including how this is provided.
- Health and safety – including hygiene procedures to prevent cross infections, risk assessments and illness.
- Medicines – including the written permission necessary for administering medication.
- Outings – including risk assessment and parental permissions.
- Smoking – how the home is kept smoke-free.
- Working with parents – how the childminder works in partnership with families.

Activity

Visit the NCMA website (www.ncma.org.uk) and view their very helpful sample policies and procedures for childminders.

There are many other situations where you may want to put in writing, possibly as part of a policy or the contract between you and the parents, your expectations: for example, not being responsible for taking children to pre-arranged birthday parties after school. It is very important that your policies and practice match up. You will find guidelines on how to write policies in Chapter 12.

Whenever you meet a new parent, you should make a point of discussing your policies and giving them a copy. All policies are working documents, setting out your intentions and how you will respond to situations. For example, you will have house rules about behaviour and this would form part of your policy.

Your policy on anti-discriminatory practice and equal opportunities needs to be spelt out, so that all parents feel secure and reassured that their children will be cared for equally, valued for themselves and will have their individual needs met.

You might think about your reasons and preparation for registering as a home-based childcarer:

- what experience you have had with caring for children
- how you will plan the daily routine
- how much your family will support you in this new venture
- the adaptations or alterations that you may have to make to your home and/or your garden so as to make sure that your home is hygienic and in good repair
- what new equipment you may have to purchase so as to meet the developmental needs of all the children, covering the whole age range
- possible changes to your lifestyle
- the importance of confidentiality
- your reliability and commitment to the job
- how you will become more knowledgeable about children and their needs
- how to make sure that your practice is anti-discriminatory
- the number and ages of the children that you will care for
- why you wish to register as a home-based childcarer.

This chapter has contributed to the following learning outcomes:

Unit 1

- providing a safe and healthy childcare environment in the home-based setting
- promoting anti-discriminatory, anti-bias practice in the home-based setting
- identifying and evaluating key factors in setting up a childcare service

Unit 2

- understanding the importance of inclusive practice and how this can be implemented in the home-based setting

Unit 3

- developing and implementing policies in the home-based setting
- understanding the importance of inter-agency work

Unit 4

- understanding the factors that have influenced the development of home-based childcare and the choices parents make
- understanding the role of the home-based practitioner when maintaining confidentiality

Want to Find Out More?

Websites

www.cache.org.uk
www.carecommission.com
www.childminding.org
www.equalityhumanrights.com
www.nicma.org
www.ncma.org.uk
www.ncmaccf.org.uk
www.ofsted.gov.uk
www.standards.dfes.gov.uk/eyfs

2 Relationships with parents

Learning objectives

Unit 1

- Introducing children and their families to your childcare service
- Starting a home-based childcare service
- Promoting inclusion and anti-bias practice

Unit 4

- Understanding the role of the childcare practitioner in the community
- Valuing families and cultures
- Promoting positive relationships with parents and understanding the importance of valuing the child's primary carer

As you have decided to embark on a career as a home-based childcarer, offering quality childcare and education, you will have realised how important it is to build good relationships with the parents of the children in your care. The words 'parent' or 'parent/carer' are used to describe all primary carers, whether they are the child's biological parents, foster carers, adoptive parents, grandparents or other relatives having responsibility for the child.

The parent as the child's primary carer and educator

From as long ago as the 1950s, it has been acknowledged that the support and aspirations of the parents play a vital part in the educational attainment of their children. All the research shows the importance of parental interests and involvement and therefore parents need to be kept well informed about their child's development and behaviour and understand your approach to their child's learning. The child will benefit most when the three elements of the triangle – parent, child and home-based childcarer – are all working together in harmony.

Parents spend time with their children and will know their strengths and weaknesses and anticipate their needs; they will have made many decisions about their child prior to placing the child with you. Therefore it is sensible to work with the parents in all aspects of care and education for the benefit of the child. It will add to the security of the child to see you and her parents working together and in regular communication.

Recent trends in parenting

The homes and lives of children in the UK have changed dramatically in the last 30 years. There are many possible reasons for this:

- increase in divorce and the number of households headed by one parent

2 chapter

- increase in mobility, so that young families do not always have the support of an extended family
- increase in the number of stepfamilies, and in the number of different relationships that the parents might have
- increase in stress, owing to uncertainty in employment or longer hours in the workplace
- increase in the number of children living in relative poverty
- increase in drug and alcohol abuse
- increase in violence on television, film and video
- increase in reporting of violence in the media, which has led to fear and to parents trying to shield their children from danger by restricting opportunities for independence outside the home
- increase in house-husbands/partners
- increase in the involvement of the father in some aspects of child-rearing
- increase in the number of much smaller families so that fewer children grow up with the opportunity to learn about babycare and childcare through direct observation.

In some ways, the home has become a more claustrophobic place. Many children do not have so much freedom to play outside and spend more time in front of computers, televisions and videos. The 2001 Census in England and Wales found 702,000 children living in flats above the ground floor and 40,000 on the fifth floor or higher. Opportunities for outside play were restricted for the 8.9 per cent of children under three living above the ground floor.

Activity

There have been many social changes during the last 30 years.
1 How do you think this has affected the lives of the children?
2 What effect have these changes had on the lives of the parents?

In the UK, families can now choose when to have their children, how many to have, how the money is earned, who stays home with the children and what childcare to choose. From April 2003, there has been:

- improved maternity rights: maternity leave is now extended to a year
- an increase in standard statutory maternity pay to £100 a week
- two weeks' paid paternity leave within eight weeks of the birth
- rights for parents of children under six and disabled children up to the age of 18 to request working flexible hours; employers are obliged to take these requests seriously
- leave for parents adopting a child, when the child is first placed with them.

A recent report by the National Centre for Research showed that a third of fathers work ten-hour days, the longest hours in Europe, and come home absolutely exhausted. In most dual-income families, one or both parents work outside the standard 9 to 5 day. More than half

2 chapter

of employed lone mothers also work atypical hours. Couples who work at unusual times tend to operate a shift system of parenting, where at least one of them is looking after the children at any time.

Some parents are starting their families at a later age. House prices are high, and people need to earn more to pay increased mortgages. Many mothers wish to remain on the career ladder for longer, so most go back to work within 13 months.

A recent survey of 1100 parents showed that:

- 53 per cent of the mothers said that they took responsibility for more of the decisions about the children
- 71 per cent of mothers said they would be more likely to stay at home if the child were sick
- 65 per cent of mothers said they spent more than 15 hours a week alone with their child, compared to 18 per cent of the fathers
- 35 per cent of the fathers spent less than 5 hours a week alone with their children
- In England, 30 per cent of children are born to unwed mothers, and the UK has the highest rate in Europe of single mothers in their teens.

Many of you will have made the decision to stay at home with your children, and not return to outside employment until all your children are much older. It is important that you respect the decision of others to return to work, even if their children are very young. If you express disapproval, it is likely to damage the relationship that you hope to achieve with the parents. If you have your own children, remember that you are a working mother too!

Parenting styles

All families are unique, but sociologists have noted that the way parents interact with their children has been influenced by their culture, class and ethnic group, and the experience of their own childhood. The birth order, temperament and personality of each child will cause parents to handle each child differently. Children from the same family who have the same style of parenting will not necessarily develop in the same way. All families have good and bad times. Children are greatly influenced by the attitudes and parenting styles used by their parents at home.

All parents have their own ideas on how to raise children, and their ways may be very different from the way you were brought up and how you care for your own children. How parents communicate with, relate to and discipline their children shows their ability and willingness to use their authority as parents. You need to understand about the various parenting styles. These may change as the children grow or if the family structure changes. Sometimes the mother and the father may not share the same approach, and children are quick to learn whom to go to for comfort, affection and security. This works as long as the parents respect each other's approach and do not seek to undermine each other.

The authoritarian style

This is the traditional view that parents have absolute control and power over their children's lives. There are hard and fast rules and punishment is swift if these are transgressed. The parents have high expectations of their children, both in aptitude and behaviour. They tend to use physical punishment, fear and threats, and are less likely to show physical affection to their children. Children are rarely allowed to question the rules.

When you are caring for children brought up in this way, you might see the following outcomes:

- fear of learning, in case mistakes are made
- not admitting to any wrongdoing and lying to cover up a misdemeanour
- restriction of natural curiosity, not wanting to test the boundaries
- low self-esteem and difficulty in making decisions
- feeling that their achievements will always be inferior
- poor social and communications skills
- inability to negotiate and resolve conflict
- being overly aggressive to others.

There can be a mismatch between the modes of discipline offered by you and those that the child experiences at home; some children may be unable to adjust to your less rigid regime and therefore behave badly whilst with you.

The permissive uninvolved style

These parents are often coping with many pressures in their lives and find it difficult to respond consistently to the needs of their children. This may be due to demanding jobs or to the pressure of coping with day-to-day living. They may not intend to be uninvolved in their children's lives, but the children pick up on the fact that their parents see them as nuisances. The parents may respond to their children inappropriately and unpredictably, swinging between harsh punishments and extravagant shows of affection. There are few routines or boundaries, and the children are left to look after themselves, frequently unsupervised.

When you are caring for children brought up in this way, you might see:

- children who appear to be able to care for themselves
- extreme risk-taking behaviour, to gain a response
- poor self-control
- over-anxiety to please
- lack of self-esteem; the child may become depressed.

The permissive indulgent style

Many of these parents may have been brought up in authoritarian homes, and have decided not to place controls on their children but to bring them up as 'free spirits'. These parents may be very involved with their children, showing them much warmth and affection but placing few controls on them. Such parents try to meet all their children's needs and avoid inflicting their own standards of values and beliefs on their children. Parents will often make elaborate excuses for their child's poor behaviour.

When you are caring for children brought up in this way, you might see:

- spoilt children, who see themselves as the centre of the universe and can be arrogant and demanding

- poor self-control
- lack of understanding and respect for the needs of others
- aggression and disobedience
- little understanding of limits and consequences.

The democratic or authoritative style

Parents using this style balance their needs with those of their children. They offer their children warm physical affection alongside clear boundaries and limits for behaviour. They take responsibility for their children, setting rules and making sure that these are adhered to. They expect their children to understand when they have broken the rules and to make amends, rather than punishing the children themselves. This family works as a unit, with each member having a share in the decision-making, taking age-appropriate responsibility and growing into

independent autonomous people.

When you are caring for children brought up in this way, you might see:

- children with a good sense of self-esteem
- understanding of right and wrong
- ability to resist temptation and accept blame
- ability to take criticism without resort to aggression
- self-reliance and self-control
- ability to make warm relationships with adults and children.

Activity

1 Look at a wide range of stories depicting parents in newspapers and magazines. How are the parents portrayed? What styles of parenting are the most frequent?
2 With a friend, role play a situation where a four-year-old is rude to an elderly relative. Using all four parenting styles, show how each type of parent deals with the behaviour. Afterwards, discuss your feelings, and how appropriate you thought each style to be.

The first meeting

As with any professional relationship, there will be a certain amount of tension and anxiety felt by both you and the parent, or parents, at the first meeting. The parents' range of emotions may include:

- guilt at leaving their child with a stranger
- anxiety about the safety of the child
- feeling that not knowing enough about childcare and education may prevent them from assessing the suitability of the home-based childcarer
- doubts about the decision to return to work
- being unhappy at the thought of parting from the child
- being upset at possibly missing out on certain milestones, such as finding the first tooth, seeing the first steps or hearing the first words
- anxiety that you will replace them in the child's affections
- anxiety about being able to cope with the logistics of running a home, doing a job, and developing a relationship with you
- worrying how they will manage if the arrangement breaks down.

As the home-based childcarer, your range of emotions may include:

- anxiety at a stranger's reaction to your home
- images of the parents as professional working people, and insecurity about your own status
- fear that you will not be able to form a satisfactory relationship with the parents
- fear that you may not like the child

- worries about cultural clashes
- worries about balancing the needs of your family with those of the child you are about to look after
- worries about whether your knowledge and skills are sufficient to equip you to do the job satisfactorily
- anxiety about discussing business matters.

Realising that the first meeting can be an emotional one for both parties, you will try to arrange it at a time when you are not overwhelmed with other responsibilities, and you can sit together discussing all the issues in a relaxed, calm atmosphere. Making the parents feel welcome, by offering a cup of tea and some biscuits, and getting them to relax, by engaging in some small talk, will help to build a positive relationship. If you manage the meeting successfully, the parents will be impressed by your professional approach.

The parents may come with a lot of questions and information for you, but, equally, you may find that they are new, inexperienced parents, who are not sure what to ask. NCMA has produced these checklists to help elicit information.

What the home-based childcarer needs to know about includes:

- other members of the child's family, including pets
- pet words and names and other vocabulary specific to the child
- any special object or toy the child uses as a comfort object
- what the child does and does not like to eat; what parents want and do not want the child to eat
- anything the child finds alarming or unsettling, e.g. dogs, people in spectacles, beards
- the family's cultural, religious or traditional background and the implications that it has for caring for their child
- the parents' attitude to the activities you plan for the children, and how they feel about your taking them out (to shops, park, drop-in centre etc.)
- whether the child can use a cup; what eating implements she uses
- information about nappies and toilet training
- whether the child still has a nap; whether there are any routines that help the child to sleep
- the hours parents work and will need your services
- the address and telephone number where parents can be contacted in an emergency
- who will be collecting the child, and if there is anyone who is not permitted contact with the child
- details of the family doctor and health visitor, the child's immunisation status and any allergies or health problems
- any new factors or special problems in the child's life.

See page 40 for a table in which to record information on the child's individual preferences.

What the parent needs to know about includes:

- where the children will spend their day; show them the rooms (and any garden) to be used
- what the children will do during the day – play activities, meals, going out, television, stories, nap
- what sort of play equipment and materials you provide
- what sort of food you provide, and your attitude towards sweets and snacks
- something about your attitude to bringing up children, e.g. setting limits to behaviour, equal opportunities for all children
- what experience and training you have in looking after other people's children
- what safety equipment you use (including, if the children are to be taken in a car, the restraints used)
- what your plans are in the event of an emergency
- when your childminding services are available and how much you charge
- details of your registration and insurance
- that you expect to use a written contract, signed by both parties
- your expectations about providing nappies, food, change of clothes, playgroup fees, etc.
- that you will not pass on confidential information about the family
- how many other children are being cared for and their ages
- your availability for taking children to and from playgroup, pre-school and school
- your policy if children are unwell
- that you will need their written permission to administer any form of medication, and for taking a child on an outing
- members of your family
- what sort of pets you keep and the children's access to them
- your non-smoking policy.

Child's individual needs

Child's name   D.O.B

Pre-school/Playgroup

School

	NOTES
Food Does the child have any allergies? Is the child given food choices? Is the child expected to finish the meal? What happens if the child refuses food?	
Dressing Can the child dress herself? Does the child like privacy? Can the child tie her own shoe laces?	
Toileting How often is the nappy changed? What is used to clean the baby? *During toilet training* How does the child indicate the need to use the lavatory? Will the child say she needs to use the potty? Are there special words or signals I should know? Is a nappy used when sleeping?	
Separation How does the child handle separation from parent? How is the child distracted? How does the child like to be comforted when distressed?	

Rituals
Is there a special way of doing things:
    at rest time
    at mealtime
    at other times?	

Preferences
What preferences does your child have for:
    food
    drink
    toys
    books
    persons
    stories
    games
    activities
    songs?	

For older/school-age children
Who are the child's best friends?
Is the child expected to do any chores?
What arrangements are there for:
    homework
    watching TV
    music practice
    outside activities?	

Medical concerns What past illnesses has the child had? Does the child have any allergies? Is there other information?	

This page may be photocopied. © Nelson Thornes Publishers Ltd

Design a statement that you can give the parents, outlining what they need to know about you and your practice.

As you develop your practice and become more experienced, you might like to build a portfolio. This would contain your registration and inspection documents, policies, insurance certificates, training certificates, any testimonials from parents, and a timetable of a typical day. This portfolio may be of interest to new parents and make them feel more secure in their choice.

During the first meeting, you might take the opportunity to introduce the new family to your own family. If at all possible, time should be spent in exploring the suitability of the partnership before a final decision is made. Then the contract should be produced, as outlined in Chapter 14, and should be completed before the arrangement begins.

Once the decision has been made and the child is coming to you, you will need to discuss with the parents how you are going to help the child settle. Ideally, if the parents are not going straight back to work, you might suggest that they bring the child for short periods of time, staying with the child and helping her to become familiar with your home environment, your family and the other children you look after. The child can be left with you for gradually longer periods. Remind the parents to bring the child's comfort object or a favourite toy in case their child becomes distressed. Use this opportunity to communicate fully with the parents, to find out all you can about the family and the way they like things done. Good communication will prevent problems arising, and any that do arise can be easily dealt with at an early stage.

CASE STUDY

Pauline is in her late twenties and is a first-time mother. She has to return to work for financial reasons and has settled her baby son of six months with Ruma, an experienced home-based childcarer. He is well, happy and thriving, but every morning Ruma observes Pauline crying as she walks down the road to the bus stop.

1 How can Ruma help Pauline?
2 Are there any outside organisations or professional workers that might be able to offer Pauline advice?

The legal framework

In recent years, there has been a great deal of legislation affecting children and their families and there have been many government initiatives. This has led to early intervention programmes to help children get a good start in life. Anyone working with children and their families must be aware of existing legislation; the knowledge will inform best practice and enable the home-based childcarer to be a professional source of information for parents.

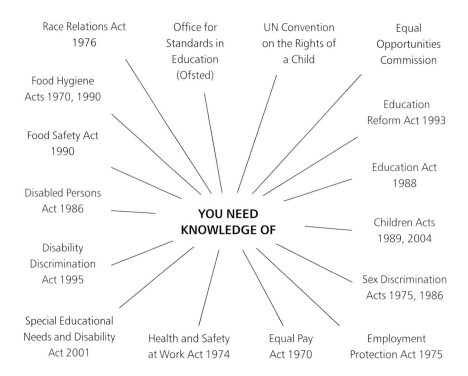

Race Relations Act 1976

Office for Standards in Education (Ofsted)

UN Convention on the Rights of a Child

Equal Opportunities Commission

Food Hygiene Acts 1970, 1990

Education Reform Act 1993

Food Safety Act 1990

Education Act 1988

Disabled Persons Act 1986

YOU NEED KNOWLEDGE OF

Children Acts 1989, 2004

Disability Discrimination Act 1995

Sex Discrimination Acts 1975, 1986

Special Educational Needs and Disability Act 2001

Health and Safety at Work Act 1974

Equal Pay Act 1970

Employment Protection Act 1975

The Children Act 1989 had a major impact on the law relating to children; it affects all children and their families. Much of the old law was abolished and the emphasis of the new law was that parents should have responsibilities for their children, rather than rights over them. Parental responsibility is defined as the rights, duties, powers, responsibilities and authority that, by law, a parent of a child has in relation to the child, and to his or her property.

The Children Act 1989 acknowledged the importance of the wishes of the child. Parental rights diminish as the child matures. Parental responsibility is a concept that is important when deciding who is in a position to make decisions about the child and who should be contacted in any legal proceedings.

Those who can hold parental responsibility are:

- the mother, who always has parental responsibility, whether married or not; she can only lose it when an adoption or freeing order is made
- the natural father, who has parental responsibility jointly with the natural mother if they are married to each other at the time of the child's birth or subsequently marry; he too can only lose it if an adoption or freeing order is made
- the unmarried father may acquire parental responsibility by agreement with the mother or by court order
- the step-parent can acquire parental responsibility by obtaining a residence order and will lose it if that order ends
- the local authority acquires parental responsibility when obtaining a care order or emergency protection order, and loses it when that order ends

others, such as grandparents, may acquire parental responsibility by court order, and will lose it when the order ends.

Parental responsibility may not be surrendered or transferred. It may be shared with a number of persons, and/or the local authority. Each individual having parental responsibility may act alone in exercising it, but not in a way that is incompatible with any court order made under the 1989 Act.

Every Child Matters

In January 2003, the Laming Report, looking at the death of Victoria Climbié, found that health, police and social services missed 12 opportunities to save her. In September 2003, the government published a green paper *Every Child Matters*, proposing:

- 150 children's trusts to be set up
- the amalgamation of health, education and social services
- a children's director to oversee local services
- statutory local children's boards to replace existing area child protection committees
- a children's commissioner for England
- an electronic tracking system for England's children.

'Child Protection cannot be separated from policies to improve children's lives as a whole. We need to focus both on the universal services which every child uses and on more targeted services for those with additional needs.'

(Laming Report, 2003)

The Children Act 2004 implemented the recommendations of the green paper *Every Child Matters*:

1. Children's commissioners are appointed in England, Wales, Scotland and Northern Ireland. The commissioners' job is to raise awareness of the best interests of children and young people and report annually to Parliament.
2. Local authorities have a duty to make arrangements to promote co-operation between agencies (social services, health, education and the justice system) in order to improve children's well-being. Key partners will have a duty to take part in these arrangements.
3. Key agencies that work with children have a duty to put in place arrangements to make sure that they take account of the need to safeguard and promote the welfare of children when doing their jobs.
4. Databases that contain basic information on young people to help professionals in working together to provide early support to children, young people and their families.
5. Local authorities required to set up statutory Local Safeguarding Children Boards and ensure that key partners take part.

6   Local authorities required to put in place a director of children's services and lead member to be responsible for, as a minimum, education and children's social services functions.

7   An integrated inspection framework and provision for regular joint area reviews to be carried out to look at how children's services as a whole operate across each local authority area.

Ofsted has responsibility for the registration and inspection of childcare. There is further information about this on pages 4–12. Local authorities still have responsibilities relating to childminding in their area. They are required to ensure that information and advice about registered childminding and other daycare is available to anyone who wants it. They must also arrange for training to be available to anyone who provides such services.

NCMA provides an online briefing sheet entitled 'Childminding and the Law', which gives a great deal of useful information.

Understanding various cultures and child-rearing practices

Family type

Children are brought up in many different types of families. These include:

- the nuclear family: a small family unit of parents and children, with no other family members living with them
- the extended family: this includes parents, children, and other family members who may live with the family or close by, and who are in frequent contact with each other
- the lone-parent family, sometimes known as the single- or one-parent family: the mother or father plus children. Roughly 90 per cent of these households are headed by the mother and 10 per cent by the father. Of the women, about 70 per cent are divorced or separated, 23 per cent are single and 7 per cent are widowed
- the reconstituted family, sometimes known as 'blended': parents have divorced or separated and remarried or are living with new partners and perhaps their children
- the homosexual family: two men or two women living together with the children of a previous heterosexual partnership or, in some gay relationships, their own children. The children may be adopted. None of the research carried out since the 1960s shows any differences in the social and emotional development of children living in these households, or in their gender orientation.

Other family types include communes, where many groups of people live together and support each other, and travellers, such as 'New Agers' and Romanies.

Various cultures

NCMA has stated that 'parents are central to children's lives and, in the interests of children's welfare, childminders should provide care which is consistent with that of home'.

Children's needs and parents' wishes may derive from a cultural or religious source or from medical reasons, or they may quite simply reflect what the parents want for their child. Parents' wishes and child-rearing practices must be respected and every effort made to comply with them.

Home-based childcarers and parents should discuss and reach agreement on matters relating to:

- food, its preparation and eating, e.g. whether it is to be meat free or certain meats are to be excluded
- personal hygiene, e.g. using the lavatory and hand-washing

- skin- and hair-care, e.g. which creams and combs are suitable for some African-Caribbean children
- the question of clothing during play, e.g. maintaining modesty in physical play, covering very curly or braided hair for sand play, or protecting skin against strong sunlight
- periods of rest and sleep, e.g. what routines, comfort objects or activities, such as massage, are expected
- any other expectations
- managing unwanted behaviour.

Do not assume that, because a family is part of a particular cultural group, they follow all the practices of that culture. It is essential to discuss all aspects of the child's care with the parents and find out what they want.

Activity

You are approached by a Muslim family who wish you to care for their three-year-old daughter and 18-month-old son.
1 What will you need to ask the parents?
2 How will you demonstrate to the parents that you can provide the care they wish for their children?

When parents explain what they want for their child, it may be necessary to discuss any compromises which have to be made in order to care for children from several different family backgrounds, and reach some compromise arrangements. Once agreement has been reached, respect the parents' wishes and stick to the practices agreed. Not to do this would represent a betrayal of the parents' trust and demonstrate a lack of respect for their views and child-rearing practices.

Building good relationships

To build a good relationship with parents, childcare practitioners need to acknowledge that:
- 99.9 per cent of parents love their children deeply and wish them to have the best care and education possible
- every family is unique with its own culture and parenting style
- carers only know their own family experience and should be careful in judging others
- the parent is the first point of contact for information about the child.

Accountability

Consistent approach to care and education

Shared understanding of children's needs

Common aims and sense of purpose

PARTNERSHIP MEANS

Mutual respect

Sharing skills

Negotiation

Discussion

Parents spend more time with their children than any professional carer and will know their child's strengths and weaknesses, anticipate her needs, and have made many decisions about their child long before the child starts any educational or care programme. Therefore, it is sensible to work with the parents in all aspects of decision making for the benefit of the child. It will also add to the security of the child to see parents and professionals working together, and in regular consultation.

Recent legislation has recognised the importance of parents as partners. The Education Reform Act 1988, the Children Act 1989 and the Special Educational Needs Code of Practice 2001 place a legal responsibility on all professionals in all sectors to work in partnership with parents. One of the ways in which the Early Years Foundation Stage promotes the *Every Child Matters* outcome is by creating a framework for partnership working between parents and professionals.

Your own attitude to the parents is crucial to building good relationships.

Activity

1 How would you describe a good parent?
2 How would you describe a bad parent?
3 Compare and discuss your list with others in your group. After discussion, would you amend your list?

1 Be sensitive to the range of family groupings that you encounter.
2 Make sure you ascertain the structures of the families of the children in your care in a tactful and open manner.
3 Do not make assumptions about the relationships within the family.
4 Be aware of stereotypical remarks and attitudes.
5 Never be judgmental about a child's family grouping.

Naming systems

You need to be aware that some cultural and religious groups have different ways of naming their children.

Most European children have a first name, possibly a middle name and a surname in that order. It is important not to impose this on other children because to do so would be disrespectful.

African names will differ from one ethnic group to another: for example, in the Igbo language of Nigeria the first daughter will be called Ada, literally 'daughter'. Other groups will name their children after the circumstances in which they were born. Traditionally, Africans do not have a family name, but most Africans in Britain will have adopted a surname that can be used for formal documentation.

The Chinese and Vietnamese communities use the family name first, followed by the middle name and then the personal name. Children take the family name of their father. Some have now reversed the order of their names to follow the British pattern, so care should be taken when filling in records.

Muslim boys of Pakistani and Bangladesh origin will often have a religious name before their personal names. Calling a boy Mohammed or Abdul, without adding the personal name, may well cause offence to observant Muslims, whereas in the Middle East Mohammed is a common personal name. Traditionally, there is no shared family name, but to conform with British naming patterns some families might adopt a surname. Many Muslim women have, in addition to their personal name, a title such as Begum, Bibi, or Nessa, which indicates that the person is female.

Sikhs place the personal name first. Common titles are Singh, meaning 'lion', for men, and Kaur, meaning 'Princess', for women. It would be inappropriate to address a Sikh woman as Miss or Mrs Singh, or the father as Mr Kaur. In Britain, some Sikh parents give their children a first name and a surname only.

British Hindus place the personal name first. The Hindu surname is a shared family name and indicates a family's traditional status and occupation.

If you are not sure how to address a child or a parent, ask. You would not like to be referred to continually by the wrong name. Remember that many names have religious or cultural significance.

Families under stress

The families of the children you look after might be feeling stress for many reasons. This might occur once the children have started with you, or be long standing. The parents may become:

- difficult to communicate with
- reluctant to fulfil the terms of their contract, such as being slow to pay you or unreliable about the time they should collect and deliver the child
- reluctant to discuss the needs of the child
- uninterested in the child's achievements
- depressed and unresponsive to offers of help
- angry and aggressive towards you.

The child might:

- be difficult to manage
- be clinging and fretful
- show anxiety at separation from the parents
- display mood swings, ranging from being withdrawn to being aggressive
- show an increase in comfort behaviour
- be reluctant to go home at the end of the day
- regress in development.

A situation in the family where the child you are caring for is obviously unhappy cannot be left to resolve itself. This is also true if the parents are taking advantage of your good nature and not contributing to a positive working relationship. If you find yourself in this position you will attempt to:

- acknowledge your feelings
- seek opportunities to communicate with the parents in a non-threatening, non-judgemental manner
- be open and assertive; state your needs to the parents
- keep calm if you have to deal with an angry parent; listen to what is being said and do not respond in an aggressive way
- keep meticulous records of the child's behaviour and incidents involving the parents
- employ stress-management techniques and persuade the parents to do the same
- advise the parents about sources of help and support in the community.

If you are unable to alter the situation and the parents continue to be stressed, making the child unhappy, you have no alternative but to contact your health visitor, local authority contact, or NCMA, making them conversant with the situation and asking for advice and support.

Tamila is a busy, experienced home-based carer who has been caring for Rosie, aged two, for the last three months. She has established a good working relationship with Rosie's mother. For the last month, Rosie's aunt has been collecting Rosie on a Wednesday. On the last two occasions, she has been very late and has smelt of alcohol. Tamila knows that Rosie's mother, who is a lone parent, has to work late on a Wednesday.

1 How do you think Tamila should handle this situation?
2 Describe any situations where a home-based childcarer might refuse to allow someone to collect a child.
3 How can Tamila support and advise Rosie's mother?

Good practice in . . . RELATING TO PARENTS

1 Respect all parents as individuals, and learn from them different ways of child-rearing. Their practice may be different from yours, but is no less valid. Be open to a variety of opinions.
2 Respect parents' values, practices and preferences.
3 Provide a welcoming and relaxed atmosphere in your home, encouraging parents to settle their children in and to spend time whenever they wish.
4 Avoid patronising parents. Remember they are the experts on their own individual children.
5 Try to communicate, at the end of the day, the important aspects of the child's day, sharing negative and positive situations alike.
6 Be professional at all times. Never gossip about parents to other parents. Refuse to listen to other people's unsubstantiated hearsay.
7 Offer reassurance and encouragement to parents, always emphasising the central role that they play in their children's lives.
8 Be clear about the service you are offering. The more time you spend in discussion with the parents prior to accepting the child, the less likely it is that there will be problems.

Reflecting on Practice

You might think about:

- how you make a good relationship with parents who have a different first language from you
- how you might work with parents to promote the child's confidence and self-esteem
- devising procedures for contact and collection, and complaints
- your parenting style and how it may differ from that of the parents you work with
- how you would recognise stress in the children or their parents
- how you might share information about their children with parents
- how you will involve and communicate with parents
- how you feel about mothers who work
- how you would handle confrontation over fees.

This chapter has contributed to the following learning outcomes:

Unit 1

- working in partnership with parents
- promoting anti-discriminatory, anti-bias practice in the home-based setting

Unit 4

- recognising different family structures and the importance of valuing different family types and traditions
- understanding how the home-based practitioner can promote positive relationships with all parents
- understanding contracts and how to deal with complaints
- understanding how to communicate effectively with parents

Want to Find Out More?

Websites

www.care.org.uk
www.everychildmatters.gov.uk
www.fatherhoodinstitute.org
www.fflag.org.uk
www.fnf.org.uk
www.oneparentfamilies.org.uk
www.opsi.gov.uk
www.parentlineplus.org.uk
www.practicalparent.org.uk
www.surestart.gov.uk

Further reading

EYTARN, *Partnership with Parents: An Anti-discriminatory Approach*, EYTARN, 1997

Hobart C., Frankel, J. and Walker M. (Series Editor), *A Practical Guide to Working with Parents*, 2nd Edition Nelson Thornes, 2009

Hylton C., *Black Families Talking,* Exploring Parenthood, 1997

Whalley M. and the Pen Green Centre Team, *Involving Parents in their Children's Learning*, 2nd Edition, Paul Chapman, 2007

Whalley M. and the Pen Green Centre Team, *Working With Parents*, Hodder and Stoughton, 1997

3

The needs of children

Learning objectives

Unit 1

- Establishing routines for home-based childcare
- Introducing children and their families to your home-based childcare service
- Promoting inclusion and anti-bias practice

Unit 2

- Providing for children's development and well-being

When caring for children, it is important to understand that a variety of needs have to be met before children are able to grow and develop satisfactorily and achieve their full potential. It is necessary to maintain a balance and adopt a holistic approach. This means taking into account all aspects of development, care and education and the interaction of one upon the other. Children belong to many diverse groups, with various values, religions, and approaches to child-rearing. All children need love and security, stimulation and education, routine physical care and the right to protection. You need to be aware of children's needs: with this awareness, and your knowledge of child development, you will be fully equipped to nurture the children's maximum growth and development.

Communicating regularly with the children's parents, building a relationship of trust and exchanging information, will keep you up to date with the changing needs of each child.

Establishing routines throughout the day and bearing in mind each child's particular needs will help to give the child confidence and security.

Developing relationships with children

You would not have become a home-based childcarer unless you enjoyed the company of children. Building trusting relationships does not happen overnight. You will have to work at it with every new child you take on.

A great deal will depend on your relationship with the child's parents. You will have spent some time getting to know them, reassuring them that you are a skilled professional worker, and that their child will be safe and well nurtured in your care. You will have gathered all the essential information that you need to know and answered all their questions about your practice. First impressions are important, and you will do your best to make sure that the parents and the child feel welcome in your home.

Settling in a new child needs a great deal of thought. Ideally, one or other of the parents will be able to stay for a while during the first week, and this will help the child to feel secure. The youngest babies will probably settle quite easily, but once babies are eight months old or so they may feel a great deal of anxiety and distress. The longer the parent can stay and share the care with you, the sooner the baby will feel secure and allow the parent to leave without fuss.

Older children vary a great deal in their response to a new environment. This is partly because of previous experiences and partly due to the personality of the child. A child who is finding it difficult to settle with you will be helped if the parent stays as long and as often as possible. It is sometimes helpful if you visit the child in his home, where he might see you as a family friend. When the parent has to go, he or she should do so quickly, as the longer the goodbyes are drawn out, the more distressing it can be for the child. On the other hand, parents must not sneak out, without the child seeing them, as this can lead to distrust and insecurity on the part of the child.

Once the parent has finally left, try to give the child as much of your attention as you can. Provide activities that are familiar to him and that do not require too much concentration and effort. In the first few days, he could perhaps bring one or two treasured toys from home. Check that he has his comfort object with him and that it is available to him whenever he needs it. He may demand cuddles and hugs, and you will need to respond to this. Remember that some children do not like close physical contact with anyone except their parents, and this should be respected.

After a little while, the new child will have fitted well into your home and this is the time to develop a loving, caring relationship. Children have many emotional needs and you will play an important part in helping them to develop emotional strengths and in enabling them to reach adulthood, confident in themselves and valuing their achievements.

From the moment of birth, the baby begins the process of attachment, bonding with the mother in the same way as the mother bonds with the baby. This love and mutual trust is the basis of emotional development, allowing the child to continue to make loving and trusting relationships with other members of the family, with you and, later, with the outside world.

Settling a child successfully into a new situation often needs careful handling. The birth of a new baby may lead to feelings of jealousy and rejection. Problems within the child's family, such as divorce, unemployment, death or addiction may distress the child and halt his emotional development, causing the child to regress and become emotionally less mature. An understanding of the stages of emotional development is a critical factor in ensuring best practice.

You can support children by sensitively preparing them for transitions in their life in a way that is appropriate to their age. Strategies can include:

- talking about what will happen as well listening to children's concerns
- arranging short visits to new settings prior to attendance in the company of a familiar, trusted adult
- reading relevant story books, leaflets, watching DVDs, etc. to become more familiar with the change (for instance, a story about going to hospital or starting school)
- allowing opportunities for children to express feelings through imaginative and expressive play
- giving children opportunities to experience increasing independence in line with their needs and abilities.

You probably feel that you know what children need, perhaps because you have had your own. Looking after other people's children requires a more professional approach, and, as you are in touch with more children, you will gain a wider knowledge and understanding of the wide range of needs that children exhibit.

Routines

Routines are regular events, organised and planned within the day, such as hygiene practices, mealtimes, nap times, exercise and play. It is impossible to generalise and describe a home-based childcarer's day, as each one will be unique. Much depends on the ages and the number of the children, your established family routines, and personal preferences. Obviously, if you are caring for a school-age child, one of your routines will be taking and collecting him from school.

In your home, television programmes may be part of your routine. When used wisely, television is a useful educational tool, which also allows you to have a short time to relax. Be very selective in the programmes you allow the children to watch. It is a good idea to record some programmes, such as *MI High* or *Roary the Racing Car*, and have them available to show the children at a time that suits you. The children will gain more from watching if you are with them to answer questions and to help them participate.

Undoubtedly, you will have to fit some domestic routines into your busy day, such as preparing food for the children and clearing up after meals. Encourage the children to help you, as this will lead to independence and teach them how to clear up after themselves. Many routine tasks can contribute to children's development and learning. For example, walking to school presents an opportunity for exercise and conversation and may expand the child's knowledge of the outside world.

Ideally, routines should take place at the same time each day, so that, knowing what to expect, the young child feels secure. A home-based childcarer who is constantly changing her daily routines, and allowing herself to be overwhelmed by events, will find the children she is caring for becoming fractious or even distressed. For this reason, you will need to arrange your routines carefully, allowing enough time for each one. Although they will be less tightly scheduled, you will also need to reflect on weekly routines, such as on what day Johnny has a music lesson; on monthly routines, which might include a major shopping trip or getting your children's hair cut;

and yearly routines, such as preparing for inspection or managing summer holidays, when everyone's holidays would have to be worked out. Time management is an issue for all home-based childcarers. A home-based childcarer's day can be very busy and complex, and time should be built in for unforeseen events and for giving 'quality time' to individual children. This must be remembered when you are considering taking on additional children.

Activity

Think about all your routines. Devise a weekly and monthly chart showing your essential routines. How do these match the needs of the children?

Physical care routines

Some routines require physical care. These include skin- and hair-care, sleep and rest, exercise, mealtimes, care of the teeth, and hygiene practices, such as hand-washing and toileting. Most children need adult help and supervision in their personal care requirements. Good standards of care are important to prevent ill health, to increase self-esteem and gain acceptance by other children. The eventual goal is for the children to become independent and care for all their physical needs themselves.

Care of the skin and hair

The skin has many significant functions, including:

- preventing injury to the internal organs

- preventing infection entering the body
- tactile awareness of hot and cold, and hard and soft
- the secretion of sebum to lubricate the hair, and keep the skin soft and flexible
- regulation of body temperature
- disposal of waste products from the body in sweat
- a role in producing vitamin D through exposure to sunlight, which is important for healthy bone growth.

Too much cleaning of the skin, particularly by scrubbing, removes the sebum and may make the skin dry and cracked.

Home-based childcarers should:

- ensure that the children wash their hands and faces before and after handling and eating food
- wash their hands after using the lavatory and after messy play
- observe the skin for any rashes or sores
- play a part in moisturising the skin of black children, taking advice from parents
- protect the skin from excessive exposure to the sun, using hats, sun block or high-factor sun-cream (after checking with parents)
- play a part in treating skin problems, such as eczema and sweat rash, following discussion with the parents.

Hair will vary in colour, texture and style. There can be strong religious and cultural practices associated with care of the hair. Rastafarians, for example, will have long strands of braided hair, tied together; the girls will cover the hair with a scarf and the boys with a hat.

Activity

In what other religions is hair of significance? Why do you think this is so?

You are unlikely to have to wash children's hair unless it becomes very dirty following messy play. If you do, use a non-stinging gentle shampoo, rinse the hair well, and avoid using the hair-dryer. Prevention is better than cure, so have at hand some shower caps for the children to wear when playing with sand, or with any other very messy material.

Care of the teeth

Home-based childcarers, in consultation with parents, play a part in encouraging good dental hygiene. They will:

- encourage children to brush their teeth after meals, using their own brush and a fluoride toothpaste
- provide a healthy diet, low in sugar, high in vitamins and calcium
- avoid giving sweet drinks, especially in a bottle or on a dummy
- restrict giving sweets to children

- not give sweet snacks between meals
- provide food, such as apples, carrots and brown bread, that has to be chewed.

One of the children may have a dentist's appointment in the near future. In partnership with the parents, prepare him carefully, discussing what is likely to happen, perhaps finding a book at the library about visiting the dentist. If you are nervous at the dentist, be careful not to pass any of your fears and anxieties on to the child.

Sleep and rest

Sleep allows the body to rest and recover from its exertions, so it is important that children are encouraged to rest after vigorous physical exercise. Sleep consists of deep relaxing sleep and, when we dream, rapid eye movement (REM) sleep. It is thought that children use REM sleep to make sense of their day, and if they are woken at this time they may become drowsy and disorientated.

Like adults, children appear to need differing amounts of sleep. You will need to discuss the sleep routines of babies and children with their parents, and, where it is compatible with your other commitments, you should attempt to follow this routine. You must remember that, as the child is having a different and possibly busier day, he might require a nap, even if this is against the wishes of the parents, and you will need to discuss his sleep needs with them.

Some children need to unwind and relax before they are able to sleep and may need a comfort object to take with them for their rest. Even if children do not sleep during the day, there should still be a quiet period when they can look at books or just have a cuddle.

Activity

How do you prepare children for their rest? Do you use any particular strategies?

Exercise and fresh air

All children need exposure to fresh air and the opportunity to exercise during the day. This will:

- increase their oxygen intake
- reduce their exposure to the risk of infection
- increase their exposure to sunlight – needed for the production of vitamin D
- develop physical skills and co-ordination
- improve muscle tone and strengthen muscles
- burn up body fat
- enable them to sleep better
- improve their digestive and respiratory systems.

Allowing children to exercise every day will help them to establish this as a habit for life and may prevent future heart disease and obesity. Access to a garden is obviously a great help in promoting fresh air and exercise, but even without one, it is possible to take the children to a park or playground regularly.

Toilet training

There are many different theories and methods of toilet training, and you will need to discuss this fully with the parents before you take on the child. Toilet training can be a cause of friction between you and the parents who often do not realise that a consistent approach is vital for success. You might find the following general guidelines useful (from Miranda Walker, *Children's Care, Learning and Development Level 3*, 2009).

It is important that toilet training does not become an issue of conflict between children and adults. To avoid conflict and stress, it is best to take a relaxed approach, waiting until the individual child is showing definite signs of being ready for training before attempting the process. Although children may have control as early as 18 months, many children will be into their second year before they show signs of readiness. Some will be older. The signs include:

- children saying they are about to soil or wet their nappy
- children telling a carer that their nappy needs changing
- children showing an interest in the toilet or potty, or in other children's use of them
- children showing reluctance to wear a nappy
- children saying they want to wear pants
- children being able to tell adults that they need to use the toilet, verbally or with signs.

It is good practice to ensure that you have the right equipment for toilet training, including:

- a child-sized toilet or potty, or a child's toilet seat that fits inside a normal toilet seat. It is advisable to introduce children to these prior to training, so have them in the bathroom. Children who already use the toilet or potty can be good role models, helping other children to understand their use

- soft toilet paper
- plenty of spare clothes
- children may wet through everything they are wearing, including socks and shoes
- materials for cleaning up both children and the environment after accidents.

Good-practice guidelines for toilet training are:

- Plan your approach to training in consultation with parent and carers. Some may ask your advice but others may be clear about the approach they would like to take.
- Be relaxed about training, and do not rush children. Otherwise children may become anxious or toilet training may become a battle. Praise children for using the toilet or potty. Deal with any accidents without fuss, and in private, getting children into clean clothes as soon as possible. Do not make children feel bad or embarrassed about having accidents by showing disapproval.
- Most libraries stock children's books that show characters using the toilet or potty. There are several that show children learning the skill and being praised. They can be useful to read with children who are toilet training, particularly if they do not have another child as a role model.

Good practice in . . . ENCOURAGING PERSONAL HYGIENE IN CHILDREN

1 Home-based childcarers should be a positive role model.
2 Establish routines that promote hygiene.
3 Make hygiene fun, by putting toys in the bath, having 'fun' toothbrushes and flavoured toothpaste.
4 Give each child his or her own flannel, toothbrush, towel and comb. Colour coding these is a good idea, to make sure they are kept separate.
5 Provide a footstool, so that the younger children can reach the basin comfortably and sit on the lavatory without fear of falling.
6 Teach children to care for themselves, and encourage independence in routines.

Nutrition

It is important for you to have a good understanding of nutrition and how to provide a well-balanced diet for the children in your care. A healthy nutritious diet plays a large part in promoting health, and in ensuring healthy development. The way you cook and eat, and the food you provide, will help the children to develop sensible eating patterns and will encourage children to try various types of food.

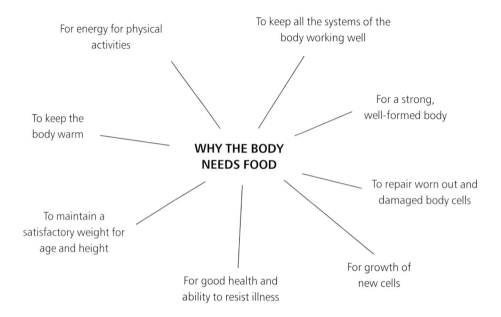

For energy for physical activities

To keep all the systems of the body working well

To keep the body warm

For a strong, well-formed body

WHY THE BODY NEEDS FOOD

To repair worn out and damaged body cells

To maintain a satisfactory weight for age and height

For growth of new cells

For good health and ability to resist illness

A healthy diet

Food consists of substances known as nutrients. Without food we could not exist. The main nutrients in food and drink are:

- carbohydrates
- fibre
- proteins
- fats
- vitamins
- minerals
- water.

Proteins, carbohydrates, fats and water are present in large amounts in our food and are known as macro-nutrients. Vitamins and minerals are only present in small amounts and are known as micro-nutrients.

Macro-nutrients comprise:

- Carbohydrates, which are sugars and starches. Carbohydrates provide the body with the main source of energy for immediate use. Examples are potatoes, flour, pasta, rice and sweet foods. Excess of these, particularly sweet foods, can lead to weight gain. When more is eaten than the body can use it is changed into body fat and stored.
- Fibre, a type of carbohydrate that we need in our diet, but which we do not digest. Fibre helps the food to pass through the body more quickly and protects the body from some diseases.

- Protein, which is needed for growth and repair of the body and forms a large part of the body's muscle tissue. It is particularly important for children, so as to build brain and muscle tissue. Protein is found in meats, fish, poultry, dairy foods and vegetables. Animal protein provides all the chemical elements (amino acids) necessary for growth and repair of the body. Vegetable proteins by themselves do not provide all the amino acids necessary, and have to be mixed. Pulses, cereals, nuts and grains all need to be eaten by vegetarians.
- Fats, which provide energy for the body in a more concentrated form than carbohydrates, and weight for weight contain more calories. Fats are needed to maintain the body's cell structures and provide warmth. They are found in meat, eggs, oils, and dairy produce. Fat found in animals is high in saturated fats (those fats that become solid at room temperature), and if too much is eaten can be linked with heart disease. Fats found in plants are liquid at room temperature and are found in oils made from seeds and fruits, such as olives and corn. We all need to eat some fat, but if adults eat too much it turns into body fat. Children must have a certain amount of fat in their diet to make sure they are getting the fat-soluble vitamins that can be stored in the body, vitamins A, D, E and K.
- Water, which is essential for life. Your body consists of 70–80 per cent water, or two-thirds of the body weight. Water helps to get rid of the poisons produced in the body. We need water to replace that lost from the body in sweat, urine, breathing and solid body waste. Water that is lost from the body must be replaced and children should be encouraged to drink several glasses of water a day. More people in the world are ill or die because of a lack of clean water, rather than from a lack of food.

Micro-nutrients comprise:

- vitamins that are needed to help your body work correctly and help to control the body systems, such as the circulation of blood, digestion, and so on (see page 64).
- minerals that help to control the body chemistry, such as the production of blood cells, and are also used in growth and repair (see page 65).

Lack of vitamins and minerals can cause deficiency diseases: for example, a lack of iron may result in anaemia.

Vitamin	Main source	Function	Notes
Fat-soluble vitamins that can be stored in the body			
A	Carrots, spinach, fish liver oils, tomatoes, butter, cheese	Good vision, healthy skin	Avoid excess if pregnant
D	Oily fish, liver, cod liver oil, egg yolk Added to margarine and milk	Healthy bones and teeth	Can be made in the skin if it is exposed to sunlight
E	Vegetable oils, egg yolk, cereals, nuts, seeds	Aids healing and blood clotting	Poorly understood at present
K	Leafy green, vegetables, liver, whole grains	Essential for blood clotting	
Water-soluble vitamins that cannot be stored in the body and must be eaten every day			
B 1, 2, 5, 6, 12	Yeast, rice, fish, meat, green vegetables, beans, eggs	Healthy nerves and muscles Needed for making red blood cells	
C	Citrus fruits, green vegetables	Needed to help hold body cells together For healthy skin and tissue Helps healing	

Mineral	Main source	Function	Notes
Calcium	Milk, cheese, fish, yoghurt, eggs, pulses, hard water	Needed for healthy bones and teeth	Works with vitamin D
Fluoride	Found in water in some areas Added to water, toothpaste	Helps tooth enamel to resist decay	——
Iodine	Water, seafish, shellfish Added to salt	Helps efficient working of the thyroid gland	——
Iron	Red meat, liver, eggs, cocoa, green vegetables, apricots	Needed for the production of red blood cells	Helped by vitamin C
Phosphorus	Most foods, especially fish, eggs, meat, fruit and vegetables	Needed for healthy bones and teeth Helps to absorb carbohydrate	——
Potassium	Leafy vegetables, fruit, liver, meat, milk, cereals	Helps to maintain fluid balance Needed for nerve and muscle activity	——
Sodium chloride	Salt, fish, meat, bread, bacon, processed foods	Needed for the production of body fluids, blood, sweat and tears	Salt should NOT be added to food for babies and young children

A balanced diet consists of a variety of foods from all the above nutrients. Care must be taken not to overeat, particularly saturated fats and sugars, but to eat sufficient to meet your needs. The more energetic you are, the more calories (units of energy) you will burn up, and the more food you will need. Energy is required by all living things to maintain the changes and chemical reactions that occur in the body (metabolism).

Foods that have little water and a high proportion of fat or carbohydrate have a high energy value. Children need more kilocalories because their bodies are growing and they use a lot of energy. The kilocalories required will vary according to age, gender, size, physical activity and climate.

The following diagram from *A Practical Guide to Child Nutrition*, by Angela Dare and Margaret O'Donovan, shows clearly how a balanced diet promotes health and development.

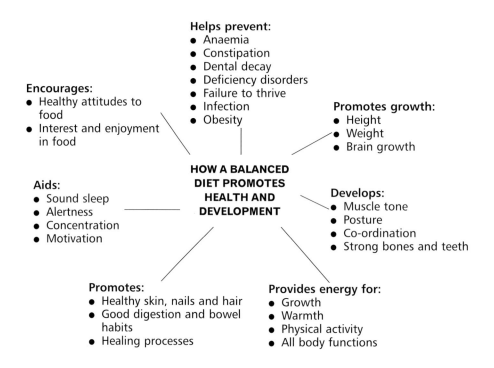

A variety of fresh foods, from the following food groups, should be offered to children every day in adequate amounts:

- bread, cereal, rice and pasta
- vegetables and fruits
- fats and sugars
- milk, yoghurt and cheese
- meat, poultry, fish, eggs, beans and pulses.

To allow for their healthy growth and development, children have different food needs from adults. No single food can supply all the nutrients required by a child.

Milk is an important food for children as it contains all the major nutrients needed, except for iron and vitamin C. Drinking too much milk may reduce the appetite for other important foods.

Children need a certain amount of fat in their diet to provide energy and the necessary vitamins. It is as well to offer less fat from animal sources and more vegetable fat: for example, by frying food with oil instead of butter. Too much animal fat in the diet may lead to heart problems in later life.

Water is an important nutrient and should be offered several times a day, instead of sugared drinks.

Fibre is necessary in preventing constipation. Fibre is found in brown rice, wholemeal bread and pasta, baked beans, pulses, potato skins, fruit and vegetables. Small children find it difficult to digest a great deal of fibre and should never be given a high-fibre diet, but it can be offered in small amounts as a snack.

Fruits and vegetables are good sources of vitamins, minerals and fibre, especially when eaten raw. A variety is necessary, as they all contain different vitamins. It is recommended that everyone should eat at least five portions of fruits and vegetables every day, whether these are fresh, frozen or tinned.

Breads and cereals, especially whole grain products, are an important source of vitamin B and iron and supply some protein.

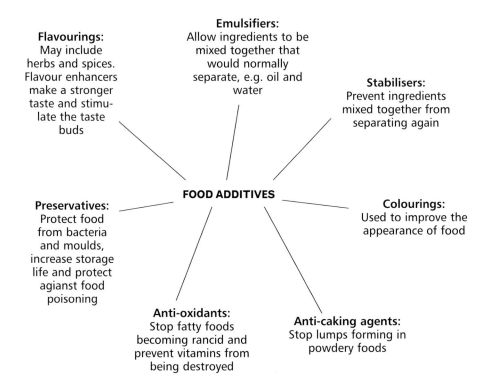

Flavourings:
May include herbs and spices. Flavour enhancers make a stronger taste and stimulate the taste buds

Emulsifiers:
Allow ingredients to be mixed together that would normally separate, e.g. oil and water

Stabilisers:
Prevent ingredients mixed together from separating again

Preservatives:
Protect food from bacteria and moulds, increase storage life and protect agianst food poisoning

FOOD ADDITIVES

Colourings:
Used to improve the appearance of food

Anti-oxidants:
Stop fatty foods becoming rancid and prevent vitamins from being destroyed

Anti-caking agents:
Stop lumps forming in powdery foods

3 chapter

Nuts provide protein but can be a safety hazard for young children, because of the risk of choking. Parents should be asked if a child has an allergy to nuts including peanut butter. Some children may be allergic to other foods, such as strawberries and shellfish.

There are concerns about the use of food additives. These are usually chemicals that are added to food to stop it from going bad and help it to look and taste good. It is thought that some additives contribute to hyperactivity and allergies. Parents should advise you if they wish you to exclude certain foods from their child's diet. Many processed foods and drinks contain a considerable number of additives, including salt and sugar. Looking at the labels will inform you of the amount and type of additives used in the product.

There is a view that some children, particularly the younger ones, or children who are unwell, benefit if they eat little and often. Snacks should certainly be offered if children are hungry, but try to discourage children from snacking less than two hours before a meal as it might spoil their appetite for the main meal. Some examples of wholesome and enjoyable snacks are:

- water, milk and fresh fruit juices (diluted with water to prevent tooth decay)
- fresh fruit
- dried fruit such as apricots (good source of iron), prunes and figs
- vegetable sticks, such as carrots, celery and cucumber
- hummus
- yoghurt
- crackers
- oatmeal biscuits
- rice cakes.

Use sugar in moderation, as sugar can lead to tooth decay and obesity. If you are cooking with the children, try to cook something other than cakes and biscuits. Salt should be used sparingly in cooking and should not be put on the table for children to help themselves.

It is quite common these days for families to be vegetarian and exclude meat and perhaps fish from the diet. There are various types of vegetarians, some of whom eat quite restricted diets:

- lacto-ovo-vegetarians eat plant foods, dairy products and eggs; this is the usual vegetarian diet
- lactovegetarians eat plant foods and dairy products, but no eggs
- vegans eat no animal product of any kind
- fruitarians eat only fruit, including nuts and seeds
- some people eat a Zen macro-biotic diet, based on whole grain cereals and pulses.

Problems rarely arise with the first two diets. A vegan diet is adequate with a supplement of vitamin B12. The last two diets are not adequate for babies and children.

During your initial meeting with the parents, they will have told you of any special dietary requirements. You will need to have a good knowledge of special diets and understand why these are necessary; this is covered in Chapter 10.

Eating is a basic human need and an activity that most people enjoy. It serves more than the need to survive and is tied into feelings of well-being. Eating at the table is a social activity, a time when relaxed conversations can take place, and news of the day is shared.

Children's eating behaviour

Children's eating patterns develop from infancy and are shaped by their experiences. The parents' and carers' attitude to food is most influential. Adults might show concern and anxiety if a child refuses food, because they worry that the child might not thrive without what they feel is sufficient food. They might feel rejected that the meal they have prepared with such loving care has been refused. The child may come to the conclusion that whether he eats or not is of very great importance and therefore has a way of manipulating adults.

Provide a range of utensils for all the children, and they should then become skilled at using chopsticks and knives and forks. 'Table manners' are more important in some families than in others. It is up to you what behaviour you tolerate at the table. Remember that some cultures do not have the words in their language for 'please' and 'thank you'.

Appetites differ in children and are unpredictable. Children know their own hunger signs and it is more sensible to offer smaller portions and provide more if the child requests it. If children say they are hungry in the middle of the morning, it is wiser to offer them a snack of fruit or raw vegetables, as filling up on milk, bread or biscuits will reduce the appetite for the midday meal.

Children have a shorter attention span than adults. Some find it very hard to sit, and it might be a good idea to allow them to leave the table when they have finished, providing a quiet activity for them so that they do not disturb the children who are slower. Allow children to eat at their own pace within limits.

Some children cause anxiety because they may:

- refuse to eat many foods
- linger for a long time over food
- refuse to swallow food
- display other poor eating behaviours.

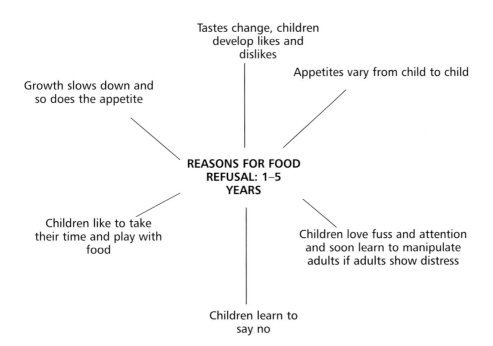

If a child is causing anxiety, make a record of what food is being refused, how he behaves at the table, such as crying, complaining or throwing food, and what food he enjoys. Evaluate this information. You may see a pattern, such as too many snacks prior to the meal, and be able to resolve the problem. If the behaviour persists after you feel the child has settled with you, and there is no obvious reason, you will need to involve the parents and discuss how he eats at home.

CASE STUDY

Summi has recently registered as a home-based childcarer and has her own child of nine months. She has started to care for Ben, aged two and a half years. She worked very hard at making a relationship with Ben's mother, and the settling-in period has gone well. There appears to be one concern: Ben sits at the table for long periods of time, chewing the same mouthful of food over and over again. He leaves the table with most of the food still on the plate; the rest is still in his mouth and is later found in various places around the house.

1 Explain why this is a worrying situation.
2 Should Summi inform the parents?
3 Why do you think Ben treats food in this way?
4 How can Summi help Ben to enjoy his food more?

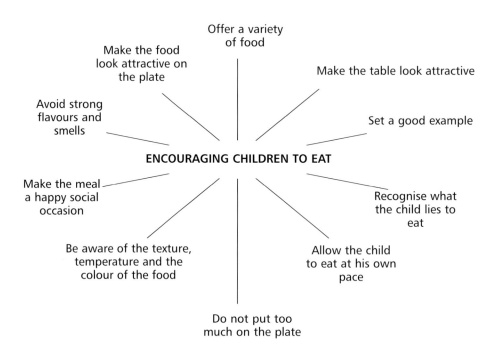

There is a fashion today for some parents to allow their children to 'graze'. This means eating continually, on demand, and usually walking around with the food. As a home-based childcarer, it is unlikely that you will be able to tolerate this, and you need to make this clear to the parents. Children are adaptable, and will probably accept your rules about eating food in your home.

How do you involve children in the preparation and clearing away of food? Why is this important?

Good practice in . . . ENCOURAGING HEALTHY EATING HABITS

1 Let children help themselves to food at mealtimes.
2 Allow children to help prepare food on occasions.
3 Encourage children to set the table and clear it.
4 Talk to children during the meal about the foods.
5 Encourage children to help mop up any spills.
6 Present food in an interesting way, mixing colours, flavours and textures.
7 Make your table look attractive, with a clean cloth and perhaps a small jug of flowers.
8 Encourage children to try new foods, presenting one new food at a time, when they are not tired or ill.
9 Set a good example by sitting at the table with the children, and showing your enjoyment of the food.

10 Never force children to eat new foods.
11 Never make children finish what is on their plates, or insist they sit at the table until they do so.
12 Make nutritious puddings as part of the meal and never use them as a reward or punishment.
13 Let children eat at their own pace.
14 Ignore fussy behaviour and praise hearty appetites.

Providing a healthy diet

When planning the meals, you must discuss the menu with the parents, as there are cultural, religious and medical concerns about certain foods and such foods may not be acceptable to the family. You should respect any requests made by the parents, showing them the weekly menus and abiding by their wishes. Do not assume, because a child comes from a certain culture or religion, that the family will necessarily pursue the prescribed food regime. If you find it difficult to provide the diet requested by the family, ask them to bring in the food for the child. Never agree a certain diet and then ignore it. See page 73 for information on dietary customs.

Activity

How do you make sure that you offer children in your care a balanced, nutritious diet?

In recent years there have been a number of health education campaigns relevant to children's nutrition, notably:

- The programme 5 A DAY. This promotes eating five pieces of fresh fruit and vegetables each day.
- The Birth to Five guide. A free booklet given to new parents. It introduces child health, safety and nutrition in the early years.
- Change4Life Campaign. A campaign to encourage and support families to make small changes to eat well, move more and live longer. Families can join online and they will then receive a welcome pack.

The government's nutrition site also gives regularly updated advice on all aspects of nutrition for everyone, from babies to adults. See page 75 for weblinks.

DIETARY CUSTOMS

Food	Jewish	Sikh	Muslim	Hindu	Buddhist	7th Day Adventist	Rastafarian	Roman Catholic	Mormon
Eggs	No blood spots	✓	✓	Some	Some	Most	✓	✓	✓
Milk/yoghurt	Not with meat	✓	Not made with rennet	Not made with rennet	✓	Most	✓	✓	✓
Cheese	Not with meat	Some	Some	Some	✓	Most	✓	✓	✓
Chicken	Kosher	Some	Halal	Some	✗	Some	Some	Some still prefer not to eat meat on Fridays particularly during Lent	✓
Mutton/lamb	Kosher	✓	Halal	Some	✗	Some	Some		✓
Beef	Kosher	✗	Halal	✗	✗	Some	Some		✓
Pork	✗	Rarely	✗	Rarely	✗	✗	✗		✓
Fish	With scales, fins and back-bone	Some	Halal	With fins and scales	Some	Some	✓	✓	✓
Shellfish	✗	Some	Halal	Some	✗	✗	✗	✓	✓
Animal fats	Kosher	Some	Some halal	Some	✗	✗	Some	✓	✓
Alcohol	✓	✓	✗	✗	✗	✗	✗	✓	✗
Cocoa/tea/coffee	✓	✓	✓	✓	✓ No milk	✗	✓	✓	✗
Nuts	✓	✓	✓	✓	✓	✓	✓	✓	✓
Pulses	✓	✓	✓	✓	✓	✓	✓	✓	✓
Fruit	✓	✓	✓	✓	✓	✓	✓	✓	✓
Vegetables	✓	✓	✓	✓	✓	✓	✓	✓	✓
Fasting (where not specified, fasting is a matter of individual choice)	Yom Kippur		Ramadan						24 hours once monthly

✓ Accepted   ✗ Forbidden

Adapted from *Nutritional Guidelines*, ILEA, 1985

Write a menu for three children, aged between three and five years, for five days. One of the children is vegetarian. Roughly calculate the cost of the food.

Some children that you care for may be on a special diet worked out by a doctor and dietitian according to the individual needs of the child. The table below shows some common disorders that require special diets.

Condition	Description	Diet
Coeliac disease	Sensitivity to gluten, a protein found in wheat, rye, barley and oats. Child fails to thrive	Exclude all foods containing gluten. Can eat fresh fruit and vegetables, fish, meat and dairy produce
Cystic fibrosis	An inherited condition, sticky thick mucus is found in the lungs and digestive system. Interferes with the digestion of food	Tablets given to help the digestion. Needs a high protein, high calorie diet
Diabetes	The body fails to produce enough insulin to control the amount of sugar in the body	Regular meals, diet carefully balanced and controlled. May need a snack before exercise, should be observed closely
Obesity	Overweight for height and age	Plan, offer and encourage a healthy balanced diet. Discourage over-eating. Encourage daily exercise
Anaemia	Lack of iron in the diet. Can also be caused by severe blood loss	A diet high in red meat, liver, eggs, cocoa, green vegetables, apricots, helped by taking Vitamin C at the same time
Cows' milk allergy: • to protein • lactose (milk sugar) intolerance	Associated with family history of allergy. Can result in wheezing, diarrhoea, vomiting, rashes, abdominal pain and tiredness	Special formula milk for babies. Substitute milks for older children. Avoid cows' milk, cheese and yoghurt

All the children in your care, whatever their age, need your affection, consistency of care, understanding and an opportunity to play and learn. Respecting children's individual needs will increase the bond between you and their family.

This chapter has contributed to the following learning outcomes:

Unit 1

- providing a variety of suitable routines for children in the home-based setting
- planning and providing appropriate play and other activities for children in the home-based setting
- promoting anti-discriminatory, anti-bias practice in the home-based setting

Unit 2

- providing for children's development and well-being from birth to 16 years

Want to Find Out More?

Websites

www.eatwell.gov.uk
www.foodcomm.org.uk
www.nhs.uk/Change4Life

www.sustainweb.org/childrensfoodcampaign
www.ukfoodguide.net/

Further reading

Beaver M. et al., *CACHE Child Care and Education Level 2 Candidate Handbook*, Nelson Thornes, 2008

Bowlby J. and Fry M., *Child Care and the Growth of Love*, New Edition, Penguin, 1990

Dare A. et al., *A Practical Guide to Child Nutrition*, 3rd Edition, Nelson Thornes, 2009

Keene A., *Child Health: Care of the Child in Health and Illness*, Nelson Thornes, 1999

Kurtz Z. and Bahl V. (eds), *The Health and Health Care of Children and Young People from Minority Ethnic Groups in Britain*, NCB with the DoH, 1997

Leach P., *Babyhood: Infant Development from Birth*, New Edition, Penguin, 1991

4

Children's development and learning

This chapter includes:

- Developmental stages
- Frameworks for understanding childcare and development
- Play
- Activities with children

Learning objectives

Unit 1

- Providing play and other activities for children in the home-based setting
- Promoting inclusion and anti-bias practice

Unit 2

- Providing for children's development and well-being

Unit 5

- Preparing, implementing and evaluating plans for home-based groups of children of different ages and abilities

Research has shown that close partnership between parent and carer encourages children's learning and development and extends their concentration and attention span. The amount of time the child spends in your care makes your role critical. A willingness to share information and discuss issues with the parents can help to identify possible concerns. Sharing your pleasure when milestones are achieved is good for the child's self-esteem, and helps to strengthen the partnership with the family.

Developmental stages

Children develop at different rates, and you may find that one of the children you look after might be advanced physically, being well co-ordinated and able to hop and jump at an early age, whereas others might be making more progress in language development than you would expect. Children vary in the age they attain a skill, but all development proceeds in stages. For example, a child learning to walk always goes through the following stages (see page 78):

- acquiring head control
- sitting with support
- sitting without support
- pulling to stand
- walking with support
- acquiring balance and walking.

Some children walk at ten months or even earlier; others may be delayed until 18 months or later, whilst the majority walk between 12 and 15 months. This is all within a normal range.

Development has been categorised under five areas: social, physical, intellectual, communication and emotional (SPICE). See Appendix A.

Social development

A human being is born without any social skills and becoming a social being is learnt initially in the family and then in the wider environment. Feral children who are brought up by animals in the wild, or those children locked away with no human contact, not only do not develop socially but do not develop physical skills, such as walking, and do not have any recognisable language. The existence of these children indicates clearly that all children need human contact to develop normally so that they can take their place in society.

Social development takes place alongside emotional development, and the importance of the environment cannot be over-emphasised. You will need to have a clear understanding of the stages and sequences of the child's developing relationships within society, the process of socialisation both within and outside the family, and the development of the child's social skills.

In our multi-cultural society, there is a variety of cultures with varying beliefs and values. Knowledge of these cultures will help you to appreciate the richness of the society and the difficulties sometimes encountered by children who are coping with more than one value system and many customs at a very young age.

Activity

Find out if any of the families you work with will be celebrating any major religious festivals during the next year. What might you do to help them celebrate?

Physical development

Physical development describes the acquisition of skills, such as the gross motor skills of running, sitting and throwing, all of which are to do with movement, and fine motor skills, such as feeding, threading and picking up objects, which are dependent on manipulation and hand–eye co-ordination.

Gaining physical skills is dependent on the opportunity for practice and the encouragement of the carer. The development of gross motor skills starts with head control and works down the body, the child learning to sit, perhaps crawl, pull up and walk. She learns to balance and then to hop and skip. Fine motor skills are linked with vision. These skills begin in the centre of the body, working outwards to the fingers, which increasingly take on more complex tasks.

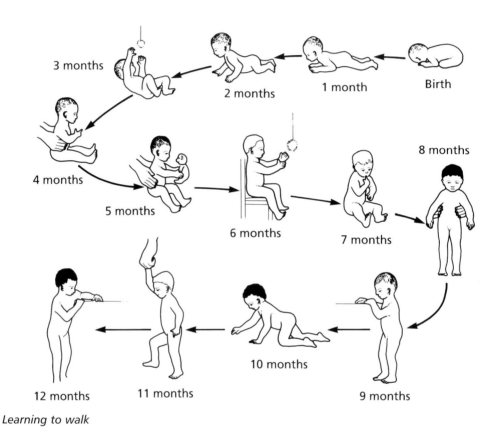

Learning to walk

Physical development is often linked with growth, which is measurable, and relates to an increase in weight, height and head circumference. Potential growth is mainly genetically determined, although the environment will play its part. Better diet has resulted in taller and heavier people in most parts of the developed world. Babies are measured at birth, and this measurement is used as a baseline for subsequent monitoring.

Intellectual (cognitive) development

Intellectual development, sometimes called cognitive development, describes the way in which we learn to think. It encompasses the ability to concentrate, memorise and understand information gained through the senses. As children develop intellectually, they are able to think logically and creatively and to relate past learning to solving present problems. There are many theories that show how this takes place, but most would agree that learning happens in stages and in a particular sequence, so it is important to recognise these stages and to encourage development in areas where learning is delayed.

Some theorists believe that most cognitive ability is inherited, whereas others think that the influence of the environment is more important. Piaget, the most influential of the theorists, argues that it is both.

4 chapter

1 Reflect on some of the children you have cared for, and perhaps your own children. Do you think that intelligence is most influenced by inheritance or by the encouragement and stimulation of the parents and others who cared for and educated the children?

2 Describe two activities that you provide for children to help extend their concentration span.

Children's learning is aided by opportunities to observe adults and other children and to observe and explore their world, by extending their language and by using their senses to the full. You will need to provide activities appropriate to the age of each child, so as to promote, encourage and extend children's learning and imagination. You will need to be conversant with the development of language and how this links with intellectual development.

Communication (sometimes called language development)

Human beings are the only organisms that can converse fluently with each other and can read and write. The ability to communicate well is a key factor in happiness and achievement. The discovery of feral children has shown us that practising and exposure to language is essential from birth and that without language it is not possible to grow and develop satisfactorily. Communication includes eye-gazing in babies, facial expressions, gestures, body language, reading and writing, understanding spoken language and speech.

In all countries and cultures, language development follows the same sequence (see Appendix B). A good knowledge of language development will help you to detect a child whose language is immature or delayed, and you will know how to help a child yourself and when to suggest that the parents seek help.

Children whose home language is not English have the enormous advantage of growing up speaking two languages fluently. When they first come to you they may need some support and additional help. Be careful not to assume that delay in acquiring English indicates that there is a delay in other areas of development. Access to books in their home language allows you and the parents to read with the children. Fluency in the home language will enable them to become fluent in English later on.

Emotional development

During your career as a home-based childcarer, you will realise how important it is to build relationships with children, helping them to develop emotional strengths, and enabling them to reach adulthood, confident in themselves and valuing their achievements. Your commitment to them will aid their emotional stability.

From the moment of birth, the baby begins the process of attachment, bonding with the mother in the same way as the mother bonds with the baby. This love and mutual trust is the basis of emotional development, allowing the child to continue to make loving and trusting relationships with other members of the family and later with the outside world. Home-based childcarers often have a part to play in giving young parents reassurance and helping them to bond with their baby. The relationship of the home-based childcarer and her charges never threatens the paramount relationships of parents and child.

There will be times in the lives of the children in your care when you will need to be particularly sensitive. Settling a child successfully into a new situation often needs careful handling. The birth of a new baby may lead to feelings of jealousy and rejection in the older sibling. Problems within the child's family, such as divorce, unemployment, death or addiction may distress the child and halt her emotional development, causing her to regress. Your love and care will help build her self-esteem and give her a positive self-image, thus building confidence and leading to independence. An understanding of the stages of emotional development is a critical factor in ensuring best practice.

Sensory development

Initially, babies learn through their senses: vision, hearing, taste, smell and touch. As children grow older, the senses of vision and hearing become dominant. Nevertheless, it is important to promote all the senses and encourage children to taste different foods, smell many different smells and develop their awareness of different textures.

Toddlers, not yet in full command of language, use all their senses spontaneously in exploratory and experimental play. It is important that this is allowed and not discouraged by caregivers telling them not to put objects in their mouths, or not to touch something which may not be completely hygienic; of course, such activities need to be closely supervised. In general, toddlers will explore everything through the senses, as this is instinctive, but there is a need to encourage children who may have some sensory impairment.

Activity

What materials and activities would you provide for a toddler who:
1 is visually impaired?
2 has a hearing impairment?
3 uses a wheelchair?

Frameworks for understanding childcare and development

The Early Years Foundation Stage

Since 2008, the Early Years Foundation Stage has been mandatory for:

- all schools
- all early years providers in Ofsted-registered settings.

It applies to children from birth to the end of the academic year in which the child has their fifth birthday.

In the *Statutory Framework for the Early Years Foundation Stage* the Department for Education and Skills tells us that:

> Every child deserves the best possible start in life and support to fulfil their potential. A child's experience in the early years has a major impact on their future life chances. A secure, safe and happy childhood is important in its own right, and it provides the foundation for children to make the most of their abilities and talents as they grow up. When parents choose to use early years services they want to know that provision will keep their children safe and help them to thrive. The Early Years Foundation Stage (EYFS) is the framework that provides that assurance. The overarching aim of the EYFS is to help young children achieve the five *Every Child Matters* outcomes.

Every Child Matters is the government agenda that focuses on bringing together services to support children and families. It sets out five major outcomes for children:

- being healthy
- staying safe
- enjoying and achieving
- making a positive contribution
- economic well-being.

The EYFS aims to meet the *Every Child Matters* outcomes by:

- **Setting standards** for the learning, development and care young children should experience when they attend a setting outside their family home. Every child should make progress, with no children left behind.
- **Providing equality of opportunity and anti-discriminatory practice**. Ensuring that every child is included and not disadvantaged because of ethnicity, culture, religion, home language, family background, learning difficulties or disabilities, gender or ability.
- **Creating a framework for partnership working between parents and professionals**, and between all the settings that the child attends.
- **Improving quality and consistency in the early years** through standards that apply to all settings. This provides the basis for the inspection and regulation regime carried out by Ofsted.
- **Laying a secure foundation for future learning** through learning and development that is planned around the individual needs and interests of the child. This is informed by the use of ongoing observational assessment.

Note
The EYFS has replaced *The Curriculum Guidance for the Foundation Stage, the Birth to Three Matters Framework* and *The National Standards for Under 8s Daycare and Childminding* which are all now defunct.

Themes, Principles and Commitments

The EYFS is based around four **Themes**. Each theme is linked to a **Principle**. Each Principle is supported by four **Commitments**. The Commitments describe how their Principle can be put into action. The Themes, Principles and Commitments are shown in the table on the next page.

Theme	Principle	Commitments
1. A Unique Child	Every child is a competent learner from birth who can be resilient, capable, confident and self-assured	1.1 Child development 1.2 Inclusive practice 1.3 Keeping safe 1.4 Health and well-being
2. Positive Relationships	Children learn to be strong and independent from a base of loving and secure relationships with parents and/or a key person	2.1 Respecting each other 2.2 Parents as partners 2.3 Supporting learning 2.4 Key person
3. Enabling Environments	The environment plays a key role in supporting and extending children's development and learning	3.1 Observation, assessment and planning 3.2 Supporting every child 3.3 The learning environment 3.4 The wider context
4. Learning and Development	Children develop and learn in different ways and at different rates. All areas of learning and development are equally important and interconnected	4.1 Play and exploration 4.2 Active learning 4.3 Creativity and critical thinking 4.4 Areas of learning and development

Additional statements are provided within the EYFS to explain each Commitment in more detail. You can see these on the Department for Education and Skills' 'Principles into Practice' poster, an extract of which is reproduced below.

Areas of Learning and Development

Theme 4, Learning and Development, also contains six Areas of Learning and Development. These are shown on the diagram below.

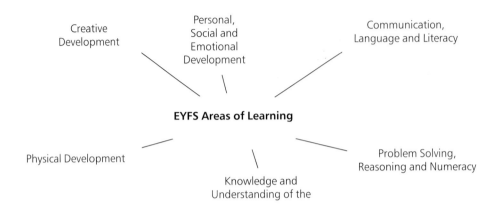

Creative Development

Personal, Social and Emotional Development

Communication, Language and Literacy

EYFS Areas of Learning

Physical Development

Knowledge and Understanding of the

Problem Solving, Reasoning and Numeracy

Each Area of Learning and Development is divided up into Aspects. You can see these on Department for Education and Skills Learning and Development card, reproduced below. Together, the six areas of Learning and Development make up the skills, knowledge and experiences appropriate for babies and children as they grow, learn and develop. Although these are presented as separate areas, it is important to remember that for children everything links and nothing is compartmentalised. All areas of Learning and Development are connected to one another and are equally important. They are underpinned by the principles of the EYFS. Each Area of Learning also has a list of early learning goals (elg). The aim is for children to reach the goals by the end of their Reception year.

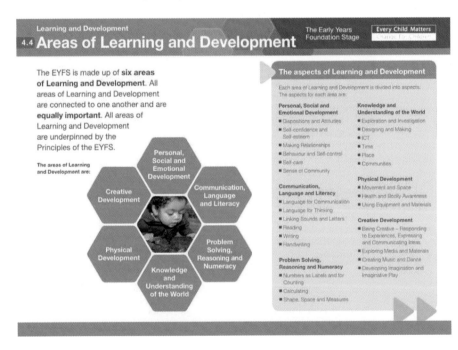

So what does all this mean?

Childcarers working in settings following the EYFS need to meet the standards for learning, development and care. Their responsibilities include:

- planning a range of play and learning experiences that promote all of the Aspects within all of the Areas of Learning
- assessing and monitoring individual children's progress through observational assessments
- using the findings of observational assessments to inform the planning of play and learning experiences
- ensuring that children's individual interests and abilities are promoted within the play and learning experiences.

In their 'Key Elements of Effective Practice' (KEEP) the Department for Education and Skills tells us that:

> Effective practice in the early years requires committed, enthusiastic and reflective practitioners with a breadth and depth of knowledge, skills and understanding. Effective practitioners use their own learning to improve their work with young children and their families in ways which are sensitive, positive and non-judgemental.
>
> Therefore through initial and on-going training and development practitioners need to develop, demonstrate and continuously improve their:
> - relationships with both children and adults
> - understanding of the individual and diverse ways that children learn and develop
> - knowledge and understanding in order to actively support and extend children's learning in and across all areas and aspects of Learning and Development
> - practice in meeting all children's needs, learning styles and interests
> - work with parents, carers and the wider community; work with other professionals within and beyond the setting.

EYFS resources for childcarers

The EYFS pack includes the following resources for providers:

The Statutory Framework for the Early Years Foundation Stage
This booklet sets out:

- the welfare requirements
- the learning and development requirements, which set out providers' duties under each of the six Areas of Learning and Development.

Practice Guidance for the Early Years Foundation Stage

This booklet provides further guidance on:

- legal requirements
- the Areas of Learning and Development
- the EYFS principles
- assessment.

24 cards

These give the Principles and Commitments at a glance, with guidance on putting the principles into practice. They include an overview of child development.

CD-ROM

This contains all the information from the booklets and cards. It includes information on effective practice, research and resources.

Activity

Visit the EYFS website at www.standards.dcsf.gov.uk/eyfs/.
1 Take the overview tour to familiarise yourself with the site.
2 Follow the links to the Areas of Learning, and read more about the Aspects.
3 Follow the links to the 'Principles in practice' for examples of how practitioners following the EYFS work with children within their settings.

The National Curriculum

The English National Curriculum sets out the minimum curriculum requirements for all maintained schools, including:

- the subjects taught
- the knowledge, skills and understanding required in each subject
- attainment targets in each subject
- how children's progress is assessed and reported.

Within the framework of the National Curriculum, schools are free to plan and organise teaching and learning themselves. Many schools choose to use Schemes of Works from the Qualifications and Curriculum Authority. These help to translate the National Curriculum's objectives into teaching and learning activities for children.

Key stages

The National Curriculum is divided into four **key stages** that children pass through as they move up through the school system. These stages are in addition to the Early Years Foundation Stage described earlier:

- Year 1 and Year 2 of primary school are known as Key Stage 1.
- Years 3 to 6 of primary school are known as Key Stage 2.
- Years 7 to 9 of secondary school are known as Key Stage 3.
- Years 10 to 11 of secondary school are known as Key Stage 4.

Subjects at Key Stage 1 and 2

The compulsory National Curriculum subjects for Key Stages 1 and 2 are:

- English
- Maths
- Science
- Design and technology
- Information and Communication Technology (ICT)
- History
- Geography
- Art and design
- Music
- Physical education.

Schools also have to teach:

- Religious education. (*Parents have the right to withdraw children from the religious education curriculum if they choose*)

Schools are advised to teach:

- personal, social and health education (PSHE)
- citizenship
- one or more modern foreign language.

There are **attainment targets** and a **programme of study** for each subject. Programmes of study describe the subject knowledge, skills and understanding pupils are expected to develop during each key stage. It is acceptable for schools to use different names for the subjects, as long as they are covering the National Curriculum.

Levels and formal teacher assessments

Attainment targets are split into **levels**. Teachers carry out regular checks on children's progress in each subject. There will also be **formal teacher assessment** at the end of Key Stages 1–3. (Pupils will usually take GCSE/equivalent exams at the end of Key Stage 4.) This indicates which National Curriculum level best describes individual children's performance in

4 chapter

each subject. Schools send parents a report telling them what National Curriculum levels their child has reached in formal assessments.

Subjects at Key Stage 3 and 4

Key Stage 3 compulsory National Curriculum subjects are:

- English
- Maths
- Science
- Design and technology
- Information and Communication Technology (ICT)
- History
- Geography
- Modern foreign languages
- Art and design
- Music
- Citizenship
- Physical education.

Schools also have to provide:

- careers education and guidance (during Year 9)
- sex and relationship education (SRE)
- religious education (*parents can choose to withdraw their child from the religious education curriculum*).

In Year 9, children do national tests and choose what to study at Key Stage 4, when they will study both compulsory and optional subjects. Most pupils work towards national qualifications. Pupils are advised to choose a balance of options to give them more choice when deciding on courses and jobs later on. Pupils may also choose from a growing range of vocational qualifications. The compulsory Key Stage 4 subjects are:

- English
- Maths
- Science
- Information and Communication Technology (ICT)
- Physical education
- Citizenship.

Schools must also provide:

- careers education
- work-related learning
- religious education
- sex and relationship education (SRE)
- one subject from each of the four 'entitlement' areas.

The entitlement areas are:

- arts subjects
- design and technology
- humanities
- modern foreign languages.

Review of the curriculum

A new secondary curriculum was published in September 2007. Its aims include cutting back on compulsory subject content and developing pupils' personal attributes and practical life skills. The Department for Education and Skills tells us that:

> The new Key Stage 3 curriculum will be brought in over a three year period. It became compulsory for Year 7 pupils in September 2008. From September 2009, it will apply to all Year 7 and Year 8 pupils, and from September 2010 it will apply across Years 7, 8 and 9. Changes to the Key Stage 4 curriculum will be brought in from September 2009.
>
> As part of changes to the curriculum for 14 to 19 year olds, from September 2008 a new Diploma qualification will be introduced alongside GCSEs and A levels in selected schools and colleges.

For more information about the new secondary curriculum, visit the Qualifications and Curriculum Authority website at www.qca.org.uk/qca_13575.aspx

Play

Children need to play, and you will be experienced in offering play activities to the children in your care. For them, stimulating play is vital as it is mainly by play that children learn.

For children, passive play, such as watching videos, is not as valuable as active play in which they participate. That is not to say that there is no place for television, but the child learns more if she watches with an adult who helps to interpret what is happening.

Children's play reflects intellectual ability and development and has been called 'children's work'. It is an integral part of the daily life and the promotion of all-round development. Through play, the child experiences life and learns to understand the world and her place in it. Play can be social, when children interact with each other; some researchers look on play as a process of socialisation.

The baby plays from birth, the first 'toy' being the mother's breast. From this stage, play develops through several stages: solitary; parallel (playing alongside another child or adult); associative play with other children, and co-operative play, involving planning and games with complicated rules.

There are many different types of play, indoor and out, structured and spontaneous. These include:

- child-centred play, where the child chooses the activity
- imitative play, where the young child copies what the adult is doing
- domestic play, such as pretending to make cups of tea and sweeping the floor
- messy play, such as finger painting and hand and foot printing
- play with natural materials, such as sand, water and mud
- imaginative play, which involves creative thought
- repetitive play, where the child feels the need to repeat an activity over and over again, until she feels satisfied
- creative play including art work and model-making
- vigorous physical play, usually taking place outside
- organised games, which include ring games and board games, and which often have rules.

Adults should avoid intervening too frequently and attempting to impose too rigid a structure on children's play. By interaction with the children, the adult can enrich the play, as long as this is done sensitively, based on observation and assessment of the child's need.

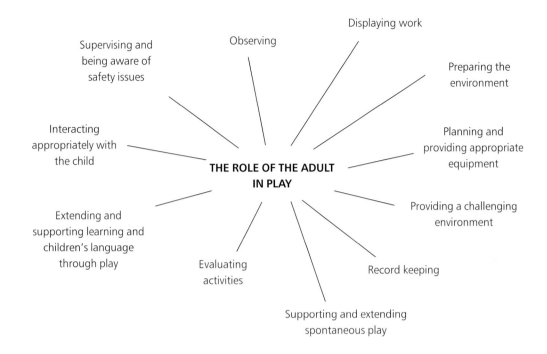

The role of the adult in play:
- Displaying work
- Observing
- Supervising and being aware of safety issues
- Preparing the environment
- Interacting appropriately with the child
- Planning and providing appropriate equipment
- THE ROLE OF THE ADULT IN PLAY
- Extending and supporting learning and children's language through play
- Providing a challenging environment
- Evaluating activities
- Record keeping
- Supporting and extending spontaneous play

Activities with children

However familiar you are with providing play opportunities for the children in your care, you will need to remember that all activities should promote the children's all-round development.

Through your knowledge of the children and of the norms of development, you will be able to plan your activities with the children's needs in mind. This will help you to be aware of what is happening and when you need to step in to move the play forward. If you are receiving funding for early years education as an accredited home-based childcarer and part of an approved network, you will be in regular contact with your co-ordinator who will help and support you. Your formal and informal observations will not only help you in discussion with parents but also form part of the planning of the activities you provide (see the following example).

There will be many occasions when you feel that unstructured and spontaneous activities will be fun for all concerned and allow children to use their imagination. There are very few activities that do not have some value. The important point is that you are aware of the value of the activities you are planning and preparing.

Play and activities should start from birth; this stage is discussed in Chapter 6. It is not always possible to provide an activity in which all children within a wide age-range can participate. You might have to wait until the younger children are napping before offering a more complex activity to the older children.

chapter 4

Let older children help you with routine domestic activities. Laying the table, preparing food, sorting the clean washing, and putting away the shopping all require mathematical skills, concentration and a good vocabulary, and are part of their social development. Growing independence gives children self-esteem and confidence, all of which aid learning in other areas.

An accredited childminder works in her home caring for three children, aged three and four, for up to 35 hours per week. Her home is in the middle of a town and has a medium sized garden with a lawn and steps leading to an area for growing fruit and vegetables.

As an accredited childminder and part of an approved network, she is visited every eight weeks by her coordinator who helps her to plan learning opportunities for the children, to enable them to progress towards the early learning goals. She keeps a notebook of dated photos, observations and significant pieces of dialogue that she has had with the children. These are used to inform her planning and are also shared with the parents/carers during informal discussions on the children's progress.

I have only recently started writing plans for the children in my care. I try to build on the children's interests to plan a variety of activities. For example, I took the children to explore the vegetable patch and pointed out the different types of fruit and vegetables that were growing in the garden. The children were intrigued by the gooseberries as they thought they had a funny name. They did not know that they could eat them.

How an observation influenced my planning

Dan pointed to the gooseberries and said, 'What's that? They prick me!' I explained that gooseberries are fruit and that I grew them in my garden every year, because I like to cook them and eat them with custard. I showed the children the rough leaves and the prickly branches telling them that unlike most fruit they were better cooked and sweetened before eaten.

The garden had obviously stimulated the children's interest so I decided to plan a week's activities around plants and, in particular gooseberries.

THEME: Fruit	Date: 3–7 July 2009
Personal, social & emotional development * encourage children to listen to others' questions & take turns * choose own utensils * safety reminders: prickly branches, use of knives, hygiene	**Knowledge & understanding of the world** * how gooseberries grow, conditions of growth, sun, soil, rain * use magnifying glass to look at the inside and outside of gooseberries * Allow to see, feel, smell, taste gooseberries
Communication, language & literacy * listen to explanations * make list of fruit growing in the garden * vocabulary: parts of plants: root, branch, stem, leaf, flower, fruit, seed. * non-fiction books on growing and eating fruit	**Physical development** * keep to the narrow path around the garden/ climb steps * fine motor skills: use of knives/magnifying glass
Problem solving, reasoning and numeracy * compare size of gooseberries and count them * order sizes * vocabulary: bigger than, more than, less than, how many	**Creative development** * colours of leaves and ripening berries * textures: smooth, rough, prickly * paint pictures of the garden * drawings of gooseberries
NOTES: * Only allow children to feel, smell and taste gooseberries under supervision * Katy explained to Jess that we have to be careful with knives because they can cut you * Dan brought a book on fruit and vegetables from home that had a picture of gooseberries in it - could also be useful for learning about vegetables/seasons * Next time we go shopping, look at the different fruits in the shop and discuss where they come from * Use photos to introduce ideas and encourage discussion	

An example of how observation can help with planning

Having drawn up the plan for the week, I fill in an activity sheet that I designed myself. I stick this into the children's notebooks, adding photographs and comments during the week. I base intended learning for each activity on the stepping stones.

An example of my activity sheet

Date: 3 July 2009	**Names:** Dean & Jess
Activity: Looking at gooseberries and kiwi fruit **Main area of learning:** KUW **Aspects/areas of learning:** KUW1, CD1	**Intended learning:** * show curiosity, observe and manipulate objects * describe simple features * examine living things to find out more about them * show an interest in what you see, hear, smell, touch and feel

Observation:
Don used the magnifying glass to look at the tiny hairs on the gooseberry, fascinated by the magnifying glass he went to look around the room for other tiny objects he could look at. Jess didn't want to taste the gooseberry but said she liked the kiwi fruit, showing likes and dislikes. We had a lively discussion about fruit she likes to eat.

Future action:
Close observations of natural and manmade objects. Encourage children to use new vocabulary - skin, pip, seed, fruit, thorn, branch.

An example of how observation can help with planning (continued)

Messy play

Some activities provided for children are not adult-directed. You will just need to provide the materials and observe how the children use them, without expecting any end product. You have to be very tolerant of mess if you allow messy play to take place inside your home, but it is possible to do most of the activities outside on a fine day.

Messy play, such as playing with cooked spaghetti mixed with liquid detergent and colouring, or experimenting with cornflour and water which becomes solid in your hand but liquid on a hard flat surface, is enjoyable for all children, but particularly so for the youngest ones. A large sheet of paper can be attached to a wall or to a fence in the garden, and paint in squeezy bottles can be squirted at it. Finger painting comes into this category of play: paints and paste are mixed together, and patterns made in the mixture with the fingers. Older children might like to print their creations.

Messy play is one of the best activities for intellectual development, as children use their imagination and creativity in planning and producing this work. Their concentration span is often extended in well-thought-out and enjoyable activities. Different materials encourage exploration and experimentation and this, in turn, leads to an understanding of design and technology. Mathematical and scientific concepts may be explored. Patterns may lead to an understanding of spatial relationships.

Natural materials

Water

Water is an indestructible material and children can bang and splash without harm. Playing with water, as with messy play, allows many mathematical and scientific concepts to be learnt. Some children will enjoy using the equipment provided and finding out about floating and sinking, while others might enjoy playing with water on its own, finding it a soothing and relaxing experience. Playing with water links the child's home with your home, as children are used to playing in their bath or at their parents' sink. Children learn that water comes in many forms – as snow, rain, steam and ice – and is essential for life.

Sand

You are unlikely to provide sand indoors in your home and, although some home-based childcarers have sandpits in their gardens, sand is generally less familiar to children than water. Dry sand is relaxing and therapeutic to play with. A great deal can be learnt with the use of various tools. Sand is not suitable for very young children, unless they are closely supervised, as they tend to throw it around and get it in their eyes and hair as well as eat it. Wet sand is suitable for all age groups. It can be used as a modelling material and can be combined with blocks and cars and other small toys to stimulate the imagination. It will lend itself to many mathematical, scientific and technological experiments. Making patterns and marks in sand is linked to early literacy.

Mud

Once children are mobile, most of them find out about mud quite quickly and should be allowed to play with it outside freely if they are suitably dressed and fully immunised. You will need to check that the garden is free from pesticides. Home-based childcarers should check their records to make sure children are protected against tetanus. Mud is one of the most enjoyable of natural materials for young children and is free and readily available in every garden. It can be mixed with water to give pleasant sensory experiences, and can be seen to dry out to revert to dry soil. Small animals found in the mud give interest and pleasure to children, who often need to be persuaded to return them to their natural habitat.

Modelling materials

Plasticine, dough and clay are all used for modelling. It is unlikely that you will use clay in your home, even outside, as it is extremely messy and needs close supervision.

Plasticine

This useful manufactured material is good for developing manipulative skills and for making models with older children. It is much cleaner and less messy than other malleable materials and is often familiar to children from their play at home. It can get hard very easily and needs storing in a warm environment.

Dough

Dough can be made in many ways and presented to children in a range of colours, and the children will enjoy participating in the mixing. By adding other ingredients (such as oil) to the essential flour and water, different kinds of elasticity can be achieved. Salt should always be added as a preservative, and it will also ensure that children do not eat the dough. Dough should appear attractive, have enough elasticity without sticking to surfaces or fingers, and should last for at least a week in a sealed plastic container, kept in a cool place. Playing with dough is a relaxing, soothing social activity and is one often chosen by children when settling in a new environment. Playing with dough often stimulates a shy child to take part in conversations, as the experience helps relaxation.

Activity

Experiment with different dough recipes using various flours, ingredients and colours. Make a note of the recipe you find most successful.
   You might like to involve the children in making dough with you.

Cooking

From a very young age, children enjoy watching and helping adults prepare and cook food. Children learn about food hygiene and balanced meals, how to make choices in the supermarkets for taste and value, and where different foods come from.

It is possible today to buy foods from all around the world, and by using recipes from various countries children learn about a range of cultures in a most enjoyable way. All children and parents feel valued and at home when an important part of their culture is recognised.

'Cooking' covers a wide range of activities, from making a sandwich to producing a complicated meal. It is important that the children do as much as possible for themselves, being involved from the preparation stage through to sharing the end product. By helping to plan the activity, children gain shopping skills, such as making lists, choosing ingredients and handling money. Listening to and following instructions aids concentration. Cooking reinforces a range of mathematical, scientific and technological concepts. It promotes an understanding of nutritional principles, home safety and hygiene. Recipes and labelling make links with reading and writing, as does the recognition of different scripts if the food is labelled in various languages. Knowledge of foods from many cultures will be gained, and children from the age of six years will begin to follow recipes from a book.

Imaginary play

Imaginary play grows out of imitative play. Babies from a very early age imitate adults in games of 'peek-a-boo', waving goodbye and copying actions. Later, children do not need a direct role model in front of them, but will start to use their memory, pouring out imaginary cups of tea for all and sundry, and pretending to eat non-existent food.

At around two years old, children start to take on roles. One will be the 'mummy' and another the 'daddy', and this will gradually extend to include the baby, the big sister, the home-based childcarer, and even a visiting aunt. As children become older, role play will be extended to other people familiar in their lives or from books, such as the nurse, and the firefighter. This is an opportunity to challenge gender stereotyping. The provision of dressing-up clothes often stimulates the imagination of the children. It is best to provide clothes that can be used in many different ways.

Activity

Make a cloak from a piece of material gathered at one end with elastic. Do you think boys and girls would play with it in the same way? Describe the different types of play.

Although it is discouraged in most homes and pre-school establishments, and to the despair of many parents, home-based childcarers and teachers, children do have imaginary shoot-outs, but they do not need toy guns, as toy bricks will do just as well. It is from this ability to symbolise inanimate objects that the readiness for reading grows, as a child starts to understand that those inky blobs on a page stand for real words in a story.

Acting out a role and pretending to be someone else allows some children to release emotions. A child who is constantly listening to adults quarrelling may find it helpful to pretend to be one of those adults and have some say of her own. This type of play can give you an insight into possible difficulties at home, but caution must be exercised, as the child could be acting out what she has seen on the television the night before.

A child waiting to go into hospital will find it very useful to be a make-believe patient, as a way of expressing emotions and fears. Some children, who may be withdrawn or shy, may still have difficulty in expressing their emotions. Puppets or a toy telephone can be a great help here, as the child uses them to voice hidden feelings. Ready-made puppets should be introduced cautiously, as small children can be fearful of a toy that seems to have a life of its own.

As children are small, vulnerable people, they enjoy acting out roles of superheroes. It makes them feel empowered and strong, and is a boost to their self-esteem.

Children play with dolls in different ways at each stage of their development. Once babies start to walk, they will use the doll as they do any other inanimate object, just holding on to it anywhere (usually the feet) and dragging it after them. At about two years, some children will start to cuddle the doll, treating it more as a baby, particularly if there has been a recent birth in the family. This doll might come in for some very hard knocks! A little later on, children enjoy bathing dolls, dressing (but mainly undressing) them and taking them out for walks in a pushchair. At about six years, groups of children might play with several dolls, having pretend tea parties or schoolroom lessons. Many girls start to collect dolls, such as Barbie, and there is often rivalry in the collecting of their clothes and artefacts. Some boys might have dolls, such as Action Man, but rarely collect them in the same way. Graded dolls and dolls' clothes help children understand concepts of small, medium and large.

Small-scale models of people, animals, vehicles, dolls' houses, and items of domestic equipment are often used in imaginary play. They are familiar to the children, and the play allows the children to relax, and extend and develop their language.

Activity

Describe what equipment you might provide to encourage creativity in children.

Domestic play, such as making pretend cups of tea or using a broom, is a link with home and is very comforting to the insecure child, or a child experiencing a new situation. You may see children using stereotypes in their role play, copying situations observed in their environment. You will have to challenge this behaviour in a sensitive way if negative attitudes are displayed.

Imaginary play allows boys to take on and dress up in perceived female roles such as the mother or the ballerina, while girls can be fathers and firefighters. It presents opportunities for children to direct and organise activities, promotes creativity, and may lead to the writing of imaginative stories. Imaginary play allows children to express and release positive and negative emotions. It gives confidence, and allows self-esteem to develop.

Painting and drawing

All children should be offered frequent opportunities to paint and draw when they feel inclined. When children are very young, before fluent speech has developed, spontaneous drawing and painting are a most valuable means of expression. This value is very much reduced if adults insist on questioning children about their paintings, suggest additions to the work, and want captions for every painting or drawing.

Adults interpreting children's paintings are quite often wrong. Children love to do all-dark, one-colour paintings at some stage in their development – this does not mean that something terrible has happened to them that they wish to forget! There are, however, many books on interpreting children's paintings and it is an interesting way to try to understand what stage of development a child might have reached.

Painting, in particular, often allows children to express emotions that they find difficult to put into words. Painting and drawing encourage imagination and creativity, and lend themselves to pattern creation. The exploration of materials, textures and techniques expands knowledge of colour and shapes. It helps children to understand spatial relationships and composition. Symbolic blobs might lead to the foundation of reading and writing.

Bricks, blocks and construction sets

A bag of bricks is the most versatile piece of equipment that any child can have access to from the age of one year onwards. Blocks can be hard and made out of wood or plastic, or they can be soft and manufactured from rubber, cotton or foam, and they can be brightly coloured or in natural wood – but they are all construction toys and are there to build with.

At first, children will play on their own, building a tower of bricks, and enjoying knocking it down again. This leads on to other skills; four-year-olds can play co-operatively and imaginatively, planning small and large constructions together.

There are very many types of construction sets on the market, the best known being Lego. Most children will be familiar with Lego from home, and it is probably the most versatile of the construction toys. Younger children will find Duplo (the large-scale version) easier to put together. Children from five years upwards enjoy Meccano, the wooden and the plastic types being easier to manage than the metal, which is more sophisticated.

Building with bricks is a first-hand experience of three-dimensional objects and spatial relationships and encourages creative thought and problem solving.

Puzzles and simple games

Jigsaw puzzles are familiar to all young children and create an excellent link with home, as children feel relaxed and safe doing jigsaws. They are essentially a solitary experience, although children may do the large floor puzzles with other children.

Jigsaws range from very simple inset boards for the youngest children to very intricate puzzles for adults. Sometimes children will choose easy puzzles when they are feeling the need for reassurance and, at other times, will enjoy the challenge of more demanding jigsaws. It is important that no pieces are missing, particularly for the younger children, as this spoils the pleasure of completing a task satisfactorily.

Board games, similarly, come in varying degrees of difficulty. Most are not suitable for the under-fours as the children will not yet have gained the concept of taking turns and may get upset at having to wait, and spoil the game for others. Most games are a variation of Ludo or Snakes and Ladders.

Matching games, such as Picture Lotto and Connect, help children to see similarities and differences, and to match like with like; this is a pre-reading skill. Such games can be played by one child alone, or by a group of children.

Card games, such as Snap, Go Fish, Pairs or Sevens, are enjoyed by children of four years upwards. Snap or Pairs cards can be made quite easily, using pictures or photographs familiar in the children's cultural background.

Doing jigsaw puzzles also helps children to find similarities and differences and is, therefore, a valuable early reading activity. Card games encourage memory and quickness of thought. Concentration, logical thought, reasoning and perseverance are necessary for all these activities.

Activities that aid manipulative skills

Children enjoy threading beads and cotton reels, and again the materials can be graded in order of difficulty, the younger children finding the larger beads the easiest. Pegboards and mosaic pieces help children to make patterns, as do sewing cards, where children are asked to thread in and out of holes with a lace or a threaded needle.

Books and stories

Enjoyment of books and stories usually starts in the home and will continue with you. Before a child is a year old, she enjoys looking at pictures or photographs while being cuddled by an adult. As a love of books is probably the key factor in the later acquisition of reading skills, nurturing it is very important.

Young children, in particular, derive great pleasure from being told stories. These can be personalised, being either tales from the storyteller's past, or stories where the listener becomes the centre of the tale. Being told or read a story is delightful and relaxing. Many parents read to their child just before settling her down to sleep, and she will enjoy the attention of a loved adult. You may wish to read to a child before she takes a nap.

Poetry will enrich older children's vocabulary and let them know that it is acceptable to express emotions. This may encourage older children to write their own poems. For younger children, humorous verse is a good introduction. Repetitive rhyming is most helpful to children with limited language skills. For all children, poetry can, like books, open up a world of fantasy and imagination.

Being able to read gives children independence. Empathising with a character in a book allows a child to understand her own feelings. On a one-to-one basis, reading with an adult is a nurturing experience, giving feelings of love and security. Being able to read gives a child self-esteem and a sense of achievement. Books and stories encourage concentration, extend the child's knowledge of the world and aid imagination.

Look at the range of books you have at home.

1 How many represent girls in strong roles? How many represent minority ethnic groups in strong and positive roles? How many show disabled people in active roles?

2 Which books are the most popular with children? Why do you think this is?

Good practice in . . . USING BOOKS AND TELLING STORIES

1 Books should always be available to the children and, ideally, an adult should always be there to read to them if required. Children enjoy reading on the floor. Books should be accessible to children. They should be kept in good condition, and children taught at a young age to treat them with respect. Children who damage books should be encouraged to help in the repair.

2 A comprehensive range of books needs to be available. The books should reflect our multi-cultural society, with some books in the home languages of the children in your care. Great care must be taken to avoid stereotyping when choosing books, whether it is in the area of race, religion, class, age, disability or gender. Positive images reflecting the diversity of culture and family patterns need to be included, together with stories portraying disabled children and girls in strong roles.

3 Children identify with characters in books, and you should be aware of the needs of all the children in your care in order to help them make sense of their feelings and to promote self-esteem and feelings of worth.

4 Remember the value of telling stories, as well as reading books. This is particularly valuable for the younger children.

5 The appropriateness of the book or story needs thinking about. The youngest children will be content with stories about familiar events, such as shopping and bedtime, and some simple tales that are happily resolved about other children and animals. As children's experience of stories is extended, longer books about imaginary events can be read, but always be aware of not frightening the children. A young child's imagination is very vivid, and fairy stories can be terrifying, as they often deal with tales of rejection, death and separation. Ogres and witches should be left for an older age group, and even then not all children feel comfortable with fantasy tales, as they may still have difficulty in discriminating fact from fiction. The way that you read stories has a good deal of bearing on how much the children will enjoy them. You should choose stories you enjoy reading and telling, and you will need to be familiar with the story you are going to read.

6 Children want the same stories time and time again, but occasionally you need to introduce new stories.

7 Some books have many words in them that are unfamiliar to the children. It is not a good idea to change the words into more familiar ones as you go along. This is disrespectful to the writer, and it deprives the children of learning new words. If the language is so difficult that the children become bored, re-introduce the book another time.

8 Allow some time for relaxed discussion at the end of the story. Children do not always want to talk about the book, so do not force them to do so. Sometimes children want to participate throughout the reading or telling of the story. It depends on your personal preference as to whether you let them do this or wait until the end of the story session. Usually the youngest children cannot wait until the end if they have something to say!

9 Reading sessions are sometimes held in local libraries. Older children should be encouraged to join the library, and the younger ones should become familiar with the building.

10 Books should represent the whole spectrum of society, not just the ideal nuclear family with no financial problems.

11 When buying new books, or borrowing books from the library, care must be taken to make sure that none of them contains elements that could offend adults or distress children, by displaying offensive attitudes. Show children that you enjoy books, as it is by your example that they will learn to value and appreciate books and stories.

12 Books are an ideal way of presenting positive images of children from many varied ethnic groups. Giving all children insights into different cultures with their own traditional stories and into varied child-rearing practices, will enable them to learn to value and respect people for what they are, and to challenge stereotypical attitudes. Check the illustrations for stereotypes of black people, women and minority ethnic groups. Make sure that disabled children are not depicted as being weak and needy. Girls should be depicted in strong roles, not as dependent, passive onlookers, and boys should be depicted as caring and thoughtful, and carrying out domestic activities.

13 Books are available from the library to help children who are having to deal with problems in their private lives, such as hospitalisation, parental separation, bereavement and so on.

Playing outside

Nearly every activity that takes place in the house can equally well be taken outside if the weather permits. Some activities can only take place outside, and it is to these that this section refers.

A safe outside-play area is a bonus for young children, to exercise and let off steam, to practise their developing physical skills and to build self-confidence. Exercise in the fresh air promotes good health. A safe outdoor play area allows children freedom to investigate and explore their environment with little adult restriction. Very young children, who are not used to playing outside, and live in a flat, may find the garden intimidating and overwhelming at first, but when their self-confidence has developed will soon enjoy being outside.

You will need to be outside with the children and make sure it is safe. What is provided will influence the quality of the play. Traditional games may be organised, either by the children, or by you, such as What's the Time, Mr Wolf?, Hide and Seek, Simon Says and Ring-O'-Roses.

Playing outside releases surplus energy and is a licence to make more noise. It stimulates the appetite, aids digestion and circulation, promotes sleep, and gives resistance to infection. It promotes a healthy skin, as well as developing muscle tone, manipulative skills, balance and

control. Children develop skills, such as stopping and starting, running, hopping, digging, planting, skipping, climbing, pedalling, swinging, steering and crawling through and under equipment. Children share and collaborate, take responsibility for sharing space, and gain an understanding of the rules governing outside play and games. They learn respect for living things.

The garden provides a stimulus for all the senses and an opportunity for a range of imaginary play experiences. Children must be dressed according to the weather, protected against the sun as well as the rain.

Activity

If you do not have access to a garden, how would you ensure that the children that you look after get enough fresh air and exercise?

NCMA suggests promoting children's development and learning by the use of the Seven Cs:

Confidence

Children who feel capable and valued by other people have the confidence to reach out into the environment and to other children and adults, and learn from exploration and discovery. A child in a secure situation in which she receives individual attention and loving care will develop self-esteem and be able to tackle new ideas and experiences. When she has opportunities to try out new skills and take new responsibilities, her confidence grows, and she is ready to move on to more new learning.

Communication

From her earliest hours, a baby is learning to give and receive communication – at first non-verbally, later with words. She develops understanding of language and the body language of facial expressions, gestures and tone of voice long before she produces her own earliest words. The toddler's frustrations diminish as she is more able to tell adults what she wants and to understand what they expect of her. The pre-school child wants explanations, and learning the words for the way she feels (sad, happy, cross) helps her deal with her feelings when they are so strong they threaten to overwhelm her. The foundation of communication skills is essential for later learning to read and write.

Co-ordination

As a child progresses from crawling to staggering to toddling to running, jumping and climbing, she is gaining control of her limbs and developing skills of directing the use of her body. The baby placing objects in a container (and taking them out again), the toddler wielding a stubby crayon, and the pre-schooler busy with scissors and threading beads are all learning to make their hands and fingers work as they want and as their eyes direct. Later, writing will depend on those skills.

Concentration

A child who is interested in and enjoying an activity so much that she becomes absorbed in it, and spends a length of time focusing on it, is acquiring habits which will underlie all her later learning. She is learning to stay 'on task' – to concentrate on the matter in hand. The nature of the activity and its end product are less important then her pleasure in doing something which holds her attention. Quiet time and space, and an activity which is based on what excites a child's interest, enable her to lose herself in her play.

Competence

Learning the skills to be a self-reliant human being begins early – walking, feeding and dressing yourself, going to the toilet and washing. Children need practice and praise for the progress they make.

Co-operation

Learning to live and work alongside other people starts early. Babies enjoy playing 'give and take' games; toddlers like to 'help' grown-ups and be thanked; pre-schoolers play elaborate games of make-believe with each taking a role. Sharing is a hard thing to learn, and taking turns is even harder. Children need opportunities to tackle these difficult social skills and become aware of the feelings and rights of others. They may need help to cope with the strongest feelings their efforts may produce.

Creativity

Play activities enable children to experiment with making and seeing how various materials behave and can be used (technology). Making up stories and playing games of make-believe are ways of exploring 'what if?' ideas. Children who will be adults in the twenty-first century need to learn to solve problems and become imaginative thinkers.

Educational research has shown that children's learning is encouraged when teachers, carers and parents work closely in partnership.

Good practice in . . . SUPPORTING CHILDREN'S LEARNING

1 Ensure that children feel secure and valued, promoting their self-esteem and self-confidence.
2 Make learning a pleasure and give all children a sense of achievement.
3 Provide parents with a statement of aims, objectives and curriculum.
4 Liaise with other professionals, such as the staff at the school the child will attend.
5 Encourage children to think and talk about what they are learning.
6 Help children to develop self-control and independence.
7 Plan activities and experiences for children, based on their achievements so far, and their interests and abilities.
8 Give children many hands-on experiences and clear explanations.

▶

4 chapter

9 Make sure children have the time to play and talk.

10 Intervene only when appropriate.

11 Assess and record children's progress, and share this with the parents.

12 Seek additional support if specific needs emerge.

13 Create a safe and healthy environment, in which space, facilities and equipment support learning.

14 Reflect on your own training needs.

(From the Schools Curriculum and Assessment Authority)

Reflecting on Practice

You might think about:

- the creative art materials you already have in your home
- your response to very messy play
- how you might encourage children to cook with you
- your collection of suitable children's books and rhymes, and where you might go to improve your stock
- how challenging your outside play area is
- drawing up daily activity plans showing why and how you plan activities
- how you will provide a comprehensive supply of toys and materials to meet the children's developmental needs and where you will store your play equipment.

This chapter has contributed to the following learning outcomes:

Unit 1

- planning and providing appropriate play and other activities for children in the home-based setting
- promoting anti-discriminatory, anti-bias practice in the home-based setting

Unit 2

- providing for children's development and well-being from birth to 16 years

Unit 5

- planning, providing and evaluating appropriate experiences and play
- understanding how you meet children's individual learning needs in the home-based setting

Want to Find Out More?

Websites
www.educate.co.uk
www.funwithspot.com
www.pre-school.org.uk
www.smallfolk.com
www.teachingideas.co.uk
www.thebigbus.com
www.theideabox.com

Further reading

Bruce T., *Developing Learning in Early Childhood*, Paul Chapman, 2004
   Learning Through Play, Hodder Arnold, 2001
Cobbold S., *The Foundation Stage at Home*, Nelson Thornes, 2006
Coleman, A., *Creative Play for Ages 0–8*, Scholastic, 2003
David P., *Young Children Learning*, Paul Chapman, 1999
Hobart C., Frankel J. and Walker M. (Series Editor), *A Practical Guide to Activities for Young Children*, 4th Edition, Nelson Thornes, 2009
Mathieson K., *Social Skills in the Early Years*, Paul Chapman, 2004
Mukherji P. and O'Dea T., *Understanding Children's Language and Literacy*, Nelson Thornes, 2000
Neaum S. and Tallick J., *Good Practice in Implementing the Pre-school Curriculum*, 2nd Edition, Nelson Thornes, 2002
QCA, *Curriculum Guidance for the Foundation Stage* QCA and DfES, 2000
Sheridan M. et al., *Play in Early Childhood*, Routledge, 1999
Sheridan M , *From Birth to Five Years* (revised and updated by Frost M. and Sharma A.), Routledge, 1997
Uppal H., *Play Activities for the Early Years*, Brilliant Publications, 2004
Wilkes A., *Activities for All Year Round*, Usborne Publishing, 2003

5 Understanding children's behaviour

Learning objectives

Unit 1
- Managing children's behaviour in the home-based setting
- Promoting inclusion and anti-bias practice

Unit 5
- Observing and assessing children's development in the home-based setting
- Meeting individual learning needs in the home-based setting

The way in which a person conducts herself in relation to other people is one aspect of behaviour and is usually the response to an action. If we want to teach children to behave in a socially acceptable way, we have to devise guidelines for ourselves in the way we carry this out. We need to be very clear about our aims and objectives, and be consistent in the way we manage children's behaviour.

Behaviour is learnt through the child observing the people closest to him and the way they react to him, both verbally and non-verbally. Rewards and punishments help shape behaviour. The reward may just be praise and encouragement, and the punishment a disapproving look, but it will have an effect.

Knowledge of the normal development of children will help you to understand what behaviour is appropriate at what age and stage of development. For example, a toddler is not

5 chapter

5

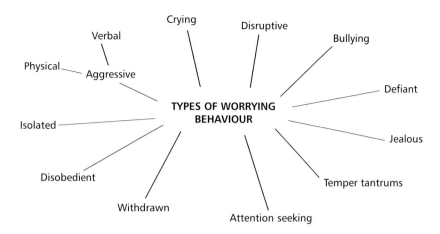

Crying
Verbal
Disruptive
Physical
Bullying
Aggressive
TYPES OF WORRYING
BEHAVIOUR
Defiant
Isolated
Jealous
Disobedient
Temper tantrums
Withdrawn
Attention seeking

expected to be completely toilet trained, but regularly wetting and soiling pants would be worrying behaviour in a five-year-old.

The children you look after will come from various backgrounds, perhaps from a variety of cultures, and their parents may well have different expectations of their children's behaviour. For example, some parents might explain in great detail to the child what he is doing wrong, while others might be more of the 'do as I say, not as I do' school. Some parents might have different gender expectations, allowing boys to be more vigorous and active and expecting girls to adopt more passive pursuits.

CASE STUDY

Berenice cares for two children and has two of her own. She was asked to look after a six-year-old, Clive, during the school holidays. She found him to be a delightful child, always happy and helpful, but his habit of never saying 'please' and 'thank you' drove her to distraction. It was clear that this was not expected of him at home.

1 What action should Berenice take?
2 Should she insist that Clive says 'please' and 'thank you'?

Once you have established your own way of managing children's behaviour, and found that it works, you will need to discuss this with the parents and make sure they are in agreement with your methods.

Factors that influence behaviour

Most of the factors that influence behaviour are family based. This is because behaviour is learnt initially in the family, and the earliest experiences have the greatest effect. These factors include:

- birth order
- siblings
- expectations of the parent(s)
- cultural child-rearing practices
- influence of the extended family
- opportunities for play within the family home
- abuse and neglect
- gender stereotyping.

Outside events that affect the whole family may also influence behaviour. These might include:

- unemployment/work pattern of the parent(s)
- moving house
- divorce and separation
- adapting to a re-constituted family
- death and grieving for people and pets
- disability within the family.

Other factors include:

- the personality of the child
- the school
- the peer group
- the media
- having a disability
- experiencing discrimination.

Common causes of challenging behaviour

Some forms of behaviour are so common that one might be concerned if a child did not at some time display one or more of them. Some of these behaviours are due to frustrated emotional needs.

Emotional causes

Attention-seeking behaviour is one of the most common forms of challenging behaviour. Children need to be reassured that they are loved and cared for, and, if they are not given attention, they may seek it by being aggressive, angry, rude, swearing, showing off, dominating conversations, and other negative behaviours.

Cecelia, an experienced home-based childcarer, has been asked by social services to care for a four-year-old boy, Edward, whose parents have recently separated. This is the third week she has been looking after him, and she is finding it very difficult to manage his constant attention-seeking behaviour. He is defiant and disobedient, frequently upsets the other children, swears and refuses to join in any planned activities.

1 Why might he be behaving like this?
2 How would you approach the parents?
3 How would you help Edward?
4 How would you minimise the effect on the other children?

Temper tantrums

About 50 per cent of two-year-olds have tantrums regularly, usually in the presence of their parents or home-based childcarer, and very seldom when on their own or when at school or playgroup. The tantrum comes about because the child feels frustrated and needs to get attention. Tantrums can be quite disturbing to observe and need to be dealt with in the same way by you and the parents. If you see one coming, it is often possible to distract or divert the child, and by leaving the room you remove the main focus of the anger. If it is already too late, or you are in a public area and unable to walk away, you will need to hold and hug the child until the tantrum is over. The child will be frightened and needs reassurance.

When the tantrum is over, cuddling the child and talking about feelings in a positive way should discourage further tantrums. It is positively harmful to smack or handle a child roughly during a tantrum, and even more dangerous to shake him. Equally, giving in to the child and allowing him to manipulate you will increase the frequency of the tantrums. Always report back to parents if the child has had a severe tantrum, and, if this behaviour is becoming problematic, ask the parents to inform you if it is happening at home, so that you both can follow the same consistent approach.

Jealousy

It is an unusual household that never quarrels, and most children will fight from time to time. A new baby will sometimes arouse deep feelings of jealousy from a displaced older child, and this may be shown by aggressive behaviour to the younger children that you look after. Often, rivalry is expressed by quarrelling over toys and attention. In general, children can sort out most of these rows for themselves and, unless they are doing serious damage to each other, it is often better to just let them get on with it.

CASE STUDY

Siobhan, a newly registered home-based childcarer, with a two-year-old of her own, agreed to care for a four-month-old baby. She was upset when, during the first week, she walked into the room to find her own child pinching the baby, and telling her to send it away.

1 Is this normal behaviour?
2 How might she have prepared her own child for the baby coming?
3 How should she respond to the situation?

Comfort behaviour

There are many forms of comfort behaviour, some more embarrassing than others. No one minds if a child drags a soft toy everywhere with him, but masturbating in public is not so acceptable. Children may suck thumbs, dummies and pieces of material to comfort themselves. They may become reliant on them at particular times of the day, usually at nap time and when confronted by a new or distressing situation. Not all children feel the need for a comfort object, but if a child has a comfort habit you will have to tolerate it in the same way as the parents do. It would be most upsetting for the child to have the object taken away, or the habit stopped, suddenly and he will give it up in his own good time.

Other children might show their need for love and reassurance by displaying anxiety or fear, and/or withdrawn behaviour, as they find it difficult to express their feelings in the usual attention-seeking ways. Children need approval from adults, so as to gain confidence that they are valued. If this is not forthcoming, their self-esteem will be low, and they will find it difficult to learn and achieve.

Physical causes

Sometimes, problematic behaviour has a physical cause. Lack of sleep can lead to irritability. Hunger can cause some children to lose concentration and become aggressive because their blood sugar level drops. Infection, particularly in the incubation period, can cause changes in behaviour patterns.

Growing independence

There are some types of behaviour that are inevitable, as they are part of the child's development.

Curiosity and exploration

As a baby becomes a toddler you will not have a cupboard that remains unexplored, or a meal that is peaceful and does not have a messy end as the toddler seeks to feed himself and enjoy the texture as well as the taste of food. Safety factors and constant vigilance are of increasing importance, as the child's curiosity knows no bounds.

5 chapter

Toilet training

There is much written about the best way to toilet train a child satisfactorily, and there are many myths around as to the time it takes and the best way to go about it. Encourage the parents not to get into any competition with their friends. It is important that you share the same ideas and go about the process in the same way; there is no point in your leaving the nappy off and offering the child the pot at regular intervals if the parents decide not to do this at weekends. The child will just get confused. Whatever regime you choose, you must make sure that you do not adopt a punitive approach to any occasional accident, and you should show pleasure in any initial success.

Activity

Remembering all the children you have cared for, including your own:
1 At what ages did they become reliably dry and clean?
2 Was there a gender difference?
3 Was there a variation in methods used?
4 Did any parent ever suggest a regime that you felt uncomfortable with?
5 How did you manage this situation?

Dressing and undressing

Some children would always rather you dressed them than have to bother for themselves, but the majority express their independence at a young age, first by undressing and then by starting to dress themselves. It can be difficult to encourage children to dress themselves when you are in a hurry to get them ready to go out. Some children are more reluctant to dress themselves than others, but at some point they have to learn for themselves or be shown up when they start school or go to stay with a friend. You and the parents will have to agree the pace you expect and the encouragement that you give.

Describe how you promote and encourage independence in the children you look after while, at the some time, keeping them safe.

Boredom

Children need stimulation and the opportunity to play and learn about the world around them. If they are restricted and frustrated, this will lead to boredom, perhaps resulting in attention-seeking behaviour.

If you have received some training, you will have learnt about the skill of recording careful and objective observations (see Chapter 13). If you are worried about any aspect of a child's behaviour, you might complete an event sample or a time sample. An event sample will show how many times in the day or week the worrying behaviour occurs, whether or not it is provoked and if it takes place at a particular time of day. A time sample will monitor a child's behaviour at regular intervals throughout the day, demonstrating, for example, how often and to whom a withdrawn child makes an approach. Sharing observations with the parents will allow you to discuss your concerns about the child and develop a consistent approach in setting boundaries.

Your role in managing behaviour

Your role with all the children, including your own, is to:

- be fair
- be consistent
- have as few rules as possible
- set clearly defined boundaries, helping the children to understand how far they can go and what behaviour is not acceptable
- understand what behaviour is appropriate for each age group
- have realistic expectations
- give brief explanations as to why you do not accept certain behaviours
- maintain communication and discussion with the parents
- prepare children to play a valuable role in society
- understand cultural variations and the different expectations that some families might have.

1 Show approval when children behave as you wish. Give rewards of hugs, smiles, praise, time to talk and play, and attention.
2 Praise children to their parents and other people.
3 Help children by offering positive choices. For example, say 'Let's tidy up' rather than 'Don't make a mess'.
4 Give the child plenty of warning when it is time to tidy up.
5 Explain why you expect certain behaviours.
6 Avoid creating confrontations and battles. Do not over-react to minor matters.
7 Give children a chance to work out minor disputes. Do not intervene too soon.
8 Be firm and do not give in to whining or tantrums.
9 Be a good role model. Behave in the way you wish the children to behave.

Managing unwanted behaviour

When children are cared for by more than one person, they will sometimes attempt to play one adult off against another. This can be a particular problem when children are being collected at the end of the day. It is helpful for parents and home-based childcarers to agree on a strategy so that this does not become a time of conflict. Consistency of care and methods of discipline help the child to know what is expected and acceptable. All children need to understand boundaries

set by their parents and home-based childcarers as to what behaviour might be tolerated. As children grow older the rules may change, but consistency is still the key for managing behaviour. Disagreements can cause a great deal of friction, and it is worth spending some time, when you first meet the parents, agreeing what is acceptable behaviour, and how this will be achieved.

Behaviour is not acceptable if it:

- is dangerous, hurtful or offensive to someone else
- is dangerous to the child himself
- will make the child unwelcome or unacceptable to other people
- damages other people's property.

Activity

You overhear a four-year-old child in your care making a hurtful racist remark to a younger child.
1 What is your immediate reaction?
2 What steps might you take to alter such behaviour?
3 How would you support the younger child?
4 How might you involve the parents?

Acceptable behaviour will be encouraged by you and the parents by:

- talking freely and frequently about the children
- discussing which rules are more flexible than others
- not allowing a child to manipulate either of you, by playing one off against the other
- treating each child as an individual; one of the children might dissolve into tears from a cross look, while another might find even a stern telling-off quite amusing
- remembering that rules should change as children become more mature and are able to understand the effects of their behaviour.

Modifying behaviour

Behaviour modification is the name given to techniques used to influence and change children's behaviour. It works by promoting and rewarding positive aspects of children's behaviour and by ignoring and discouraging negative aspects. There is a spectrum of behaviour modification techniques, from the practice of firmly holding children with autism so as to force interaction upon them, to the frequent giving of praise and encouragement for 'good' behaviour.

Research done at the University of Wales, in Bangor, in 1998, looked at a way of encouraging children to eat fruit and vegetables. More than 200 children between the ages of 2 and 7 were shown videos outlining the adventures of some street-wise children called Food Dudes who are locked in combat with General Junk and his Junk Food Junta. He is trying to take

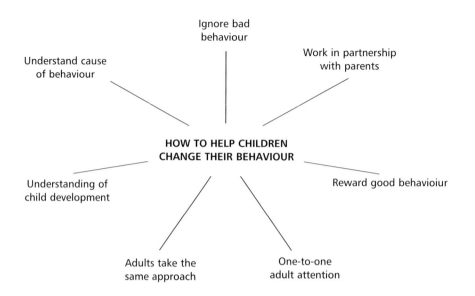

Ignore bad behaviour

Understand cause of behaviour

Work in partnership with parents

HOW TO HELP CHILDREN CHANGE THEIR BEHAVIOUR

Understanding of child development

Reward good behavioiur

Adults take the same approach

One-to-one adult attention

over the world by tricking children into eating unhealthy food, but the Food Dudes eat fruit and vegetables to keep their 'life force' strong, enabling them to outwit the baddies.

At the end of the film, our heroes encourage children everywhere to join the fight, and stickers and other small rewards are offered to those who eat fruit and vegetables. The results were quite amazing. The researchers had not been expecting a behaviour change that was so marked. Schools and nurseries showing the video had made fruit and vegetables available in the few weeks before the video was shown. After the video had been viewed, fruit and vegetable consumption rose from 35 to 70 per cent. Home-based studies of children known to be faddy eaters showed that fruit consumption leapt from 4 to 100 per cent after viewing the video. This improvement in eating habits continued, and the children were eating at a similar level six months later.

Encouraging children to cook their own meals is one way of getting them to eat foods that they might otherwise refuse. Helping to prepare vegetables and peel potatoes has been shown to increase their enjoyment and consumption of healthier foods.

Good practice in . . . MANAGING UNWANTED BEHAVIOUR

1 Distract the child by providing more attractive alternatives.
2 Remove the child from the situation. Do not humiliate him or shut him away on his own.
3 If a child is having a tantrum, restrain him gently until he calms down, and then cuddle him and offer reassurance.
4 Ignore swear words.
5 When you are saying 'No', make sure your whole body shows that you mean it.
6 If there is danger, grab the child and say 'No!'
7 Do not reward unacceptable behaviour with your attention.

8 Do not argue with a child in a tantrum.
9 Show disapproval, and make it clear that the behaviour is not acceptable.
10 Make it clear that it is the behaviour that is not wanted, rather than the child.
11 If the child is old enough to understand, explain why the behaviour is unacceptable.
12 Limit punishments, but any sanctions used must be immediate and appropriate.
13 Never smack, shake, bite or humiliate a child.
14 After any incident, show affection, and offer cuddles.
15 Stay calm and in control of yourself.

How to manage separation

It is normal behaviour for children to be upset when they are first left by their parents, but in most cases this is of very short duration, and, after an initial protest, the children will soon settle with you. If the children are old enough, you will probably have encouraged the parents to prepare them well in advance. If they are very small, it will be more difficult for them to understand, and you may find they take longer to accept the situation.

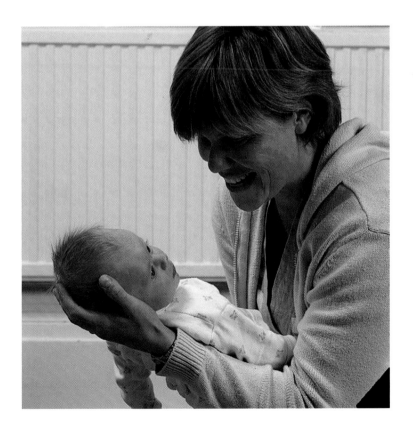

If the children are upset when the parents are leaving, the best way to handle it is to ask the parents to leave as quickly as possible; hanging around and inquiring if the children are 'all right now' will only prolong the distress. On the other hand, if the parents sneak out without saying goodbye, this may make the children feel insecure, as they will never be sure when the parents are suddenly going to disappear. Stress the importance of collecting the child on time so that he knows, for example, that his parents will be there by the time he is having his tea.

Issues that cause conflict

We all want children to eat well, go to bed on time, and live in peace with their siblings and peers, but mealtimes, nap times and sharing toys and space can all cause conflict and ignite challenging behaviour. Occasionally, home-based childcarers and parents can have conflicting views about managing these situations.

Mealtimes

Because we invest a great deal of love and thought in what we provide for children to eat, we may take the rejection of such food personally, and react to food refusal. This reaction and over-anxiety on the behalf of the adult gives the child power, and may encourage later food disorders.

Sensible rules as to when and where food is eaten need to be kept by both you and the parents. Agreement about the type of food provided, how it is cooked and presented, the size of the portion, second helpings, and the time allowed to eat the food all have to be sorted out when you first meet the parents, and up-dated as the child develops.

Rest time

If a child has a regular rest time, and the parents want you to keep to this, you will need to discuss it with them. The possible difficulties are:

- the child may have different rest needs when with you compared with his needs at home
- it is more convenient for you if the children can all nap at the same time, but this may not be possible to achieve
- a child who becomes very tired and fractious needs a nap, even if the parents request that this does not take place
- a child might not want to rest, but the parents wish him to, so that they can enjoy his company in the evening
- rest needs change as the child grows older.

Swearing

Children are excellent mimics, and enjoy new words. They get a great deal of pleasure from repeating words that get a response. The best way to deal with swearing is to ignore it.

Good Practice in Childminding

Masturbation

Some children masturbate as a comfort habit, particularly when bored, watching television or settling to sleep. The best advice is to ignore it, particularly in the younger child. Older children will soon learn from their peers that masturbating in public is unacceptable.

When children's behaviour causes concern, the question you need to ask is whether this is a normal stage in their development, or if there is a more serious problem. Most problems sort themselves out in time, and the quarrelsome child becomes charming and manageable. If this is not the case, you may have to encourage the parents to seek other professional help.

The smacking debate

Smacking is seen as a negative way of dealing with behaviour problems, as the main thing children learn is that larger people can hurt them, and when they grow up they will be able to hurt smaller people. It seldom resolves the problem. Sir William Utting (author of the report on children and violence, 1995) puts it succinctly: 'Hitting people is wrong. Hitting children teaches them that violence is the most effective means of getting your own way. We must develop a culture which disapproves of all forms of violence. All the lessons of my working life point to the fact that violence breeds misery. It does not resolve it.'

If parents smack their children (and the UK is one of the last European countries where it is legal to do so), it may be harder for you to correct their behaviour by other means.

Why should home-based childcarers never use physical punishment?

As a professional person looking after other people's children, it is never correct for you to administer physical punishment whether the parents request it or not. A light slap is one end of the continuum of beating a child and causing injury, and there would never be any reason why a home-based childcarer should hit a child. In your working career you may come across parents who choose to use physical chastisement to discipline their children. You must use your judgement as to when you feel it is necessary to intervene. Parents sometimes need help in understanding that there are alternative modes of control. This is explored more fully in Chapter 11.

Activity

How might you manage the following situations?
1 An older child deliberately provoking his younger brother into losing his temper and throwing food onto the floor.
2 A three-year-old refusing to rest, although obviously very tired.
3 A three-year-old refusing to put on his coat to go outside in very cold weather.
4 A six-year-old taunting and teasing children from a different culture.
5 A child demanding sweets in a supermarket.
6 Three children quarrelling and fighting in a car.
7 Seeing a mother hit her child as she walks along the road.

If you have cared for a child from babyhood, it is unlikely that you will experience too many difficulties in managing his behaviour. It may be more challenging to start to look after an older child, whom you do not know so well. With very few exceptions, all children respond to affectionate care in a secure, consistent environment, where it is obvious that their interests are paramount.

Reflecting on Practice

You might think about:

- how you would manage a two-year-old having a temper tantrum
- what mode of control you use with your own children
- how you might reconcile your disciplinary methods with those that parents might wish you to use with their children
- writing a statement for prospective parents describing how you will manage challenging behaviour
- how your home will accommodate a curious mobile toddler
- your view of the smacking debate
- your opinion on the use of dummies.

This chapter has contributed to the following learning outcomes:

Unit 1

- evaluating a range of techniques for the management of children's behaviour in the home-based setting
- promoting anti-discriminatory, anti-bias practice in the home-based setting

Unit 5

- using a range of methods of observation and assessment to support your work with children
- meeting children's individual learning needs in the home-based setting

Want to Find Out More?

Websites
www.childrenareunbeatable.org.uk
www.practicalparent.org.uk

Further reading
Brain C. and Mukherji P., *Understanding Child Psychology*, Nelson Thornes, 2005
Bruce T. and Meggitt C., *Child Care and Education*, 4th Edition, Hodder Arnold, 2006
Mukherji P., *Understanding Children's Challenging Behaviour*, Nelson Thornes, 2001
Rodd J., *Understanding Young Children's Behaviour*, Allen and Unwin, 1996

6 Caring for babies and toddlers

This chapter includes:

- Understanding the additional demands of babies and toddlers
- Partnership with parents
- Routines
- The development of the small baby and the need for stimulation
- Encouraging development in the toddler

Learning objectives

Unit 1

- Establishing routines for home-based childcare
- Providing play and other activities for children in the home-based setting
- Promote inclusion and anti-bias practice

Unit 2

- Providing for children's development and well-being

Unit 4

- Promoting positive relationships with parents and understanding the importance of valuing the child's primary carer

Some people become home-based childcarers because they adore babies. Their own family may be growing up, having another baby of their own may not be an option and looking after babies is something they enjoy and are competent at, so they can provide the consistent care and stimulation that all babies need. Other home-based childcarers will see babies as too much of a responsibility and too time consuming.

Understanding the additional demands of babies and toddlers

Babies are attractive and provide their carers with constant rewards. A baby who is loved and given as much attention as she demands will reciprocate with smiles and cuddles. Caring for babies takes much time and energy. Routines have to be established, such as feeding, winding, rest times, play times and changing and disposing of nappies. If the baby is prone to colic she will be difficult to settle, and you may have to walk around with her while you are managing your other commitments. Every time you leave the house, you will need to take a great deal of equipment with you, such as nappies, food, toys, and clothes. Small babies are very vulnerable to infection, and in addition to sterilising any feeding equipment, you will need to be extremely vigilant in preventing cross-infection.

A calm and equitable temperament helps when looking after very small babies, as they can be trying. Caring for a baby who continually cries for no apparent reason can be an upsetting and frustrating experience if all your efforts to pacify her are fruitless. If you find you are reaching the end of your tether, as an experienced home-based childcarer you will know to place the baby somewhere safe, and to remove yourself from the situation until you feel able to cope once more.

As the child matures and becomes mobile, you will have to provide close supervision throughout the day. As the child explores her environment, you will have to make sure she is safe, and try to protect your belongings and those of the older children. A toddler is very messy, with her food and with play materials, and it requires patience to allow her to explore.

Settling the baby and the toddler into your home

A baby will show her personality from the start. She may be placid or excitable, easy or difficult to feed or to settle for sleep, need constant attention or be content on her own, she may cry rarely or a great deal or may display a mixture of all of these behaviours.

Some babies appear not to mind who handles and cares for them and will welcome new people and new experiences. This makes it easier for the parent to share the care with you, knowing that the baby will be happy as long as her needs are met. Other babies are slower and more reluctant to accept change and have to be coaxed until they are more familiar with a new carer. A few babies are extremely difficult and will protest loudly at every change. Many babies will exhibit a mixture of these responses.

When a baby is very young, it is important that you and the mother care for the baby together for a while, so that you can be aware of the baby's fussy moods and be shown the best way to respond to her. Small babies need warm consistent care that promotes emotional security, and encouraging the mother to spend some time in your home caring for the baby with you will reassure the mother before she returns to work.

It may be easier to settle a very young baby with you than one of seven months or so. At this age, babies start to miss their mothers and become very aware of strangers, and with some babies this may continue for some time. Between 7 and 15 months, babies feel 'stranger anxiety', becoming anxious in the presence of strangers and strange places, and experience 'separation anxiety', not wishing to be separated from the primary caregiver.

Partnership with parents

Many parents prefer to use home-based childcarers, rather than group care, because they want consistent, individual care for their baby in a family home. You should feel pleased that they have chosen you for what could be the start of a long relationship, stretching over many years.

You will be able to appreciate how difficult it is for many parents to separate from their babies, and you will need to support them by welcoming any visits or telephone calls during the day and by working hard to establish a strong, trusting relationship.

Communication with parents is important whatever the age of the child you are looking after, but if you are caring for babies and toddlers it is vital. They are unable to speak for themselves and to tell the parents what they have achieved during the day. They are also very vulnerable to infection and ill health, and the parents and home-based childcarer should note any changes in appetite, behaviour, excretion or sleep pattern and exchange information in the morning and the evening. At the end of the day, the parents should be informed of any changes that have occurred.

Right at the start, the mother will need to tell you how she expects to feed the baby. If she is using formula milk, you will need to discuss who makes up the feeds and is responsible for sterilising equipment. If the mother is breast-feeding, she may wish to visit your home during the day to feed the baby and you may wish to store some frozen expressed breast milk for emergency use. This will keep for up to forty-eight hours in a fridge, or up to three months in a freezer. Do not use a microwave to thaw or warm milk; it heats the milk unevenly, and the milk may scald the baby's mouth. As the baby matures, her feeding needs will change, and you and the mother will have to work together in introducing new tastes and foods to the baby. You will also need to find out about the baby's preference for:

- sleeping times and routines
- sleeping position
- comfort objects.

You will need to discuss what type of nappies the mother prefers and make arrangements to ensure you have a constant supply. The mother will also wish to tell you about the baby's skin care. This is particularly important if the baby is from a culture different from your own. Dry skin is common in black children and should be given special attention.

Routines

Before leaving the baby with you, the mother will have established certain routines with her baby. It is important that these are discussed, and an attempt is made to continue the established routines. All feeding, sleeping and nappy-changing routines should take place in accordance with the child's individual needs and not as part of the home-based childcarer's routine.

Care of the skin

There are some very common skin conditions that are not infectious but nevertheless need careful handling. To prevent cradle cap, heat rash and nappy rash:

- wash the baby's hair only once or twice a week and rinse it very thoroughly
- look out for any crust on the scalp, and apply olive oil to the crust, washing it off after a few hours
- do not allow the baby to become too hot by over-dressing her, or leaving her in a hot room with a great many bed coverings
- change nappies frequently and wash the baby's bottom at each change
- be aware that creams and washing powders can cause allergies
- ensure that terry-towelling nappies are adequately rinsed, if used
- expose the baby's skin to the air at regular intervals during the day.

Bathtime

If you are responsible for bathing the baby, it should be an enjoyable, rewarding and relaxing time, but you need to be fully aware of the following potential safety measures:

- the bath should not be too full
- the cold tap should be run before the hot tap
- the temperature should be checked before putting the baby into the bath
- a non-slip mat should be put in the bath
- the baby should be put in at the end without the taps
- the room should not be cold
- all equipment and clothing should be gathered together before the bath
- the baby should never be left unattended in the bath.

Bathtime should be fun and an opportunity for the baby to splash, make bubbles, play with bath toys, and enjoy the sensation of the warm water against her skin and the freedom of playing without clothes on. If the baby should be frightened of the water, do not have a confrontation. It is better for the baby to go without bathing for a while until she is ready to enjoy it. A fear of water developed as a baby could inhibit learning to swim at a later date.

Sleep

First of all, you must ensure that you have a cot that is exclusively for the baby, because of the risk of cross-infection and so that the baby has access to the cot whenever she needs to sleep. Sleeping patterns vary considerably in babies. You need to ask the mother the baby's pattern, and understand the importance of allowing the baby to sleep when she wants to and not when it is most convenient for you. You will probably want to check on her once or twice during her nap. A baby-listening device is a useful investment. Other safety factors include:

- cots and prams that meet British Standard Institute safety regulations and display the Kite mark
- a mattress that is firm and well fitting
- pillows and duvets should not be used
- cot bumpers should be avoided
- the baby should not be put down to sleep wearing anything with a string or ribbon round her neck
- sleeping babies should be checked frequently.

You will soon know the amount of noise the baby can tolerate and whether loud sudden noises disturb her or not. As the baby grows and matures, other routines such as tooth brushing and story-time will be established and sleep time will be shorter.

Sudden Infant Death Syndrome (SIDS)

This is the sudden and unexpected death of an infant, usually found dead in her cot or pram with no obvious cause. It occurs in babies between the ages of one week and two years, peaking at three months and it occurs more frequently in the winter months. It has been linked with smoky environments, untreated minor ailments, over-concentrated formula feeds, and multiple births. To reduce the risk:

- always place the baby on her back in her own cot or pram
- always place in the feet-to-foot position, so that the baby cannot slip down under the covers
- avoid overheating; use blankets, not duvets, and avoid cot bumpers
- be sure to report any minor ailment to the parent when the baby is collected.

Prevention of infection

Small babies are very vulnerable to infection and you must be scrupulous in your personal hygiene when sterilising feeding equipment, making up formula milk, changing and disposing of nappies and bathing baby.

Hands should be washed prior to and after each nappy change. It is recommended that disposal gloves be worn during each nappy change. If you have older children in your care, they may need to be taught that they should always wash their hands after using the lavatory and before eating or preparing food. They should also wash before handling the baby, and any cuts on their hands need to be covered.

Crowds and overheated rooms might expose the baby to the risk of illness, whereas a brisk walk in the park will expose her only to fresh air. As the baby develops and becomes more sociable and meets more people, she will be more exposed to possible infection, but by this time her immune system is more able to cope with it.

1 Wash the bottles, teats and other equipment in hot water and detergent. Use a bottle brush for the inside of bottles. **Do not rub salt on the teats.** Squeeze boiled water through the teats.

2 Rinse everything thoroughly in clean running water.

3 Fill the steriliser with clean, cold water. Add chemical solution. If in tablet form, allow to dissolve.

4 Put the bottles, teats and other equipment (nothing metal) into the water. Ensure everything is covered completely by the water, with no bubbles. If necessary, weight down. Leave for the required time according to manufacturer's instructions.

Sterilising feeding equipment

Food and nutrition

The giving of food and nourishment is a key factor in your relationship with the baby. Take your lead from the mother. She may have very definite ideas about how you will feed her baby, when to wean her from milk to solids and what type of foods she wishes you to offer her baby. The mother will be reassured by observing how you hold the baby close, maintain eye contact, talk to the baby, and in general show an understanding of how to feed and interact with a baby.

Breast-feeding

Some mothers will wish to continue to breast-feed either by expressing milk, or returning to the home-based childcarer's during the day. The desire to do this must be respected, but it can be stressful as babies do not necessarily match timetables or recognise lunch breaks. Make sure there is plenty of expressed breast milk in your freezer, to use in an emergency.

Bottle feeds

If the baby is being bottle fed, most parents will deliver the feeds along with the baby. These will be stored in the fridge until required. In the unlikely event of your having to make up a feed, the approximate guide to calculating the amount of formula milk required by a baby is 75 ml of fully reconstituted feed for every 500 g of a baby's weight (2½ fluid ounces per pound body weight) in 24 hours. The total is divided into the number of bottles the baby is likely to take in that time. Like a breast-fed baby, the bottle-fed baby should be allowed to dictate her feeding requirements to allow for changes in appetite and growth. Babies should never be left to feed themselves whilst propped up in the cot, as they may choke and suffocate. Always hold the baby when she is being bottle-fed and use this time to interact with her.

Studies have shown that bottle-fed babies are frequently given feeds that are over- or under-concentrated, so always read and follow the instructions on the packet as manufacturers often develop and change their products. Most home-based childcarers will be familiar with sterilising equipment and preparing bottle feeds.

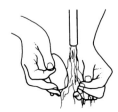

1 Check that the formula has not passed its sell-by-date. Read the instructions on the container. Ensure the container has been kept in a cool, dry cupboard.

2 Boil some **fresh water** and allow to cool.

3 Wash hands and nails thoroughly.

4 Take required equipment from sterilising tank and rinse with cool, boiled water.

5 Fill bottle, or a jug if making a large quantity, to the required level with water.

6 Measure the **exact** amount of powder using the scoop provided. Level with a knife. **Do not pack down.**

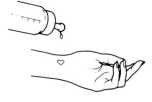

7 Add the powder to the measured wateer in the bottle or jug.

8 Screw cap on bottle and shake, or mix well in the jug and pour into sterilised bottles.

9 If not using immediately, cool quickly and store in the fridge. If using immediately, test temperature on the inside of your wrist.

10 Babies will take cold milk but they prefer warm food (as from the breast). If you wish to warm the milk, place bottle in a jug of hot water. **Never keep warm for longer than 45 minutes** to reduce chances of bacteria breeding.

Note: Whenever the bottle is left for short period, or stored in the fridge, cover with the cap provided.

Preparing feeds

What are the risks associated with over- or under-concentrating formula milk?

Weaning

You will have discussed with the parents when to introduce mixed feeding and when the baby is ready to start solid foods. You will want to agree a routine so that the baby experiences continuity.

All mealtimes, especially those for a baby, should take place in a quiet calm atmosphere, and you should encourage her to enjoy new tastes without ever forcing them upon her. If the baby dislikes something on a Monday, she may well enjoy it the following Friday. It is always worthwhile reintroducing foods, as the baby's tastes become more mature.

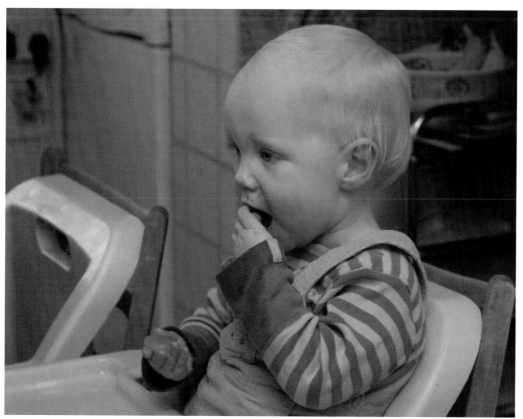

Health checks

It is possible that the parents will ask you to take the baby to the clinic for her regular developmental, hearing and health checks and for her immunisations. Written permission will be needed before the immunisations can be given, and the doctor will wish to have a full medical history, which only the parents can provide. If there are any anxieties about the baby's development or health, it is essential to encourage a parent to attend the clinic. The health visitor's name and telephone number will be recorded on the medical information chart and it may be useful to establish a relationship with her.

Illness develops faster in a baby than in an older child, and any disease can progress quickly, in some cases becoming life threatening. If you are at all worried about the baby, you should contact the parents as soon as possible at an early stage, and then, with their permission, telephone the doctor. Signs of ill health to cause concern are:

- refusal to feed over several feeds
- a rise or fall in temperature
- noisy or laboured breathing
- convulsions or fits
- excessive crying that continues despite cuddles and feeds
- a sunken or bulging anterior fontanelle (the soft spot on the crown of the head)
- a rash
- a persistent cough
- discharge from the ears, or if the baby pulls on the ears and cries
- changes in the stools or urine
- a very quiet, pale baby, difficult to rouse, and refusing to feed
- vomiting and diarrhoea
- poor muscle tension (the baby is very 'floppy').

The development of the small baby and the need for stimulation

Babies learn and develop as soon as they are born, quickly learning to recognise the smell, taste, voice, feel and face of the mother, thus using all the senses to ensure survival. In addition to love, protection, shelter and food, the baby also needs stimulation. At first, the mother provides all the stimulation the baby requires through gentle handling and stroking, speaking in a soft voice and feeding. As the baby develops, the interaction between the mother or the main caregiver and the baby becomes increasingly important. As routines become established, there is time to play when feeding, bathing and changing nappies. Many babies are spending longer parts of the day awake, and you will have fun interacting and playing with her and making sure that she is not left alone or bored.

Encouraging development

By six weeks, most babies are smiling, showing that they are responding to a stimulus, usually during a conversation whilst maintaining good eye contact. This is a good time to introduce mobiles and rattles. The mobiles which will interest her most will have horizontal pictures, so that she can gaze at them when lying on her back in a cot, or supported in a bouncing cradle. Bright colours add interest, and some mobiles have a musical attachment.

Many toys are taken to the baby's mouth, so that she can learn, with one of the most sensitive parts of her body, the shape and substance of the object. This should not be discouraged, but checks must be made for safety. Everything needs to be durable, well made, non-toxic, washable, too large to swallow and have no sharp edges.

By far the most important stimulus is still the consistent contact given to the baby by parents, family and home-based childcarer. Interacting with songs and cuddles and talking to the baby will aid emotional, intellectual and language development. The first response will be facial: smiles and intense looks. Be sure to take turns and listen to the baby when she begins to vocalise. After changing the baby's nappy, allow time for her to play with hands and feet unrestricted by clothing. Most babies enjoy their bathtimes, getting pleasure from the warmth of the water and the freedom to kick and splash. This aids all-round development.

At approximately six weeks, a baby can be seen occasionally moving her hands towards objects in her field of vision and sometimes accidentally succeeding in touching them. At three months, the baby discovers her hands and begins to engage in finger play. By six months, this area of hand–eye co-ordination is usually well established and babies can reach out for a desired object and grasp it. Initially, toys such as an activity centre, which hang suspended just within the baby's reach, will help develop this skill. Play mats with a range of different sensory activities will help stimulate the baby's interest.

Increasingly, the baby's responses are no longer just reflex actions to sensory stimuli, but become selective, and she chooses which stimulus to react to. Lightweight rattles and toys that can be easily held in the hand help to develop hand–eye co-ordination.

Once the baby is able to sit up, supported by cushions, other toys may be offered. An exciting assortment of objects gathered together for her to explore will encourage her all-round development. Bricks can be built into towers and knocked down. Objects can be banged together. Singing to a baby comes naturally to most adults. From action songs to finger rhymes, from nursery rhymes to lullabies, the baby will get pleasure from them all and enjoy a sense of security and comfort. Singing helps babies to recognise different sounds and anticipate repetitive actions.

At this age too, the baby will start to enjoy books. Sitting with you and looking at pictures of familiar objects can start as young as six months and will lay the foundation for a life-long enjoyment of books.

The treasure basket

All areas of sensory development can be encouraged by the use of a treasure basket as described by Elinor Goldschmied. The baby is offered a container filled with objects made of natural materials, chosen for their interesting shape as well as texture. About twenty items are needed to stimulate the five senses, such as a baby mirror, an orange, a fir cone, a piece of pumice, a small natural sponge, tissue paper, small cloth bags containing lavender or cloves, a brush, a piece of velvet, clothes pegs and a bunch of keys. All the equipment needs to be kept clean, and perishable objects such as fruit should be discarded and replaced as necessary. Select items that have no sharp edges. Do not put in any items that are small enough to be inserted into noses or ears. A comfortable and safe position for the baby must be found, so that she does not topple over and become distracted. She should be allowed to explore the items on her own. You should keep an eye on her from a distance and not talk or interact with her as she plays and explores, as this will interfere with her concentration. You need to be alert to when she becomes bored, or has had enough.

Plan a treasure basket. List five items for each of the senses.

Safety factors

- All toys and equipment given to the baby should be clean and washable, to avoid infection.
- They should be durable to avoid accidents from broken edges, and any painted items should be covered in non-toxic paint.
- Small babies are vulnerable to suffocation, so avoid using pillows and cushions and ensure that any plastic bags are stored out of the baby's reach.
- Anything with strings should not be near the baby as, if the string becomes wrapped around the neck or other parts of the body, the blood supply could be cut off, or the child could be hanged.
- Be careful with heavy toys or objects near the baby.

- Always use a harness when the baby is in the pram, or high-chair.
- Avoid small items that the baby might swallow or choke on.

Encouraging development in the toddler

Toddlers are challenging and they may often use the toys and activities provided by you very differently from how you expect, but this is acceptable as learning is still taking place. Toddlers should be given every opportunity to explore and set their own agenda within a safe environment.

Social development

During the second year, the child begins to understand more, and she has to learn how to fit happily into the household and the larger outside environment. A whole set of rules has to be learnt about acceptable behaviour. At this stage, play is solitary, but the presence of a familiar adult provides reassurance and security. The toddler is not interested in playing co-operatively with other children. She has just learnt the meaning of 'mine', and the concept of sharing does not usually occur until the third year.

Taking toddlers to the park, shopping, and visiting friends, parent and toddler groups, drop-in centres, the local library and the clinic, where other small children are likely to be found, will enlarge her social circle and allow her to play alongside other children. Provision of small-scale household equipment, such as brooms, tea sets and telephones, promotes domestic play and the beginning of role-play.

Physical development

During the first year of life, the baby will have developed physical control. Some will be walking confidently by their first birthday, while others may need encouragement to get started and develop balance and co-ordination.

If you have stairs in your home, the gate may be removed on occasion, and the toddler shown how to climb up the stairs and, more importantly, how to crawl down. Strong supermarket cartons, which are sturdy and large enough for toddlers to climb in, promote such skills as getting in and out of objects, co-ordination and balance.

Fine manipulative skills
During the first year, babies start to practise handling and manipulating small objects, reaching and grasping, holding and letting go, moving objects from hand to hand, passing objects, poking and pointing with one finger, and picking up objects with finger and thumb.

Equipment and activities that aid physical skills
There are many materials that will help develop manipulative skills and hand–eye co-ordination, such as bricks for building towers that can be knocked down; cups and beakers for stacking; posting boxes; hammer sets; dolls that are easily undressed and simple inset jigsaws. You can even improvise with small tins and cartons available in the house.

6 chapter

Outings to parks where the playground will have swings, seesaws, climbing frames and rocking toys are enjoyable and will aid balance and co-ordination as well as strengthening arm and leg muscles.

Physical skills are encouraged by ball play, pull-along toys and small-scale climbing and sliding equipment. Other toys and equipment that you might find she enjoys at this age include wheeled toys to push along or sit on and move with the feet, rockers, and tunnels and boxes to climb in and out.

Playing with stacking beakers, posting boxes, barrels, bricks and small model toys will be good for the toddler's manipulative skills. Child-sized tea sets and cooking and cleaning equipment encourage her to imitate you, and this type of play is a spur for later, more creative and imaginative play.

The contents of the lower kitchen cupboards, where it is sensible to store only safe sturdy equipment such as saucepans, plastic storage containers, baking tins and wooden spoons, can be played with. So can small bouncy balls, Duplo, large threading toys and screw toys. Playdough, crayons and finger-paints can be used.

Intellectual development and communication

Children learn at an amazing rate, and during the first year the baby has learnt, among other things, to become mobile, to understand a great deal of what is said, to speak a few words, to identify people with whom she is in regular contact, and to recognise food she enjoys. The next year shows an acceleration of learning as the toddler becomes more proficient with language.

The toddler spends an increasingly large proportion of time in exploratory and experimental play. She will enjoy looking at books, listening to and taking part in songs and rhymes, learning that objects have names as do parts of the body, and realising that using language enables needs to be met without her having to point and cry. Children's minds develop at different rates and in different ways, and they often have individual preoccupations, such as wrapping things up, making 'nests', taking toys around and around and arranging objects in straight lines over and over again.

One good way of promoting language development is to sit down with a toddler, with a book or a toy, and have an enjoyable conversation, making sure you take the time to listen to her responses and to enlarge on her replies. This can be difficult in a busy household, but is rewarding for the child and for you.

Emotional development

During the first year, the baby progresses emotionally from total dependency to an understanding that there are some things she is able to do on her own, and this increases during the second year. You will need to have patience as the toddler tries to help you with her own care, or assist with the chores.

Tantrums can be caused by the toddler being bored, frustrated, hot or cold, hungry or feeling anxious. Sometimes, they just cannot cope with their angry feelings. It is often possible to avoid confrontations but, if these do take place, toddlers are usually quite amenable to diversions. Some feelings are so strong and overpowering that you just have to wait until the storm has passed; then cuddle and comfort her, as she may well be frightened by the immensity of these emotions.

A great deal depends on the developing personality of the child as to how happy or sad she may be. Comfort objects may play a large part in her life and no attempt should be made to remove them. It is best to have as few rules as possible and to make sure that the environment is safe and offers security. Toddlers still need the love and support of a familiar adult and find new emotional demands difficult to deal with. You need to be aware of this when first building a relationship with a child of this age and proceed slowly and sensitively.

This is the age when toddlers really get into messy play. This allows them to express their frustrations and is relaxing and soothing. It is not always easy to organise this in the home but, if it is at all possible, let painting and water play take place outside. It is possible to buy water-based paints and markers that wash out of clothing. Parents should be asked to bring children in clothing that is durable and easily washed. The garden offers such opportunities for messy play as making mud-pies and digging for worms, and, as long as she is not wearing her best clothes, the toddler will be quite easy to clean up after a soak in the bath.

Sensory development

Very young children learn mainly through their senses. As they grow older, learning in this way becomes less dominant. Toddlers, not yet in full command of language, use all their senses spontaneously in exploratory and experimental play. In general, toddlers will explore everything through the senses as this is instinctive, but you may need to encourage children who have some sensory impairment.

6 chapter

1 What materials and activities would you provide for an 18-month-old toddler who is visually impaired?

2 What areas of development are extended and promoted at mealtimes?

3 What particular messy play activities help promote emotional development?

Working with babies and toddlers can be challenging, but it is immensely rewarding, and you may make relationships that endure for life.

Local authorities should now be offering training to home-based childcarers to support the implementation of the 'Birth to Three Matters' Framework as outlined in Chapter 1.

Reflecting on Practice

You might think about:

- your familiarity with making up bottle feeds and sterilising equipment
- satisfying the needs of the babies and toddlers as well as those of their parents
- the hygiene needs of a small baby
- the equipment needed to stimulate physical development of babies and of toddlers and what activities you will plan
- how you will quickly recognise illness in babies
- how you would participate in a weaning programme in partnership with the parents
- where the baby will sleep and how you will organise the daily sleep time
- recognising particular safety hazards when looking after babies and toddlers.

This chapter has contributed to the following learning outcomes:

Unit 1

- providing a variety of suitable routines for children in the home-based setting
- planning and providing appropriate play and other activities for children in the home-based setting
- working in partnership with parents
- promoting anti-discriminatory, anti-bias practice in the home-based setting

Unit 2

- providing for children's development and well-being from birth to 16 years

Unit 4

- communicating effectively with parents

Want to Find Out More?

Websites

www.gtce.org.uk
www.peep.org.uk
www.raz-kids.com
www.zerotothree.org

Further reading

Dare A. et al., *A Practical Guide to Working with Babies*, 4th Edition, Nelson Thornes, 2009

Goldschmied E. and Jackson S., *People Under Three: Young Children in Day Care*, 2nd Edition, Routledge, 2003

Rowlands H., *Making 'Birth to Three Matters' Work for You*, QEd Publications, 2005

Silberg J., *Games to Play with Babies*, Brilliant Publications, 2004
  Games to Play with Toddlers, Brilliant Publications, 2005
  Games to Play with 2-year-olds, Brilliant Publications, 1999

7 Caring for the school-age child

Learning objectives

Unit 1

■ Establishing routines for home-based childcare
■ Promote inclusion and anti-bias practice

Unit 2

■ Providing for children's development and well-being

Unit 5

■ Preparing, implementing and evaluating plans for home-based groups of children of different ages and abilities

Home-based childcarers are frequently employed to care for children before and after school, and in the school holidays. You may have cared for the children when they were babies or toddlers, or they may be the older siblings of children you are caring for now. They may be children who have been at home with their parents, or used other forms of daycare, and who now need looking after before and after school, as their parents are working. Some children may require more attention than others, and may take time to adjust to the home-based childcarer and new routines. Government initiatives in recent years have led to more children requiring after-school care.

Looking after mixed age groups can be challenging as careful planning is needed to ensure that the care and learning needs of all the children in your care are met.

Development and growing independence

Once one of the children you look after starts school full time he will have reached a stage of growing independence and his peer group will become increasingly important and dominant. Judith Harris (*The Nurture Assumption*, 1998) proposes that, at this age, the peer group and inheritance factors have more influence on the child than the parents do. In spite of this, he will still need care and stimulation from you and an understanding of his different status.

Children have a busy day at school and need to have their routine firmly structured. Going to bed at a reasonable time, dressing themselves as quickly and efficiently as they can manage, having time to eat a nutritious breakfast, cleaning teeth and combing hair, and being ready on time all take practice. You can play your part in preparing the child by making sure that in the holiday before school starts he can dress and undress himself and see to all his toilet needs. You can talk to him about the school day and how it will be more structured than the pre-school. Without frightening him, you could explain that the playground will be noisier than he is used to and the dining room will be larger.

Whoever is collecting the child from school will need to make sure that he is not kept waiting. Even a few minutes wait after the other children have left can have a very negative effect on a child. After school, he will need some time to unwind and perhaps have a snack before starting his homework or attending any extra-mural activities. It needs a fair amount of self-discipline for him to ignore the younger children who may be playing outside or watching television and you may have to persuade him to stick to his routine.

Communicating with the parents is just as important at this age as it was with the younger children. You will need to keep up to date with the changing rules in the parent's household, in respect of the child's growing independence, so that you can offer the same consistent approach. A five-year-old might assure you that he is allowed to play outside before doing his homework, as his mother always lets him do so. This needs to be checked!

He understands that his parents and his home-based childcarer do not know exactly what has been happening during the day and that it is possible to keep secrets from them. When he does wish to confide in you, he demands your undivided attention.

From about the age of eight, the child's growing independence should be encouraged and his carers need to let go gradually, trusting him to make his own mistakes within a framework of respect, and valuing him as an autonomous person. This works both ways, and you will expect him to become increasingly considerate, and adhere to the rules of the house. As he grows older, rules may have to be revised, and agreed between the parents, the child and the home-based childcarer.

Activity

1 Describe how you give added responsibility to the older children that you care for.
2 How do you encourage school-age children to express their feelings?

You will have discussed with the parent the routine that is required after school, and the child will be quite aware of what is expected. Children these days have very busy lives, full of extra-mural activities at the weekend, extra classes and coaching, parties and team games, Cubs, Brownies or Woodcraft Folk. You may be involved in taking and picking up children from these activities. There will be little time for organised activities in your home during the school year, and there is a lot to be said for identifying some time for 'free play'.

The child's circle of friends will become increasingly important to him and his regard for their opinion will start to displace his wish to always please you or his parents. When you arrive to collect him, you might be told that he has been invited to his best friend's for tea that day. You will have to explain to the best friend's parent that the parents expect you to collect their child and suggest that any social arrangements are made through the parents, giving you adequate notice. While in your home, children often ask to go out to play with friends or ride a bike around the block, and such requests can be a major cause of friction. The Children Act 1989 requires children to be supervised at all times by you while in your care, and this cannot be delegated to any other adult.

School-age children become more aware of their special identity and gender, due to peer-group influence, and will need your reassurance to bolster their self-esteem. Unfortunately, you may find some of the children in your care absorbing the prejudiced attitudes of their peers at school, and you will have to be alert to this and challenge name-calling and stereotypical attitudes. You will have to make it clear that this behaviour is not acceptable and that if it continues you may have to discuss it with the child's parents. By always using equipment that reflects positive images of all racial groups, religions and cultures and does not discriminate on the basis of disability or gender, you will be playing your part in ensuring equality of opportunity for all.

Developing skills

Physical development

Children of five learn to write, and this skill is developed and improved all through their school days. Tying shoelaces and colouring in perfectly are indicators of better hand–eye co-ordination.

By six or seven, they can usually make themselves a snack, skip with a rope and ride a two-wheeler bike skilfully. Ball skills develop and often take up a large part of their leisure time. Physical skills continue to improve and develop. Muscles become stronger and outside play can become more energetic. Team games help social development. Swimming is learnt. Regular sporting activities and exercise encourage these skills and are the foundation for an interest in keeping fit and healthy in later life.

Intellectual development

Starting school will obviously encourage intellectual development, as the young child is keen to learn and ask many questions about events outside his family. By eight years of age, most children will be able to read quite well and write short stories; they will have some mathematical skills, tell the time and perhaps start to learn a musical instrument, act in a play, and paint and draw. Between the ages of 8 and 12 children begin to think in a more abstract way. They do not need to have, for example, actual counters in front of them to calculate numbers.

The ability to think logically becomes increasingly developed throughout the school years. Language and vocabulary is often as good as an adult's; this will depend to some extent on the language abilities of the family and the other adults with whom the child mixes.

Social and emotional development

When children first start school, their emotional development may appear to go backwards. They might become fussy about food, demand help with putting on outside clothes and play with toys that are old and familiar. This is just an adjustment to having to be a 'big boy' whilst at school, and is a perfectly normal stage of development. A full school day is physically tiring, and this might also affect his behaviour.

On some days, the child may be full of news and expect your undivided attention as he relates the exciting events of the day. At other times, perhaps after a day when things have not gone so well, he may be silent and sullen, and just want to flop down on the couch and watch the television. He begins to have his own private world separate from his family and carers. Sometimes this leads increasingly to fights and squabbles with younger children as he needs his own privacy and a place to think.

From about the age of eight, the child's growing independence should be encouraged and his parents and carers need to let go gradually, trusting him to make his own mistakes within a framework of respect, and valuing him as a more independent person. School-age children become more aware of their special identity and gender, because of the influence of their friends.

Adolescence

Adolescence describes the period of time from puberty, at about 12 years of age, to adulthood. This is a time of physical change and growth. Up until now, boys and girls of the same age are quite similar in height, weight and strength, but at puberty differences become obvious. As girls reach puberty before boys, for a year or so they are often taller and stronger, but once the boys catch up their growth spurt is even more apparent. Boys develop larger muscles and less fat than girls. This gives them greater speed and strength of movement. They tend to be superior in sports that demand strength and speed. Both boys and girls may develop spots, sometimes leading to acne, due to over active hormones.

As well as a physical growth spurt there is also an increase in intellectual ability, and abstract thought becomes more complex. It is thought that, because girls reach puberty before boys, they often do better in exams and tests at 11 years of age. As there is more equality of opportunity these days, girls have more opportunity to study traditional 'male' subjects such as mathematics, physics and technology. The wider world beckons, and adolescents become interested in the local community and in national and international affairs. They can develop an intense interest in religion or politics. Boys and girls go on to higher education in about the same numbers.

This period is a time of change in emotional behaviour. By testing their feelings against authority adolescents find out their true identity and discover their own codes of behaviour. Parents often find it difficult to cope with the mood swings of their children, loving and caring one day, difficult and argumentative the next. This can be a difficult time for all concerned, but most issues are resolved during this period.

It is a time when an interest in sex begins. Friends become even more important and have a great influence on general behaviour. Adolescents can become depressed quite easily and can lose confidence in themselves, becoming shy and embarrassed. Eating disorders often start during this time.

Road safety

You will probably be involved in taking and fetching children from school, and will have to take all the children you are caring for with you. If you are using the car, appropriate restraints will have to be fitted and used on every occasion. If you are walking, you will apply the rules of road safety, teaching all the children how to cross the road safely, and following the rules yourself at all times.

There is a certain discipline the children will have to obey if they are to be totally safe when out with you. If you are caring for children of varying ages, from babies to school age, the baby should be strapped in the harness in the pram, the toddler should wear reins, and be held firmly by you, and the older children should walk close to the pram and never be allowed to run too far ahead. When you arrive at the school, you will have to take all the children in with you and never for one minute leave the baby in the pram unattended.

Liaison with the school

The parents will have made the initial contact with the school, met the teachers and seen the classroom. Once you start to take and collect the child from the school, you will begin to make relationships with the staff team and will be informed of any concern or achievement that has taken place during the day. The school will need to understand that the parents trust you and have given you permission to discuss their child and convey messages back to them. Some teachers find this difficult because of the professional rules of confidentiality, and you may need to take the parents' written consent. Make sure parents receive all written and practical information given to you by the school and do not rely on the children to do so – they often forget!

Activity

How might home-based childcarers encourage teachers to accept them as professional carers and educators?

If you are asked to help with homework, all the information the parents receive from the school about curriculum planning needs to be shared with you, so that you understand what is required. There are some practical issues, such as:

- finding a quiet place for the child to work
- agreeing with the child and the parents how much time should be given to homework
- what homework needs to be done on which night.

As this will be a very busy time of day for you, it may be difficult to offer intensive one-to-one support. Encourage the parents to share the information they receive at parents' evenings with you, so that you can further help the child.

If you do not have children at school, you may not be fully aware of the National Curriculum, which is taught to all children from 5 to 16. All primary schools have to provide a literacy hour and a numeracy hour every day. The National Curriculum is divided into Key Stages, and children are tested at 5, 7, 11 and 14 to make sure they have attained the required targets.

Bullying

The child you are caring for might be unfortunate enough to be one of the number of children who are the victims of bullying. Bullying is rare among under-fives, but can occur even though young children are usually well supervised at all times. In the infant school, some forms of bullying may take place, such as name-calling, fighting, excluding a child from his peer group, sending to Coventry and racial abuse.

Dan Olweus, an expert in the prevention of bullying, defines bullying as involving:

- deliberate hostility and aggression towards the victim
- a victim who is weaker and less powerful than the bully or bullies
- an outcome which is always painful and distressing to the victim.

Bullying is the main cause for school refusal and can result in emotional scars that remain for life.

There are some behavioural indicators in children that might alert you to the fact that a child is being bullied. These indicators may be:

- reluctance or refusal to attend school or nursery
- saying he feels unwell in the mornings
- coming home with torn clothes
- being hungry, having had his lunch stolen
- withdrawal, unhappiness or showing signs of poor self-esteem
- crying frequently
- parents report that the child has frequent nightmares
- aggression
- starting to bully other children
- reluctance to talk about what is happening.

Children who bully others may:

- have low self-esteem
- have little sense of their own worth

- be in families where they are not encouraged to show or express their feelings
- have experienced bullying or even abuse from others (this may still be occurring).

Home-based childcarers have a responsibility to tackle bullying alongside parents and schools. If you are caring for a child who is being bullied, you will comfort and reassure the child and discuss the issue with the parents and, if the parents request it, with the school. If you discover that the child you are caring for is bullying others, the strategies you might use include:

- getting the facts clear, finding out from the teachers and the child's parents what has been happening
- talking to the child with the permission of the parents, about the consequences of his actions
- discussing any problems that the child feels he has at school or at home
- building up his self-esteem and valuing his achievements
- agreeing with the child's parents on how to reward the child's good behaviour.

Activity

If you suspected that a child that you care for was being bullied at school:
1 What steps might you take to help the child in the short term?
2 How might you support the family in the long term?

CASE STUDY

Sylvia, an experienced home-based childcarer, was preparing the tea in the kitchen, when she overheard David, aged seven, being racially abusive towards Ashid, aged four. When David saw Sylvia, he stopped. Sylvia decided to ignore it for the time being, and planned to talk to David's mother about it when she came to collect him.
1 Was this the right approach?
2 How could she prevent such behaviour in the future?
3 What should she do to support and comfort Ashid?

Out-of-school activities

You may be asked to care for school-age children for all or part of the holidays. You will need to establish if and when the parents are taking them on holiday, so that you can work out a suitable programme. It will need careful planning to meet the needs of all the children of various ages in your care.

There is no pressure on home-based childcarers to follow a curriculum with the school-age child. Your role is to provide a safe, secure but challenging environment and to make available appropriate resources for play. When you are planning activities you may have to take into account a wide age range, often from 5 to 12 years, and sometimes up to 16 years, as well as babies and pre-school children.

School today makes many demands on children, and the holidays should be a more carefree time to pursue their own interests and have fun. You will need to adjust the way in which you work to suit the needs of older children and young people, and so it is worth taking a look at the Playwork principles which explain the values playwork is based on. The principles themselves appear below; it is good practice to promote them in your work with older children.

Playwork principles

These principles establish the professional and ethical framework for playwork and as such must be regarded as a whole. They describe what is unique about play and playwork, and provide the playwork perspective for working with children and young people.

They are based on the recognition that children and young people's capacity for positive development will be enhanced if given access to the broadest range of environments and play opportunities.

1   All children and young people need to play. The impulse to play is innate (built in). Play is a biological, psychological and social necessity, and is fundamental to the healthy development and well being of individuals and communities.
2   Play is a process that is freely chosen, personally directed and intrinsically motivated. That is, children and young people determine and control the content and intent of their play, by following their own instincts, ideas and interests, in their own way and for their own reasons.

3 The prime focus and essence of playwork is to support and facilitate the play process and this should inform the development of play policy, strategy, training and education.

4 For playworkers, the play process takes precedence and playworkers act as advocates for play when engaging with adult-led agendas.

5 The role of the playworker is to support all children and young people in the creation of a space in which they can play.

6 The playworker's response to children and young people playing is based on a sound up-to-date knowledge of the play process, and reflective practice.

7 Playworkers recognise their own impact on the play space and also the impact of children and young people's play on the playworker.

8 Playworkers choose an intervention style that enables children and young people to extend their play. All playworker intervention must balance risk with the developmental benefit and well being of children.

The activities you provide for children as a home-based childcarer will depend to some extent on the restrictions of the home and the number and ages of the children in your care.

You might consider some of the following activities:

- physical games and the chance to use physical skills, such as climbing and building
- craft and creative activities
- cooking with you
- board games or cards
- enjoyment of books and story time
- selected use of television or video
- imaginative play
- opportunities for free play and the encouragement to do this
- trips out, either locally or more special trips further afield.

Here are some suggestions for older children:

1 When using clay with the children, ask them what they might like to make. The ideas should come from them. When the object is finished, allow the clay to harden. The child may then paint it, and, after varnishing, the finished article should last for some time.

2 Read a book without pictures to the children. Ask the children to draw some scenes from their imagination, and make these drawings into a book.

3 Buy some grass seed with the children. Choose different media on which to grow the grass, such as sand, earth, cotton wool, blotting paper and cardboard. Ask the children to measure and record which grass grows the fastest and which looks the healthiest? Why?

4 Take the children shopping with you. Having let them decide what they want to cook, let them buy the correct amount of ingredients, pay for them, and make sure they have the right change. They will be able to weigh and measure everything themselves.

Sometimes the older children may be booked into playschemes or sports camps, and you would be looking after them at similar times as in term-time. Other children may be spending the day with you, and the activities that you would normally provide for the pre-school children will have to be extended and made interesting for the older children. For example, if you have introduced a junk-modelling activity, ask the older children for their ideas for a theme and allow it to continue until the project is complete. You may need to extend the range of equipment that you have available.

Most local authorities provide a range of activities and entertainment in their parks and libraries. Your newspaper will also give information as to what is available. Many museums mount special interactive exhibitions for children during the holidays. It may be useful to design a large chart, displaying details of what is available for each day as a reminder of where you might take the children. Many home-based childcarers get together in the holidays, arranging outings together and pooling resources.

Reflecting on Practice

You might think about:

- how you encourage children to become independent
- how much privacy is appropriate for this age group
- how you might liaise with your local schools
- suitable holiday outings
- your role in supervising homework
- how to support a child who is being bullied.

This chapter has contributed to the following learning outcomes:

Unit 1

- providing a variety of suitable routines for children in the home-based setting
- planning and providing appropriate play and other activities for children in the home-based setting
- promoting anti-discriminatory, anti-bias practice in the home-based setting

Unit 2

- providing for children's development and well-being from birth to 16 years

Unit 5

- planning, providing and evaluating appropriate experiences and play

Want to Find Out More?

Websites

www.ipl.org/div/kidspace
www.londonplay.org.uk/home
www.minedu.govt.nz
www.naturegrid.org.uk
www.playtrain.org.uk
www.show.me.uk
www.4children.org.uk

Further reading

Bonel P. et al., *Good Practice in Playwork*, 3rd Edition, Nelson Thornes, 2009
Davy A., *Playwork – Play and Care of Children 5–15*, Thompson Learning, 2000
Mosley J. and Thorp G., *All Year Round: Exciting Ideas for Peaceful Playtimes*, LDA, 2002
Phinn G., *Young Readers and Their Books*, David Fulton, 2000

The safe environment

This chapter includes:

- Types of accidents
- Checking hazards inside and outside the home
- Planning in case of an emergency
- Hygiene in the kitchen and bathroom
- Medication
- Recording accidents

Learning objectives

Unit 1

- Establishing a safe and healthy childcare environment in the home-based setting
- Promote inclusion and anti-bias practice

Children are the responsibility of the adults who care for them. An accident is something that happens that is not anticipated or foreseen, and may be preventable with care and thought. Sometimes, accidents occur because the carer is in a hurry, is experiencing stress due to personal problems, or is feeling tired and is therefore less alert.

The National Standards require all home-based childcarers to be aware of the need to provide a hazard-free and safe environment in the home. This allows children to explore safely, and in turn aids all their areas of development and promotes independence. It is not always easy to find the balance between allowing too much independence and being over-protective. The younger the child, the more supervision is necessary. If a group of children becomes very quiet, it is always sensible to investigate!

Information from the Royal Society for the Prevention of Accidents (RoSPA) and the Home Accident Surveillance System (HASS) shows that the most serious accidents happen in the kitchen and on the stairs, and the largest number of accidents happens in the living room/dining room area.

Types of accidents

Falls

Twenty children die as a result of falls each year, some from windows and balconies, the remainder mostly on stairs. Forty-two per cent of all accidents involve falls. The worst injuries occur when children fall from a great height or land on something hard, sharp or hot. Most falls result from falling between two levels, such as falling out of a pram or falling from a bed.

Burns and scalds

Seventy-one per cent of these injuries happen to children under five. Most of the scalding injuries are caused by mugs or cups of tea or coffee being knocked over. Tea or coffee is still hot enough to scald 15 minutes after being made and it is therefore not best practice to leave cups of coffee or tea around, or to sit children on your lap while you are drinking. Burning injuries are caused from contact with hot surfaces, such as fires or cookers, or by playing with matches.

Cuts

There has been an increase in glass-related accidents, because of the fashion for patio doors, large windows and glass tabletops. As many as five children might die in one year following an accident with glass. Accidents involving all types of glass account for nearly 40,000 injuries to children a year.

Poisoning

Most poisoning accidents involve medicines, followed by household products and cosmetics. Every year, approximately 15,000 children receive in-patient treatment and 43,000 children receive outpatient treatment.

Other causes

Other accidents may be caused by foreign bodies in the ear or eye, choking, mainly on food, and drowning either in the bath or garden pond. The number of accidents involving family pets is increasing.

One child in 12 will be treated for a home accident each year. Half the children are under four years of age. Boys are more likely to have an accident than girls. Children in lower socio-economic groups are more likely to have a fatal accident than those in higher groups. Such factors as divorce, death in the family, chronic illness, homelessness and moving home increase the likelihood of a child having an accident, due to the stress caused to the main carer.

To prevent accidents to children, a combination of factors is required:

- improvements in the planning, design and manufacture of products to create a safer environment
- an increasing awareness of risks, hazards and safety equipment
- education and training to improve knowledge and skills.

Activity

Suffocation and choking is the third most common cause of death in young children. What steps can you take to prevent this happening to the children in your care?

A professional approach to safety might involve you in carrying out the following checks on a regular basis:

- examine each room of the house for obvious hazards
- test and maintain all safety equipment
- make sure that all the children's equipment, such as high-chairs, pushchairs and prams, is clean, has attached harnesses, and is well maintained
- make sure the garden is safe
- ensure that the car is regularly serviced, and has appropriate restraints and car seats fitted
- carry out a fire drill at least once a month, making this into a game so as not to alarm the children.

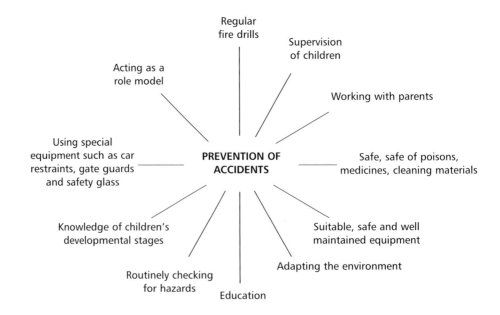

Checking hazards inside and outside the home

Keeping your home safe is not just a matter of checking for hazards, and being sure that there is nothing dangerous around. It entails constant vigilance and imagination whilst inspecting and maintaining all equipment on a daily basis. You will find yourself as a role model and educator, not only with your own children, but also with the children in your care.

Good practice in . . . PREVENTING ACCIDENTS IN THE HOME

1 Check domestic and play equipment regularly for sharp edges, splinters and loose pieces. Do not give children under three small playthings, such as marbles or small Lego pieces.
2 Always buy toys and equipment from reputable shops. Look at the label, and check for the Kite mark.
3 Keep the following objects out of sight and out of reach of children:
   - medicines and tablets, which must be kept locked in a high cupboard
   - matches
   - sharp objects, such as knives and razor blades
   - plastic bags
   - household cleaners and chemicals
   - alcohol
   - cigarettes.

4 Ensure that safety gates for stairs or doorways are secure.
5 Never use baby walkers as there have been serious accidents when using this equipment.
6 Do not use pillows for any child under 18 months. Use a firm mattress with no gaps between it and the cot.
7 Always supervise children in the kitchen where there are many hazards. You must be sure to:
   - turn saucepan handles away from the edge of the stove
   - keep all hot and sharp objects away from the edge of units
   - use short, coiled flexes on electrical equipment
   - have a fire blanket, and know how to use it
   - keep chest freezers locked
   - keep the doors to washing machines and tumble dryers shut
   - avoid using tablecloths that hang down
   - use a harness fitted to the high-chair and see that it is always secured.
   - always supervise children when they are eating or drinking and never leave a baby propped up with a bottle.
8 Avoid giving nuts or hard-boiled sweets to children.
9 Remove rugs from highly polished floors and try to keep floor space free of obstruction, as much as possible.
10 Make sure cords are not trailing from curtains or blinds.
11 Avoid anything around babies' necks, such as anorak strings, dummies on strings and ribbons on hats.
12 Fit child-resistant locks on all windows, keeping keys readily available in case of fire.
13 Use safety glass or safety film for large areas of glass and for low-level glass.
14 Highlight large glass doors with stickers.
15 Secure doors leading to cellar, balcony and any unsupervised outside area.
16 Do not leave a hot drink unattended, and never sit a child on your lap while drinking something hot.

To prevent fire:
- make sure all fires have securely fitted safety guards
- have your water-heating and heating equipment regularly inspected and maintained.

In case of fire:
- have smoke alarms fitted and keep them maintained
- plan how you would escape from your home, particularly if you have sealed windows or permanently locked doors
- practise fire drill with the children regularly.

To prevent electric shocks:

- cover all power points with child-resistant socket covers
- check all flexes regularly for fraying and replace those that are worn
- never put electrical appliances in the bathroom
- make sure new electric appliances come fitted with a plug.

Good practice in . . . PREVENTING ACCIDENTS IN THE GARDEN

1 Keep garage and shed doors locked, and keep all equipment and materials locked away out of sight and out of reach of children.
2 Secure garden gates and fences so that children cannot get out and people and animals cannot get in.
3 Cover or fence off any area or equipment containing water.
4 Cover sandpits when not in use to avoid soiling by animals.
5 Destroy poisonous plants.
6 Check all outdoor play equipment such as slides and climbing frames regularly for safety, and make sure that any new equipment is correctly installed and that the space underneath has either mats or wood chippings to ensure a soft landing.
7 Avoid trailing clothes lines.
8 Supervise animals when children are in the garden, and put a cat-net over a baby's pram.
9 It is safer to avoid ponds and water butts in gardens, but any that you cannot remove need to be securely netted. A young child can drown in two inches of water.

Activity

1 You are caring for a six-month-old baby and an active four-year-old. Which hazards in the house and in the garden are particularly dangerous for each age group?
2 Devise a safety checklist for your home and garden.
3 Identify indoor and outdoor plants that might be poisonous.

Further afield

You will be taking children out very often, going shopping, posting letters, collecting older children from school, and visiting libraries and friends. You may find yourself having to manage a baby in a pushchair and an active toddler.

With very young children, it is prudent to avoid places where:

- there are very large open spaces and a child might wander off
- there is a lot of traffic and pollution
- animal droppings are not cleared up promptly
- there is a great deal of litter dropped, such as in some markets
- the children have to be quiet and keep still for a long time
- it is difficult to supervise more than one child safely, such as in a playground with swings, high obstacle courses and slides, and unsupervised water play
- there are sandpits that are not covered at night to prevent animals from fouling them.

It is a good idea to take a small emergency First Aid kit on any outing. It is never too early to start teaching children basic rules of safety, and making sure that they know their address and home telephone number. When in parks and on beaches, always identify a highly visible point, such as a café, where children should go if they are lost.

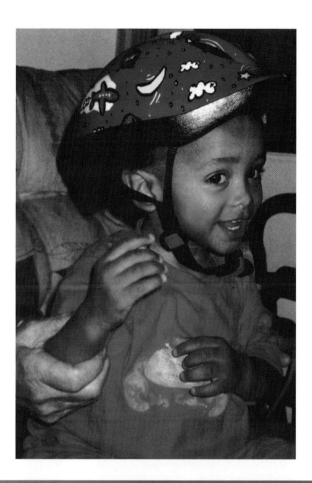

1 Maintain prams and pushchairs in good working order and check brakes regularly.
2 Fit harnesses to prams and pushchairs and always use them.
3 Be a good role model when crossing the road, teaching children road safety from an early age. Always use zebra or pelican crossings if available. Make sure that children are holding your hand, or the pram.
4 Never push the pram or other conveyance into the road first, so as to stop the traffic.
5 Be alert when in shopping centres and other busy areas. Use personal restraints, such as harnesses or reins.
6 When in a park, use the 'children only' areas and exercise constant supervision in the playground.

▶

7 If you are taking children further afield, you will need to plan the trip carefully and well in advance. Consultation with parents is essential, and you will need to make sure you have their written permission. Do double check that your insurance covers all the activities you are planning.

8 Children should never be left alone outside shops or schools. Prams must either be taken into shops with you, or you must carry the baby.

Activity

1 Plan a picnic in your local park, with children aged one, three and six.
2 What would it be essential to have with you so as to make sure the children are protected and you are prepared for any emergency?

Always be alert to danger, and aware that children are small, vulnerable beings. Knowledge of children's development should allow you to anticipate some potential hazards and risks, and understanding the children's personalities will help you to predict how they will react to situations. Part of your role is to teach children about dangers, and how to protect themselves.

Good practice . . . **WHEN USING THE CAR**

You might find yourself using your car to transport the children from place to place. There are certain checks you need to make and rules to establish:

1 Check that your car insurance is valid for business purposes and fully comprehensive.
2 All adults in the car must wear seat belts, whether in the front or in the back.
3 All children in the car should be secured in child restraints appropriate to the size of the child, with the younger children in the back.
4 Make sure that child-locks are activated when you have the children with you.
5 Do not allow the family pet in the car when you are transporting children.
6 All child restraints should be professionally fitted.
7 Never allow the children to stand up on the seats, between the front seats, or travel in the back section of an estate or hatchback.
8 Make sure that children alight on to the pavement, and not the road.
9 Make sure that all the children are properly secured in the car before you get in. If you are carrying a number of children, count them, to make sure you have not inadvertently left one behind!
10 Be a careful and alert driver, a good example to the children.

In the Easter holidays, Anita, a newly registered home-based childcarer, took her two children and the two she looked after to the zoo with her friend Jessie, who has three children of her own. They had to take two cars. All the children were playing up, wanting to sit in particular seats, next to friends. When they met up at the ticket office, Anita was horrified to find that her son, Jamie, who is seven, was not with them. Anita thought he had gone with Jessie, and she thought he was with Anita.

The day was ruined, as they all had to return home, and they found Jamie in tears in the back garden.

1 What could Anita have done to prevent this situation happening?

2 How would you have dealt with Jamie?

Planning in case of an emergency

There are many types of emergencies that might arise during the day and you need to be prepared. Each child should have an individual record form (see www.ncma.org.uk).

As you complete this form with the parents, it will be an opportunity to discuss how you handle any crisis. For example, if a child is prone to asthma, some parents might wish the child to be taken straight to hospital, where they will meet you, while others might like to come to you from work.

There might be other emergencies where you are unable to look after the children. You will need to think about back-up help, someone who would take over at short notice. Reassure the parents that the children will never be left with anyone who is not a registered home-based childcarer, except in a real emergency where there was not any choice. You need to have access to a telephone, together with a list of essential telephone numbers. If you do not have one at home, do you know where the nearest public telephone is? Do you always have coins or a phone-card available? Many of you will have your own mobile phone; it should be fully charged at all times.

The 'House information' table on page 165 may be useful to someone who takes over from you and is not as familiar as you are with the house.

HOUSE INFORMATION

Your stand-in carer has been informed:	Tick for Yes
how to secure the house (doors, windows, shutters)	❏
how to set the alarm	❏
where to find a spare set of keys	❏

Where to find the:	
fire extinguisher	....
torch	....
candles	....
fuse box	....
First Aid kit	....

Emergency telephone numbers:	
Gas	....
Electricity	....
Water	....
Vet	....
Local authority	....

Arrangements for disposal of rubbish	....

How to use domestic equipment:	
Washing machine	....
Drier	....
Dishwasher	....
Microwave	....
Cooker	....
Central heating	....

Other essential information	....

First Aid

It is a requirement to complete a First Aid course when regisering as a home-based childcarer. Courses should be taught by those with expertise, such as the St John Ambulance or the British Red Cross or a trainer approved by NCMA. All First Aid certificates need to be updated regularly. First Aid is the immediate action taken to treat a person who has been injured or has suddenly become ill. Knowing what to do can save life and prevent further injury, but it is important to know your limits and do only what you are competent to do. Urgent care requires you to:

- remove the victim from the source of danger
- check breathing and give artificial respiration if necessary
- control bleeding
- place the child in the recovery position if she is unconscious
- call for help, giving accurate information, and keeping any substance that might be relevant to diagnosing the condition.

Many hospitals now offer two-hour resuscitation sessions, which you might like to attend, prior to taking a full First Aid course. NCMA recommends that the full range of emergency action skills requires at least a 12-hour course.

Many accidents cause shock in children, and you will need to recognise the signs, which are:

- pale, cold, sweaty skin
- rapid pulse, becoming weaker
- shallow, fast breathing
- restlessness, yawning and sighing
- thirst
- loss of consciousness.

If you think one of the children is suffering from shock, you should summon medical aid.

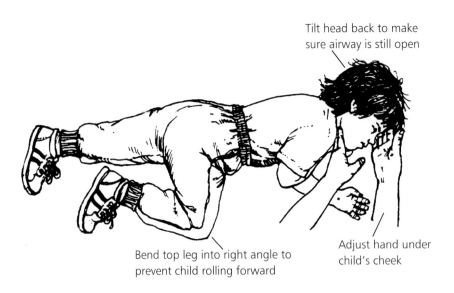

Tilt head back to make sure airway is still open

Bend top leg into right angle to prevent child rolling forward

Adjust hand under child's cheek

Anaphylactic shock

This is a generalised allergic reaction that may occur a few minutes after:

- eating a particular food, such as peanuts
- being stung by an insect or a sea creature
- the injection of a particular drug.

This is a rare occurrence, but one where a knowledge of First Aid is essential. The air passages become constricted and swelling of the face and neck increases the risk of suffocation. The signs are:

- anxiety
- red blotchy skin
- swelling of face and neck
- puffy eyes
- wheezing
- a fast pulse
- difficulty in breathing.

If you think a child might be suffering from anaphylactic shock, you must act immediately and call an ambulance. If the child has a known allergy, there may be medicine to take in case of an attack. Give this as soon as the attack starts, following the directions carefully. Keep calm and reassure the child, putting her in a position that relieves her breathing difficulty.

Concussion

Concussion is not always easy to recognise. After a bump to the head, a child might be concussed if there is:

- a brief loss of consciousness
- dizziness
- nausea
- mild headache
- loss of memory of events immediately preceding the accident.

An unconscious child who is breathing and has a pulse should be put into the recovery position to keep the airway clear by preventing choking on the tongue or vomit. Check for breathing and pulse until medical aid arrives.

Contents of a First Aid box

Your First Aid box should contain:

- cotton wool
- prepared bandages in several sizes
- gauze squares in several sizes
- a triangular bandage
- crêpe bandages in several sizes and lengths
- tubular gauze with applicator
- surgical spirit
- plasters in several sizes
- surgical tape
- disposable plastic gloves

- safety pins
- small mirror to check breathing
- tweezers
- scissors
- thermometer, preferably a fever strip that can be applied to a child's forehead.

We have suggested a basic kit, but you would need to discuss with the parents any possible allergies to plasters. You will probably keep medication available to treat your own family. You should not prescribe these medicines for other children you are looking after.

The box should be airtight and clearly labelled. It should be accessible to adults but not to children. Store the box with the accident book so that you remember to fill the book in immediately. Replace items as you use them.

Hygiene in the kitchen and bathroom

It is particularly important for home-based childcarers to have high standards of personal hygiene, as they have to carry out intimate tasks for the children, as well as teaching them the rules of hygiene.

Infection is spread by touch, food and water, animals, droplets in the air and through cuts and grazes. All children are vulnerable to infection and it is important that you understand how disease is transmitted in order to minimise children's exposure to bacterial, fungal and viral infections. The rooms that harbour most germs are the kitchen and the bathroom and, as you will be having other children using these, they need to be scrupulously clean.

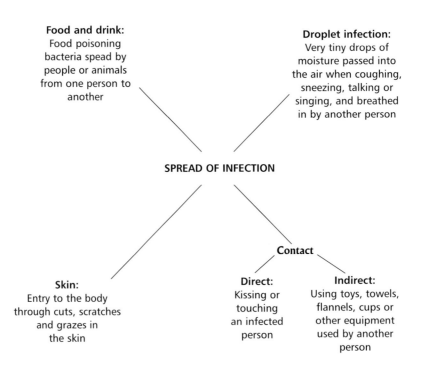

Food and drink:
Food poisoning bacteria spread by people or animals from one person to another

Droplet infection:
Very tiny drops of moisture passed into the air when coughing, sneezing, talking or singing, and breathed in by another person

SPREAD OF INFECTION

Skin:
Entry to the body through cuts, scratches and grazes in the skin

Contact

Direct:
Kissing or touching an infected person

Indirect:
Using toys, towels, flannels, cups or other equipment used by another person

Good practice in . . . THE PREVENTION OF INFECTION

1 Make sure that you and the children wash your hands after using the lavatory, handling animals and their equipment, coughing or sneezing, and before eating. In addition, you need to wash thoroughly after changing nappies, wiping noses, wiping bottoms and handling raw food.
2 Keep the kitchen work-surfaces, utensils and implements clean.
3 Always keep food covered when it is left out on the work-surface.
4 Never refreeze food that has already been defrosted.
5 Never store raw meat alongside other food. Keep it well wrapped at the bottom of the refrigerator.
6 Do not allow the refrigerator to become over-crowded, as this will impede the circulation of air.
7 Never eat meat and fish that has been refrigerated for more than three days.
8 Make sure the refrigerator is no more than 5 degrees centigrade and that the freezer is set at minus 18 degrees centigrade to prevent bacteria multiplying.
9 Sterilise feeding bottles and teats, as milk is an excellent medium for bacteria.
10 Keep rubbish bins covered and scrupulously clean.
11 Keep animals out of the kitchen.
12 Use disposable paper towels to dry hands, wash faces and wipe surfaces.

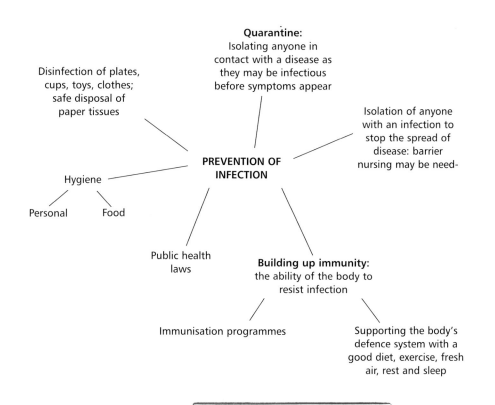

Quarantine:
Isolating anyone in contact with a disease as they may be infectious before symptoms appear

Disinfection of plates, cups, toys, clothes; safe disposal of paper tissues

Isolation of anyone with an infection to stop the spread of disease: barrier nursing may be need-

PREVENTION OF INFECTION

Hygiene

Personal   Food

Public health laws

Building up immunity: the ability of the body to resist infection

Immunisation programmes

Supporting the body's defence system with a good diet, exercise, fresh air, rest and sleep

The safe environment

1 Suggest two hygiene routines that will help to prevent infection.
2 Describe how you dispose of waste products and soiled items hygienically and safely.

Someone in your family, or one of the children you look after, may be suffering from:

- impetigo (a highly infectious skin disease)
- cold sores
- fungal skin infections such as ringworm
- conjunctivitis.

These are all contagious and easily transmitted by touch and other parents should be notified.

Keeping a clean home will prevent germs from multiplying. The use of soap and water, fresh air and sunlight will destroy many germs. Chemical disinfectants, such as carbolic or strong bleach, will destroy germs but are potentially harmful to children and pets, and need to be locked away after use. Antiseptics are weak disinfectants that prevent the growth of organisms but do not destroy them. They are equally dangerous to children.

Those keeping any kind of pet should know about its food and habits, and how to care for it.

Good practice in . . . CARING FOR PETS

1 Children should be taught the importance of looking after animals, feeding them and cleaning out cages.
2 They must be told the importance of washing hands after handling a pet or cleaning a cage.
3 Children should be discouraged from kissing pets or letting pets lick their faces.
4 Sick animals must always be seen by a vet.
5 Disinfectant should be used to wash floors soiled with animal excreta.
6 Animals' foods and plates should be kept and washed separately from those used by humans.
7 Puppies and kittens should be wormed when very young, and, before this, children should not handle them. The animals should be wormed again at regular intervals.
8 No family should have a pet that is not tolerant of young children.
9 All animals need space and exercise and a person who is devoted to their care.

Activity

1 Investigate two diseases that are associated with pets.
2 What action would you take to ensure that the children you care for are not put at risk?

Medication

For your own protection, you should have written permission from the parents before administering any medicine; ask them to complete the form: 'Permission to administer short course of medication or treatment daily'. Each time you give medication, note the time and dose and ask the parent to sign the form when the child is collected.

Some children require routine medication for a chronic condition. For example, a child might suffer from asthma and would need some form of inhaler to prevent attacks, as well as medicine to have at hand if she should become ill. In this situation, you will need to complete the form: 'Permission to administer medicine or treatment over an extended period of time'.

All medicines should be stored in the original container and be properly labelled. They must be in a secure place, out of the reach of children. Most medicines should be kept in a cool, dry environment, and out of sunlight. Many medicines need refrigeration and should be kept separate from food, in a secure box, labelled 'medicines'. You should not prescribe medication yourself, not even paracetamol for a raised temperature. If you become concerned, you should follow the instructions on the child's personal record form (see www.ncma.org.uk).

Recording accidents

Any accident requiring hospital treatment should be reported to a registration officer within 24 hours of the accident occurring. A detailed account of the accident should be recorded by the home-based childcarer at the earliest opportunity.

Fill in an accident record book sheet (see www.ncma.org.uk) carefully and, after informing the parents, ask them to sign to confirm that they have been informed.

Every accident, however slight, should be recorded in the accident book, as some seemingly minor accidents can result in more serious concerns, and accurate recording of information can be vital. The accident book may also show regularly occurring hazards.

Every parent wants his or her child to be safe and healthy at all times. This does not happen just by chance, and it takes a great deal of effort to make sure that there are no hazards in your home and garden. Children need to be protected against infection and appropriate care should be taken to minimise accidents and illness. You and the parents will share the same objectives.

Reflecting on Practice

You might think about:
- any possible hazards in your home and garden
- the contents of your First Aid box and updating your First Aid knowledge
- writing a fire procedure, recording arrangements for an emergency evacuation of the house
- making sure all dangerous substances are locked away
- door and window safety
- car safety
- how to keep children safe when out of the house and how to maintain good supervision
- preventing cross-infection
- how to keep your pets clean and healthy
- whether your safety equipment is in good repair, and if you need to purchase any new items
- gaining a Food Hygiene certificate
- making sure all your equipment conforms to British and European safety standards.

This chapter has contributed to the following learning outcomes:

Unit 1

■ providing a safe and healthy childcare environment in the home-based setting

■ promoting anti-discriminatory, anti-bias practice in the home-based setting

Want to Find Out More?

Websites

www.capt.org.uk
www.ncma.org.uk
www.redcross.org.uk
www.rospa.org.uk
www.sja.org.uk

Further reading

British Red Cross, *First Aid for Babies and Children Fast*, Dorling Kindersley, 2006

Dare A et al., *Good Practice in Safeguarding Children*, 3rd Edition, Nelson Thornes, 2009

Holtzman D.S., *The Safe Baby, Expanded and Revised*, Sentient Publications, 2009

NCMA, *Guide to Children's Safety*, NCMA, 2005

Raatma, L., *Safety at Home*, Bridgestone Books, 1999

Wolfe L., *Safe and Sound: Complete Guide to First Aid and Emergency Treatment for Children and Young Adults*, 2nd Edition, Health Education Authority, 1995

9

Disabled children

Learning objectives

Unit 1
- Promote inclusion and anti-bias practice

Unit 2
- Working with disabled children and their families

Unit 5
- Observing and assessing children's development in the home-based setting
- Meeting individual learning needs in the home-based setting

All children have the same needs: to be loved, valued, feel secure and protected, to receive routine physical care and to have enough stimulation to achieve their potential. Disabled children may have additional needs and require extra help, but the important thing to remember is to view the child as a person in his own right, and not see just the impairment. Impairment becomes disability only if the environment is not adjusted to enable the child to function effectively; for example, the majority of people with sight impairment are not disabled because they wear spectacles.

Defining disability

The Disability Discrimination Act 1995 (DDA) defines a disability as 'a physical or mental impairment which has a substantial and long-term adverse effect on a person's ability to carry out normal day-to-day activities'. Long-term is usually taken to mean 12 months or more. This definition covers physical and sensory disability, mental health problems and learning disability, and a range of medical problems such as diabetes, epilepsy, and severe allergies. An estimated 700,000 children in England meet this definition which also includes children with:

- medical conditions, such as asthma, sickle cell, eczema or thalassaemia
- a need for special diets, such as milk-free, nut-free, gluten-free or sugar-free
- behavioural and emotional difficulties, including hyperactivity
- HIV positive status.

Medical and social models of disability

The medical model of disability sees a disabled child as a problem and focuses on what the child cannot do. It labels the child as ill and in need of treatment, leading to dependency on others, which, in turn, can lead to overprotection and isolation. The phrase 'suffering from' is frequently used. The medical model reinforces reliance on others, giving disabled children no control over their lives and denying them opportunities for choice.

The social model came about from the disability movement, which sought equal rights and opportunities for disabled people. This focuses on the child as an individual and not on his impairments. It rejects the medical model of disability but does not deny the need for medical care. According to the social model, it is society that is the problem, not the disabled child.

Problems are seen to lie with:

- the way society is organised, segregating special provision, funding treatment rather than resources to reduce the effect of disability, excessive influence of healthcare professionals and costly special equipment
- the way the environment is constructed – physical barriers to mobility, and communication barriers with little access to Braille and sign language
- people's attitudes and assumptions.

The social model acknowledges disabled people as people first. It emphasises the need for environmental and social change to allow disabled people to live in a society that is inclusive, accessible and supportive of personal rights. Impairments are a fact of life, but, if they are planned for and resources allocated well, they do not have to become a problem.

Special educational needs

The legislation concerned with children with learning difficulties uses the term 'special educational needs'. The law states that children have special educational needs if they have a learning difficulty that requires special educational provision to be made for them. Home-based childcarers working within a network should be aware of the Code of Practice 2001 for the identification and assessment of children with special educational needs and may work together

9 chapter

to develop a special educational needs policy. The role of the special educational needs co-ordinator (SENCO) may be carried out by the network co-ordinator, sometimes sharing this with individual home-based childcarers.

Activity

Obtain a copy of SEN Code of Practice from teachernet. Telephone: 0845 602 2260, reference 581/2001, or download from www.teachernet.gov.uk/wholeschool/sen/

Deciding to care for a disabled child

The DDA has introduced new laws aimed at ending the discrimination faced by many disabled people. From October 2004, anyone who offers goods, facilities or services to the general public may have to make reasonable adjustments to their premises to overcome physical barriers to access. It is illegal to refuse to provide a service to a disabled person for a reason related to their disability. You are not required to make changes or adaptations to your service, which are too unreasonable or expensive. Philippa Russell, Disability Rights Commissioner, suggests that, when considering whether you can offer a service to a disabled child you need to take into account:

- cost
- your available resources
- practicality
- the implications for your childminding service
- health and safety
- the interests of the other children in your care.

She also points out that it is only when you have accurate information about the child's needs that you will be able to say whether 'reasonable adjustments' will allow you to care for the child.

All home-based childcarers need a calm and patient disposition, a good sense of humour and a firm, fair and consistent approach to the children in their care. If you are considering looking after a disabled child, there are additional skills, attitudes and knowledge that you may need to have. These include:

- being optimistic about the child's physical and intellectual potential
- seeing the child rather than the impairment
- being physically strong, as you may have to lift a child or manage a child having a fit
- having knowledge from the parents, as well as doing your own research, about the possible effects of the impairment
- being responsible for administering medication, as instructed by the parents
- being willing to undertake a short course of specialised training, if one is available
- being prepared to research and contact organisations
- being willing and competent to carry out necessary therapies
- being competent in using any necessary aids

being willing to liaise with specialists, therapists and support groups.

Part of the process in deciding your suitability for looking after a disabled child is to consider whether:

- you are being realistic – you may need a good deal of strength and stamina, both physically and emotionally
- you have adequate experience in caring for disabled children, and for those without disabilities
- you have some experience or knowledge of this impairment
- you have sufficient space in your home for additional equipment, such as wheelchairs or large pushchairs if required
- you are willing to learn about therapies, such as physiotherapy and speech therapy if necessary
- you have knowledge of the aids and the maintenance that might be needed
- you are aware of the length of time the child is to spend with you, as consistent care is so important
- you are willing to learn about any programmes he might be following and to help him undertake such programmes.

Not all these factors will be relevant for every disabled child. For instance, not all disabled children need medication or use special equipment. You will have to think about each child as an individual when deciding whether you are ready to meet the child's needs and requirements.

As with all children, you will need to have:

- ideas for encouraging his development
- observation skills and be able to maintain written records
- awareness of the child's specific needs and be willing to provide appropriate care
- adequate communication skills with the child, parents, and outside agencies.

Some common worries, apart from a general fear of the unknown, may include:

- managing nutrition and mealtimes
- how to give enough time to all the children in your care
- making sure he is included in all routines and activities
- the possible additional wear and tear on the home.

With some disabled children, you might be concerned about:

- how to communicate with the child

- coping with an incontinent child
- lifting the child in a skilled way
- dealing with unfamiliar patterns of behaviour
- managing a child with epilepsy.

Having a sympathetic nature is not enough. You must be sure not to over-protect the child, see that he is encouraged to reach his full potential and be ready to support him in integrating himself with friends and family. You may find yourself having to challenge the negative and discriminatory attitudes of adults and children. Your assertiveness techniques (see Chapter 12) will be invaluable here!

Meeting individual needs

As you know, it is best practice to observe, assess and meet the individual needs of all the children in your care. Some disabled children will need little additional support, whilst others with more complex needs will require more support and care. Prior to accepting any child you will have discussed his individual needs with the parents (see page 38).

You will need to ascertain if the child is already part of an Early Support Programme or holds a Statement of Special Educational Needs. The parent-held Child Health Record is an invaluable source of information for all children and you might ask the parents to show it to you.

Resources

The local authority has a duty to promote disability equality. It may provide support to home-based childcarers and others who care for disabled children, by making the services of the area special educational needs co-ordinator (SENCO) readily accessible, and may run a toy library and specialist equipment loan scheme. The authority should also provide training.

Additional support, advice and resources may also be available from:

- the local childminding network co-ordinator or development worker
- health professionals
- disability charities.

The needs of other children

It has sometimes been found that the needs of the other children in a domestic setting are not always met, if carers have to give more attention to one child.

Other children may experience:

- anxiety, leading to disturbed sleep
- resentment and jealousy
- fear of 'catching' the condition
- emotional swings, from being loving and protective, to disturbed behaviour such as regression or attention seeking.

On the other hand, children are introduced to the concept of caring for others, sometimes at a younger age. They will see the person rather than the disability and in later life be able to value all people that they come in contact with.

Children are aware of how much time and focus is given to the needs of the disabled child, and need some special time to talk about how they feel. You will need to:

- find time to give them individual attention every day
- reassure them that they are loved and valued
- be honest with them, and give them information appropriate to their level of understanding
- encourage them to care for the disabled child as part of the routine of the day, talking to him and including him in all activities.

CASE STUDY

Lauren cares for two children, Andrew, four, and Whitney, two, and has two school-age children of her own, twins Patricia and Henry, aged six. Andrew is new to the family and is very demanding. He is with Lauren two days a week to give his mother a break. He is hyperactive, has little speech, is frequently aggressive, particularly towards Henry, and takes up much of Lauren's time, but lately he has been showing some improvement and his mother says Andrew is much better behaved at home than he used to be.

Lauren has noticed that Henry avoids Andrew, refusing to sit at the table with him and spends most of the afternoon in his room when Andrew is there. Lauren is distressed to be told by Henry's teacher that he frequently confides in her that he dislikes Andrew and is frightened of him.

1 How might Lauren help Henry?
2 Should Lauren discuss the situation with Andrew's mother?
3 How could Henry's father be involved?

Planning suitable activities

All children learn through play and are naturally curious. Some disabled children may need more help and encouragement to become involved in play. It is important to have realistic expectations of the abilities of all the children in your care, but in particular it would not be best

9 chapter

practice to expect a disabled child to succeed at something that his impairment makes impossible. For example, to expect a hyperactive child to sit at a table concentrating on an intricate task for more than five minutes would be unrealistic. On the other hand, do not fall into the trap of expecting too little. A child with a physical impairment is likely to be just as intelligent as any other child – think of Stephen Hawking! It is important not to make assumptions and be over-protective. You should allow children to face appropriate challenges.

Your observation skills will be a key factor in deciding what to offer individual children. In assessing their needs, you will be able to plan a programme of activities to promote their development. All children need a great deal of praise and encouragement in order to succeed and feel confident. Breaking down a task into small steps may be necessary to help some children succeed.

Children with sensory impairments particularly benefit from play with natural materials, such as water, sand and clay, as an end product is not required and all the experiences are pleasurable and therapeutic, increasing self-esteem and confidence. The activities are adaptable and can be used by children in wheelchairs or played with on the floor.

Music is a part of all our lives and all children find simple repetitive songs and rhymes relaxing and soothing. Percussion instruments are fun and special grip pads and stands are available. Children with hearing impairments enjoy listening to the vibrations of low-pitched sounds. Visually impaired children need highly developed hearing skills to compensate for poor vision. Movement to music on a one-to-one basis can be particularly useful for children with multiple disabilities. Some music calms children with behavioural difficulties.

Promoting the child's self-image

All parents hope for confident, well-adjusted children who feel good about themselves and become independent, autonomous members of society. This may be harder for disabled children, and they very quickly learn to compare themselves with other children, as there are so many activities from which they are cut off and excluded. Any activities that you plan should be accessible to all the children you are caring for, at individual levels of achievement. No child should be made to feel that he is unable to join in because of his particular disability.

To foster a disabled child's self-esteem you will need to:

- handle his physical needs with sensitivity
- praise any achievement, however small
- offer choices where possible, and allow the child to make decisions
- be positive and not underestimate his ability
- be sensitive to his body language (this may be his main form of communication)
- break down all planned activities into small steps, so that he can achieve
- if just looking after the one child, find a suitable group of children, where he has the opportunity to develop his social skills and make friends
- always use positive language and challenge any inappropriate language or behaviour from other adults or children
- encourage any sign of independence, and do not over-protect the child.

The needs of parents

Parents of disabled children may need a great deal of support themselves, and you may have to set aside some time for offering them a listening ear and allowing them to express their anxieties to you. Most conditions have support and information groups, and the parents will most likely be aware of these. Any information they have should be communicated to you.

Parents may experience negative feelings about their children's situation, such as:

- confusion (how can I cope with this?)
- anger (why me?)
- guilt (it's my fault; where did I go wrong?)
- grieving (for the able-bodied child that might have been)
- blaming (partner, in-laws)
- shame (attitudes of neighbours, friends and even family)
- fear (about the future)
- rejection (of the child).

Parents may also experience denial and disbelief, especially if they secretly feel that they have contributed in some way. Bringing up a disabled child can be a tremendous strain on the marriage or partnership and can be a contributory factor to marital breakdown. Some parents experience increasing isolation from their neighbours and family.

How you might support parents

Parents of disabled children may need your support on a day-to-day basis. You should try to:

- listen sympathetically and allow time for them to talk
- give positive, truthful feedback about the child's day, his achievements and behaviour
- be interested and praise the parents for their work with the child
- ask the parents about any programmes they are carrying out at home
- gather information from any support groups, and share this with the parents.

CASE STUDY

Margaret cares for three children from one family: Lisa who is seven years old, Tom aged four and Simon, aged nine months. Simon has just been diagnosed with a severe hearing impairment, and the parents are very upset. All their attention seems to be focused on the baby.

Margaret has time to spend with Tom during the day whilst Lisa is at school, but finds it difficult to give Lisa enough attention when the other children are there. Lisa seems withdrawn, and often bursts into tears for little or no reason saying that she hates Simon.

1 How might Margaret help Lisa?
2 Should Margaret speak to the parents about her concerns?
3 What support might Margaret offer the parents?

Activity

As a home-based childcarer, you have recently been asked by social services to care for a three-month-old baby born with only one hand. It is apparent to you that the mother is having difficulty in relating to and accepting the child, the youngest of six children.

1 How might you help and support the mother?

2 How will you plan to help the child?

By emphasising the child's positive aspects and achievements, you can go a long way in supporting and reassuring the parents as someone outside the family who values their child. There are many people who have surmounted difficulties to achieve a great deal in later life, writing books, running support groups, being ministers in government and becoming the number one scientist in the country.

In 2005, a new statue was unveiled in London's Trafalgar Square.

Alison Lapper sculpture by Marc Quinn/Justin Kase/Alamy

Alison Lapper was born with no arms and very short legs. Brought up in an orphanage, she overcame her disability and became an artist. She also became a mother and when she was eight months pregnant, Marc Quinn took a cast and began work on a marble statue of this most courageous lady. He said he had sculpted his friend Ms Lapper because disabled people were under-represented in art.

This chapter has contributed to the following learning outcomes:

Unit 1
- promoting anti-discriminatory, anti-bias practice in the home-based setting

Unit 2
- explaining the importance of inclusive practice and understanding how this can be implemented in the home-based setting
- providing for children's development and well-being from birth to 16 years

Unit 5
- using a range of methods of observation and assessment to support your work with children
- explaining how you meet children's individual learning needs in the home-based setting

Want to Find Out More?

Websites

www.asbah.org
www.bcodp.org.uk
www.bda.org.uk
www.circleofinclusion.org
www.downs-syndrome.org.uk
www.equalityhumanrights.com
www.inclusion.org.uk
www.scope.org.uk
www.sense.org.uk

Resource packs

Learning for Life – Early Years. Published by SCOPE. Telephone: 0808 800 3333, for a free copy.

Play Talks, published by SCOPE to help pre-school children with communication difficulties, comprising fact sheets and a CD-ROM.

DVD: *Every Child is Unique: Childminding Disabled Children*, produced by NCMA, £5.75 (free to NCMA members).

Further reading

Dare A. et al., *Good Practice in Caring for Children with Special Needs*, 3rd Edition, Nelson Thornes, 2009

Mortimer H., *Special Needs Handbook*, New Edition, Scholastic, 2004

Mortimer H., *Speech and Language Difficulties*, Scholastic, 2007

NCMA *Inclusive Childminding – Working with Disabled Children* (CD-ROM for tutors), NCMA, 2005

10

The sick child

Learning objectives

Unit 1

- Establishing a safe and healthy environment in the home-based setting
- Promoting inclusion and anti-bias practice

Unit 2

- Providing for children's development and well-being

To make sure that the children in your care are healthy, you will be working in partnership with their parents. A home-based childcarer can be regarded to some extent as a health educator who wishes to promote the health of children by understanding health issues and setting a good example. You will understand the importance of routine health surveillance and screening programmes, and encourage parents to participate.

Caring for children who are unwell

Sick babies and children need to be with their main carer if possible, and you will certainly wish to avoid the risk of cross-infection, but there may be times when you find yourself caring for a child who is sick whilst waiting for the parents to collect her.

If the child's temperature suddenly rises, it is important to take action so as to prevent a convulsion. The child needs to get rid of excess heat, so keep the room cool and airy, remove excess clothing and bedding, and give frequent drinks of water. Sponging with lukewarm water may help to reduce the temperature. You may have discussed the possibility of this situation with the parents, and have their written permission to administer medication.

Giving medication

You should never administer medication to a child unless you have the written permission of the parents. With any prescribed medicine it is essential to know:

- when to take it, and for how long
- what the medicine should do
- how long it will take to work, and how you can tell it is working
- what to do if it does not seem to be working
- what to do if you forget a dose
- what the possible side-effects are.

Most medicines for children are in liquid form: shake the bottle thoroughly before giving a dose. Tablets are more concentrated than liquid medicines, and may need to be crushed to a powder. Slow-release and coated tablets must be swallowed whole. Eye, ear and nose drops are designed to coat the affected surface.

When giving medicine, it is a good idea to sit the child on your lap and have a towel and damp cloth handy in case of spills. Measure the medicine into a non-spill tube spoon. Gradually tip the medicine into the back of the child's cheek. Chase it down with a favourite drink. Never mix medicines into a drink or bottle, as the child may not finish the drink and therefore take less medication than the prescribed dose. It may also present a hazard to other children.

As soon as you have given the medication, record it on the child's chart (see Chapter 8), with the date and time and amount. You must do this, even if you have been unsuccessful in administering the full amount, indicating the difficulty. Ask the parent to sign the form when they collect the child. All medicines should be stored in the original container and be properly labelled. They must be kept in a secure place, out of the reach of children. Most medicines should be kept in cool, dry conditions and out of sunlight. Medicines needing refrigeration should be kept in a secure plastic box, away from the food, and labelled with the child's name.

If one of the children in your care suddenly becomes unwell, you will need to contact the parents and care for the child until the parents can take the child home. You should have discussed with the parents how you would cope in such an eventuality, and you may have been given their written permission to give proprietary medication if necessary. When you contact them you should offer accurate information. You can help parents by remaining calm, and reassuring them that appropriate action has been taken, as you will appreciate how concerned they are. When they collect the child, you may find you can offer some support and practical help and advice.

The parents' reluctance to return from work, or stay at home when their child is ill, can cause conflict. At the time of signing the original contract, it is helpful if you make it clear that:

- the terms of registration do not allow home-based childcarers to care for children who have an infectious illness

- their own home environment is more suitable for children who are unwell
- parents should be available in case of illness
- you will act responsibly, and not exclude children unnecessarily, but the decision lies with you
- if the parents' employment means that access and availability is difficult, a plan should be devised for alternative care
- you cannot authorise treatment.

It may be necessary to inform the parents of other children that one of the children in your care has an infection or infestation, so that they can take steps to protect their own child's health and well-being. Confidentiality is important, but it may be quite obvious to the other parents who the child is. As a professional person you will divulge only what is necessary.

Activity

How do you inform parents if one of the children you care for has an infectious illness?

Infection

Infection is the most common cause of illness in young children and, if frequent, can cause developmental delay and slow down growth. As a home-based childcarer, it is important that you know the different types of infection, how they are communicated to others, and how to prevent the spread of infection.

Infection can range from the common cold to meningitis and, as you gain experience, you will find it easier to diagnose the symptoms of the illness. If you are in charge of a child who suddenly becomes ill, you must contact the parents and if you have any serious concerns you must seek medical advice. You can encourage parents to participate in immunisation programmes so as to reduce incidence of childhood diseases, which can be very dangerous.

In addition to the common childhood complaints, there is one other infection that you must be aware of. Meningitis can develop within hours into a life-threatening illness. The signs and symptoms are variable, which makes both the viral and the bacterial forms of this infection so difficult to diagnose. If the child has a raised temperature combined with a severe headache, vomiting, painful neck, confusion, dislike of light, irritability or a purplish rash, which does not disappear when you press the skin with a glass tumbler, you should seek urgent medical attention and contact the parents immediately.

Infection results from invasion of the body by pathogenic (disease causing) organisms. The main organisms are:

- bacteria
- viruses
- fungi
- protozoa.

To grow and multiply, these organisms need moisture, warmth, food and time. Once in the body, they multiply rapidly: this is called the incubation period. Although children are infectious during the incubation period, they only begin to display signs and symptoms and feel unwell at the end of this time.

Infection is spread:

- by droplets: sneezing and coughing
- by touch: contact with people or equipment
- by eating or drinking infected food and water
- through cuts and grazes on the body.

Good practice in . . . PREVENTING CROSS INFECTION

1 Wash hands before handling and eating food.
2 Wash hands after using the lavatory.
3 Provide paper towels for yourself and for the children.
4 Well ventilate rooms, avoiding over-crowding.
5 Wash and disinfect toys and equipment regularly.
6 Discourage parents from bringing unwell children into your home.
7 Clean the lavatory and bathroom daily.
8 Clean up all spills immediately.
9 Use disposable gloves for First Aid, cleaning up body fluids and changing nappies.
10 Provide regular trips out of doors.
11 Keep pets clean and healthy.
12 Use tissues for wiping noses and dispose of them at once in a covered bin.
13 Select, store and prepare food carefully.
14 Clear the table immediately after meals; do not allow food to be left about

The quarantine period is the time when a person with an infection is capable of transmitting that infection to another person. Hygiene, isolation and exclusion, and immunisation all play an important part in preventing the spread of infection.

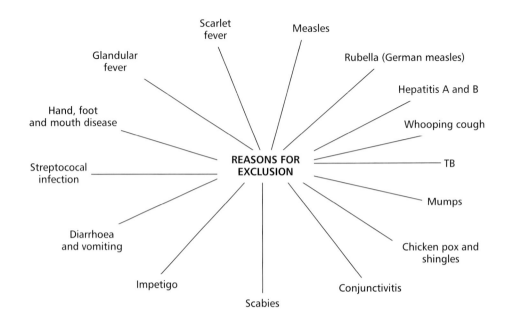

Scarlet fever

Measles

Glandular fever

Rubella (German measles)

Hepatitis A and B

Hand, foot and mouth disease

Whooping cough

REASONS FOR EXCLUSION

TB

Streptococal infection

Mumps

Diarrhoea and vomiting

Chicken pox and shingles

Impetigo

Conjunctivitis

Scabies

Minor ailments

You need to be clear in your own mind whether you will exclude children with some minor ailments and to discuss it with the parents at your first meeting.

Signs of poor health:

- signs of injury and/or neglect
- rashes, spots or sores
- abnormal stools or urine
- unresponsive to others
- quiet and lethargic
- fretful
- complains of feeling unwell or pain
- poor appetite
- sleeps badly
- raised temperature
- frequent worrying behaviour
- under- or overweight
- poor posture/muscle tone
- dry spotty skin
- unhealthy hair or scalp
- poor colour
- tooth decay

- expected milestones not achieved
- regression.

Action if child is unwell:
- observation
- partnership with parents
- prompt diagnosis
- loving care
- fluids
- care of skin
- light diet
- medication
- rest and sleep.

You need to consider the risk of cross-infection even with minor ailments, for the sake of the looked after child, your own family and yourself. If you become unwell, your services are no longer available to the family.

Upper respiratory tract infections

The areas of the mouth, nose and throat are the first to be attacked by viruses as they are breathed in. Children are very prone to colds because they are frequently in contact with new organisms and have yet to build up their own immune systems. The main sign of a cold is a runny nose. The discharge is thin at first, becoming thicker after a day or two. The nose can feel blocked, and the child may wish to pick and scratch it. The lining of the nose is more fragile, and will bleed easily. Care will consist of offering the child plenty of fluids, checking to see whether she has a fever, teaching her to use disposable tissues and to blow her own nose, and keeping her warm within a well-ventilated room.

A cough can be caused by direct infection of the throat or by nasal mucus dripping from the back of the nose. Coughs cause anxiety but serve a purpose in pushing back infected mucus that threatens the lungs. A cough indicates a more serious illness when it presents with other symptoms such as:

- difficulty in breathing
- pallor or blueness
- thick sticky mucus coming from the lungs
- traces of blood
- choking
- vomiting.

The parents should be urged to seek medical advice.

A sore throat may develop on its own, or be accompanied by a cold; many only last a day or two. It is often present in childhood infections. If a child refuses to drink, has swollen pus-covered tonsils, has a high temperature or is drowsy or dizzy, the parent should be contacted and the GP consulted by the parents.

Lower respiratory tract infections

Infections that spread into the lung tissue are more serious than upper respiratory tract infections. Croup occurs in children between the ages of six months and four years. The child is usually hoarse, with a barking cough, may have some difficulty in breathing, and will appear distressed. A doctor should see all children with croup.

Smoking

Passive smoking is now acknowledged to be a serious health risk to babies, children and adults. Smoking is no longer allowed in many public places and in all schools and nurseries. Currently in England (although not in Wales and Scotland), home-based childcarers are allowed to smoke with the written permission of the parents but, apart from the effect that smoking might have on you and the children, you may find it difficult to find parents who are willing to leave their children with you.

All early years organisations, including NCMA, continue to challenge this permission to smoke, and want home-based childcarers to be treated the same as other childcare providers.

Rashes

A rash is a sign that the child's body is reacting to an irritation or an infection of some type. Refer to page 194 for descriptions of common rashes. As long as there are no other symptoms, a rash on its own is rarely a sign of serious illness and usually disappears as quickly as it comes. How a rash looks is generally less important than where it is on the body. There are three main types of rash.

- The rash may be all over the body accompanied by other symptoms, such as a cold and a raised temperature. This usually indicates a viral infection.
- The rash may be all over the body with no signs of ill health. This rash will often irritate the child and is an allergic reaction to something. It needs to be discussed with the parents, as, if the cause is discovered, it can be eliminated. The child may need to be referred to the GP.
- The rash may be on only one part of the body: for example, nappy rash and cradle cap. The rash's cause will often be suggested by where it is sited. If it does not heal within a few days, encourage the parents to seek GP advice.

Stomach aches and pains

Stomach aches are a symptom of an upset somewhere in the body, not necessarily the abdomen. Children with tonsillitis, urinary tract infection or middle ear infection may well complain of stomach ache. Stomach aches may have different causes, from mere over-eating to more serious conditions such as appendicitis. In most cases, there is nothing to worry about but, on rare occasions, stomach ache is the first sign of a real emergency, so it is best to play safe.

In children, the pain is generally caused by an infection, an inflammation or a change in the activity of the bowel. Many school children complain of stomach ache in response to stress. It may not have a physical cause, but the pain is real, as the disturbed central nervous system, which controls the contractions of the stomach and intestines, intensifies the contractions. The pain can be so severe that the child cannot eat or drink.

You should contact the parents if:

- the child cannot be comforted, and is refusing food and drink
- there is any swelling, or she refuses to let you touch where it hurts
- she vomits, but the pain continues
- she vomits greenish, yellow matter
- she has crying spasms, turns pale and vomits
- there are other signs of illness, such as raised temperature or diarrhoea
- she is lethargic
- the pain is mild, but it is mentioned repeatedly over several days.

The child's behaviour is the best guide to the seriousness of the stomach ache. Cuddle and reassure the child. Give her small sips of plain water to drink. Encourage her to rest on a sofa or a bed. She may prefer to lie against a pillow. Have a bowl ready in case she vomits. Warmth may help, so you could offer a well-covered hot-water bottle. It is best not to offer anything to eat. If the pain is severe or continues for more than 20 minutes, contact the parents.

RASHES	
Condition	**Description of rash**
Hand, foot and mouth disease	A sparse rash of greyish white, tiny blisters with a red halo. It is seen inside the mouth, on the tongue and on the palms of the hands and the soles of the feet. It lasts 3 to 5 days and then fades rapidly. Occasionally it spreads to the buttocks.
Cold sores	Sore, painful blisters near the lips and nose that crust after 2–3 days.
Impetigo	Starts as a small blister generally near the mouth and nose as this part is more vulnerable to infection. Number and size increase, the surface of the skin breaks down, leaving a raw, moist surface that becomes a thick, yellow crust over a reddened, sore area.
Nettle rash	Pale, swollen patches and spots with a red border.
Scabies	Raised, blistery spots and raised, red, discrete spots, generally with scratch marks as it is intensely irritating. Greyish ridges of scabies mite tracks may be seen. Generally between fingers, inside wrists, under the arms, waist and groin.
Eczema	Dry skin, patches of red skin often with small, blistery spots. Inflamed by scratching. Starts on face or skin creases. May become sore or weepy.
Rubella (German measles)	Pale pink spots that start on face and spread to chest and back, perhaps the limbs. On 2nd or 3rd day they become an overall flush. Can last between a few hours and up to 5 days.
Measles	A blotchy rash of dark red spots that spreads from behind the ears to the face, body and limbs over 3 to 4 days. Up to 2–3 days koplik spots (small white spots) can be seen on the inside of the cheeks at the back of the mouth. Rash fades after 4 days.
Scarlet fever	Small spots of intense red colour that are rough to the touch. It begins with the face and spreads to the neck and chest and then the limbs over 4–5 days. It leaves a pale patch around the mouth.
Chickenpox	3 stages: 1) raised, red, discrete rash of tiny pimples starting on chest and face 2) spots develop into blisters 3) after 2–3 days the fluid in the blister becomes cloudy and yellow. It will then form a crust, which is intensely irritating. By the third day it will spread to the limbs. In severe cases it can be found on the mucous membrane of the body orifices.
Seborrhoeic eczema	Inflamed, scaly rash behind ears or neck. Associated with cradle cap. Does not irritate.
Heat rash	Small, irritating blisters or pimples on the chest, neck or groin.

Vomiting

Hold the child's head over a bowl, while supporting the upper body with your other hand. Be reassuring.

After the vomiting, wipe the child's face with a sponge or cloth wrung out in tepid water. Encourage the child to sip a drink of water slowly to replace fluid loss and remove the taste from the mouth. Try to get her to lie quietly on a bed or sofa, keeping the bowl handy. A small baby who vomits can dehydrate quickly, so ask the parents to consult a doctor.

Ear infections

Earache can follow a cold, flu or a throat infection, or develop by itself. The child may have a raised temperature, complain of pain, refuse to drink and may be seen rubbing or pulling her ear. Encourage the parents to seek medical advice as soon as possible.

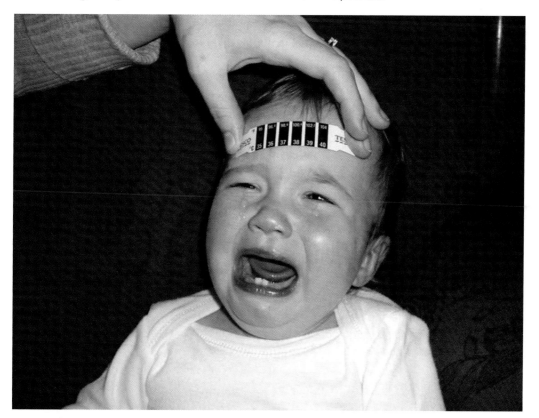

Stools and urine

As a home-based childcarer, you are frequently wiping bottoms and emptying potties. The table on page 196 will help you to identify any concerns that should be communicated to the parent.

STOOLS AND URINE	
Condition	**Description of stool**
Underfeeding in a baby	Small, frequent, green stools
Diarrhoea	Frequent, loose watery stools. May contain blood or mucus
Straining	Bright red blood may be seen on the stool
Taking iron medicine	Very dark stools
Bleeding in upper intestine (rare)	Very dark stools
Cystic fibrosis	Large, watery, foul-smelling stools
Constipation	Hard, dry stools, difficult to pass. Hard, dry pellets in a baby
Jaundice	Very pale stool
Inability to digest fats	Large, pale, fatty stool
Threadworms	Worms that look like threads of cotton 1–2 cm. Seen in stool
Normal stool	Soft, clay-like, easy to pass
	Description of urine
Normal	Pale, straw-coloured, no smell
Child lacking fluid	Very dark fluid
Jaundice	Very dark fluid
Urinary tract infection	Frequent passing of small amounts. May smell fishy and child may complain of pain
Diabetes	Frequent passing of urine containing sugar

A minor illness is becoming serious if the child:

- has a fit
- has a temperature and a stiff neck
- has a temperature and a severe headache
- has a temperature and photophobia (dislike of light)
- has a headache and sickness and dizziness
- is drowsy
- is becoming dehydrated
- becomes quiet or limp
- is in pain
- loses consciousness
- has difficulty breathing
- develops noisy breathing
- begins to turn blue.

You should immediately seek medical attention as a matter of urgency for any child in your care presenting any of these signs and symptoms.

Infestations

Infestations are caused by animal parasites that live on and obtain their food from humans. All children are likely to be affected at some time.

Head lice

Head lice are small insects that live in human hair, close to the scalp where they can bite the skin and feed on the blood. Many children are infested by coming into contact with children who are already carrying head lice, and lice show no preference between clean and unwashed hair. The lice lay eggs, called nits, close to the scalp and cement the eggs firmly to the hair. You may think the child has dandruff, but if you try to dislodge it you will find the nits are firmly fixed. The first indicator of head lice may be the child scratching her head and complaining of irritation.

Tell all the parents immediately and suggest they seek advice from the local chemist. Many people are unhappy now with the chemical shampoos and treatments. The current method recommended by many schools is to apply a conditioner to the child's head, and use a nit comb to remove the nits and lice. Regular brushing and combing will discourage lice.

CASE STUDY

Sylvia is a newly registered home-based childcarer, caring for Alex aged three who has a six-year-old sister at the local primary school. One day after lunch, she noticed her own daughter Helen, aged two years, scratching her head. On examination, she discovered that Helen had nits.

1 What should Sylvia do at once?
2 What should she say to the parents of the children in her care?
3 Who might check Sylvia's hair?
4 What steps should Sylvia take to get rid of the nits?
5 How can she protect herself and the children in future?

Threadworms

Threadworms are small white worms that live in the bowel. They resemble small pieces of white cotton and can often be seen in the stools. They come out of the bowel at night to lay their eggs around the anus. This causes severe irritation and the child will scratch herself. If the fingers are then placed in the mouth, the cycle of infestation will continue.

Constant sleep disruption will cause the child to become drowsy during the day and lack concentration. Inform the child's parents, so that they can seek medical advice, as the whole family will have to be treated. Apply the rules of personal hygiene stringently, encouraging careful hand-washing, disinfect the potty each time the child uses it, and be alert to the signs in other children.

chapter 10

Fleas

Fleas are small insects that jump from host to host and feed on blood. Fortunately, human fleas are rare in the UK but many children are sensitive to fleas that live on cats and dogs. A flea bite will leave a red mark that irritates and swells. Pets need to be treated regularly to avoid this problem.

Ringworm

Ringworm is a fungus infection of different types that may affect the skin or nails. It is seen as a red circle with a white scaly centre. It spreads in increasing circles while healing in the centre. The active edge is raised into small bumps. On the scalp, ringworm will result in bald patches. It causes much irritation. The parents must seek medical advice.

Scabies

Scabies is a skin infestation caused by the scabies mite which burrows under the skin, causing severe irritation. The mites feed on the skin and lay their eggs. Characteristic lines may be seen on the skin. The child will scratch, causing redness and infection. The mites can crawl from one person to another. The child must be seen by a doctor who will prescribe a lotion to kill the mites and eggs.

Ticks

Ticks live on animals and feed on blood. They are often found on deer and, although deer are relatively rare in the UK, if children have been to an area where deer roam, they are at risk from tick bites. These are very dangerous as, if untreated, they can cause Lyme's disease. The symptoms are like a bad dose of flu, but can result in brain damage. Children should be examined for tick bites whilst being bathed, and, if any are found, medical attention should be sought immediately by the parents.

Chronic medical conditions

Many children now spend nearly half their waking hours in the care of a home-based childcarer. About 10 to 15 per cent will have a known medical condition that may affect their physical health, their ability to learn, their relationships and their emotional well-being. It is important for you to have some knowledge and understanding of these conditions. There is danger in knowing a little about a condition and assuming that all children are affected in the same way. Parents are the best source of information. At the initial meeting with the parents, you will need to establish:

- how the child is affected by the illness
- whether there are any significant signs and symptoms you should look for
- what actions you should take if any problems arise whilst the child is in your care
- precise instructions and written permission to administer any medication or therapy required by the child

- knowledge of any side-effects of medication
- whether there are any physical or dietary restrictions placed on the child.

You will, of course, have an emergency contact number for the parents.

Working with parents

Minding a child with a chronic medical condition has additional rewards, such as the feeling of satisfaction, the use of all your skills, and the self-esteem you will gain from meeting the challenge. If you decide to care for a child with a chronic illness, it is important that you reach this decision after discussing the following points with the parents:

- the cause (where known) and the effect of the condition
- details of all routine medication and therapy required by the child
- possible side-effects of any medication and therapy
- any possible emergency that may arise, and your ability to manage the situation
- possible hospital appointments and admissions
- the need for any special equipment.

You would need to assess how much support the parents might demand of you and whether you are willing to take on this responsibility, which will take up your time and energy. You should also consider the effect on and the reactions of other children in your care and the impact on your own family. It might be wise to suggest a probationary period, when you can assess how everyone is coping.

If any child that you look after has a chronic medical condition, you must:

- have full knowledge of the condition and its effect on the child
- liaise closely with the parents
- be very familiar with any treatments and medication.

Diabetes

Diabetes is an endocrine disorder where the pancreas gland fails to produce the insulin that controls the amount of sugar or glucose released into the bloodstream. The high level of blood glucose is too much for the kidneys to cope with, and it is discharged in the urine. Signs of diabetes include:

- excessive thirst
- frequent passing of urine
- loss of weight in children.

Children may complain of headache and abdominal pain, and may vomit. Sugar will be found in blood and urine samples. Most children with diabetes require insulin by injection. Each child will have her own diet plan providing a balanced diet, controlling the intake of carbohydrate. Exercise burns calories, so you may need to offer a sensible snack after any vigorous activity. Normal growth is an indication of good diabetic control.

If you care for a child with diabetes you must:

- make sure the child is wearing a diabetic identity disc
- provide meals promptly

- teach other children in your care about diabetes
- help the child to behave as normally as possible
- be very clear about emergency procedures
- understand hypoglycaemia (a drop in blood sugar that may lead to a seizure or the child becoming comatose). Always have an emergency supply of glucose in the house
- understand hyperglycaemia (a rise in blood sugar, which may mean that the child needs insulin).

Asthma

This is an increasingly common, distressing condition, where the muscle walls of the lungs constrict. Excess mucus is produced that blocks the already narrowed passages. Breathing becomes difficult, the child will wheeze and cough, and may choke. Asthma is often associated with allergic conditions, such as eczema and hay fever. It may be triggered by exercise, viral infections, smoke, pollen, fur, house-dust mites, yeast, dairy food, anxiety and stress.

It is treated by medication, both preventative and curative. Inhalers and nebulisers are often used to administer the medication. Physiotherapy and a well-balanced diet may also form part of the treatment.

If you are caring for a child with asthma you must:

- know the individual triggers
- be very familiar with the medication used by the child, and know how to keep inhalers and nebulisers clean
- encourage normal activities
- observe for any chest infections
- be fully aware of emergency procedures.

Reducing allergens in your home

- Damp dust all surfaces regularly.
- Put soft toys in the freezer for 24 hours twice a month, and then wash at 60 degrees centigrade or above to kill the mites.
- Invest in a high-filtration vacuum cleaner.
- Regularly air the house and keep the house well ventilated.
- Replace upholstered furniture with leather, wood, plastic or cane.
- Wash cushions once a month, and never use feather-filled ones.
- Choose short-pile carpets or wooden or tiled floors.
- Avoid carpets in kitchens or bathrooms, where they can become damp.
- Dry all clothing out of doors when the weather is good.
- Use bleach to kill any fungus present in the bathroom.
- Have heaters and central heating serviced regularly.
- Take advice about plants and trees in the garden.
- Avoid compost heaps.

If you are asked to take a child with asthma, and you have a pet, you should discuss this with the parent.

Eczema

Children with eczema usually have very dry skin that becomes inflamed and cracked, making the skin vulnerable to infection. It causes intense irritation and can be very painful. The irritation is made worse when the child is warm, and this can disrupt sleep, leading to tiredness, irritability and lack of concentration. There are times when the skin flares up and is badly affected and other times when it is completely clear. It can be triggered by infection, irritants, such as soap and washing powder, environmental factors, certain foods, exercise and anxiety, medication and handling pets.

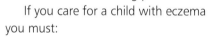

If you care for a child with eczema you must:

- know the triggers that cause the allergy
- understand the special attention you may need to give the skin
- keep the child cool when she is showing signs of irritation
- limit messy play if the eczema on the hands is infected; an older child might be willing to wear gloves
- discourage petting strange animals
- teach the other children about the condition, stressing that it is not contagious.

Epilepsy

There are many different types of epilepsy. Grand mal (tonic/clonic seizure) produces a typical fit, with loss of consciousness, convulsive movements and frothing at the mouth. Petit mal (absences) is less dramatic, and may go unnoticed. The child may look as if she is daydreaming. There is no cure, but modern treatment reduces and prevents frequency of fits.

Children with epilepsy need a normal environment, but if you care for a child with epilepsy you must:

- be alert to the signs of an epileptic fit and how to respond
- make sure the child is wearing a medical identity disc
- not leave the child alone for long periods of time
- restrict television viewing, as flickering lights can sometimes result in a fit
- observe the child closely if she is unwell
- teach the other children about epilepsy
- supervise very closely if the child is swimming or cycling.

Blood disorders

Haemophilia is an inherited blood disorder in which excessive bleeding results after even a minor injury, often causing bleeding into the joints and a great deal of pain.

Sickle cell is a chronic genetic condition, commonly found in people of African-Caribbean and African descent and sometimes in people from the Middle East, India and Pakistan. Abnormal haemoglobin is produced, assuming a sickle cell shape that is not fully oxygenated. It is an extremely painful, distressing condition.

Thalassaemia is a general term for a number of genetic blood disorders in which there is insufficient haemoglobin. It is found in children whose families came from the southern Mediterranean and the Middle East.

If you are caring for a child with an inherited blood disorder you must:

- try to avoid over-protecting the child, but be aware of hazards
- be aware of the child's need to attend hospital regularly
- understand any possible side effects, which might include lack of concentration, pain, infection, anaemia, fear of rough and tumble play and dehydration
- be aware of emergency procedures.

Cystic fibrosis

This is an inherited disorder, found mainly in children of North European descent. It produces problems in the lungs and digestive system. Over-production of sticky mucus secretions clogs the lungs and blocks the pancreatic ducts, preventing the flow of enzymes needed for digestion of food. The severity of symptoms will vary but can include repeated chest infections, failure to thrive, and large, watery, foul-smelling stools that are difficult to flush away. A sweat test will show a high concentration of salt.

This is a life-threatening condition, but the prognosis has much improved over the last few years. Treatment includes:

- antibiotics
- physiotherapy
- a high-calorie diet
- additional vitamins
- immunisation.

If you are caring for a child with cystic fibrosis you must:

- try to avoid contact with infectious children
- observe closely for signs of infection
- encourage the child to develop as normally as possible, including her in all activities
- supervise the child at mealtimes, with regard to medication, and encourage her to eat well
- understand that physiotherapy may be painful and distressing
- try to boost the child's self-confidence, as she may be shorter and lighter than average
- be aware of the child's need to attend hospital on a regular basis.

Coeliac disease

This is caused by an inability to digest gluten, found widely in various cereal products. It is diagnosed when the baby is weaned from a milk to a mixed-feeding diet. The baby may begin to refuse food, fail to thrive, become lethargic, irritable and listless, pass abnormal stools, vomit and look malnourished. The only treatment available is a gluten-free diet. All foods containing wheat and rye flour and oat and barley products must be excluded. Rice and maize products are acceptable. This diet must be maintained throughout life. Many products in the supermarket indicate if they are gluten free.

If you are caring for a child with coeliac disease, you will have to liaise closely with the parents, particularly concerning the child's diet.

Phenylketonuria

This is a genetically inherited disease that causes an excess of phenylalanine (an essential amino acid), which cannot be broken down and absorbed by the body. It accumulates in the bloodstream, causing brain damage and learning delay. All newborn babies are screened for this disorder. Treatment is a life-long restricted diet. Children will have routine blood tests.

If you care for a child with phenylketonuria you will have to liaise very closely with parents and be extremely knowledgeable about the diet.

Activity

A little boy of three that you look after is constantly thirsty, needs to empty his bladder often, and does not appear to be thriving.
1 Why might this be?
2 What steps would you take?

Children with HIV (human immune deficiency virus)

It is possible that you may be caring for a child who is HIV positive and you may or may not be aware of this. Many children who are HIV positive remain well and healthy, displaying no symptoms of AIDS (acquired immune deficiency syndrome). Children with an impaired immunity system may have a greater risk of catching infections and may also experience severe complications from common childhood infections, such as measles and chickenpox.

HIV has been isolated in many body fluids. Sufficient amounts of the virus to cause infection have been found in:

- blood and blood products
- semen
- vaginal and cervical secretions
- amniotic fluid (the fluid that surrounds the baby in the uterus)
- breast milk.

It is not thought the virus can be passed on through:

- saliva
- sweat
- tears
- urine
- faeces.

The virus is extremely fragile, and is unable to survive long outside the body. It cannot be carried through the air. It is destroyed by heat, light, bleach and detergents. The main routes of transmission are through sexual contact, blood to blood through sharing needles and syringes, and mother to baby. There is no known case of HIV being transmitted in any childcare setting. Most pathogens, such as hepatitis B, are much more infectious than the HIV virus.

Good hygiene practice plays an important part in providing a safe and caring environment for children. All children, including your own, should be treated as if they were HIV positive, and this will ensure best practice and equal treatment for all.

In addition to the good hygiene practices pointed out in Chapter 8, you should always:

- wash blood, faeces and urine off your skin with warm, preferably hot, soap and water
- regularly clean and disinfect floors, equipment, toys and cups
- clean up any spilt blood or faeces with a bleach solution (1 part household bleach to 10 parts water)
- cover any open wounds on your skin or on a child's skin
- wear disposable gloves when dealing with faeces, urine or blood if you have cuts on your hands
- rinse with running water for several minutes if blood is splashed on your face or in your eyes
- soak any blooded clothes, or implements used for First Aid in a 1:10 bleach solution for 5 to 10 minutes
- wipe the nappy-changing pad with a 1:10 bleach solution after each use
- double-wrap all waste that contains body fluids, and put in plastic sacks.

There is no obligation for the parents to tell you that they, or their child, are HIV positive. Adults and children can become infected in different ways and it is important not to make assumptions about how a child might become infected. If a parent does confide in you, you must respect this confidence and tell no one. Many people will not be as knowledgeable as you and may feel their children to be at risk.

Ninety per cent of children are healthy most of the time. Nevertheless, it is prudent to be able to recognise illness, however minor, so steps can be taken to prevent cross-infection, to relieve symptoms and to ensure that the child receives the care she needs.

Reflecting on Practice

You might think about:

- storing, recording and administering medication to children in your care
- how you will manage children with minor ailments
- how you will recognise more serious conditions
- when it is necessary to exclude children because of illness, and for how long
- how you will work in partnership with parents to manage infestations
- how you will work in partnership with parents to manage chronic conditions
- how to update your knowledge of HIV.

This chapter has contributed to the following learning outcomes:

Unit 1

- providing a safe and healthy childcare environment in the home-based setting
- promoting anti-discriminatory, anti-bias practice in the home-based setting

Unit 2

- providing for children's development and well-being from birth to 16 years

Want to Find Out More?

Websites

www.allergyuk.org

www.asthma.org.uk

www.bbc.co.uk/health

www.eczema.org.uk

www.ich.ucl.ac.uk/gosh-families/information_sheets

www.sicklecellsociety.org

www.teachernet.gov.uk/wholeschool/healthandsafety/medical/

Further reading

Briffa J., *Natural Health for Kids: How to Give Your Child the Very Best Start in Life*, Penguin, 2007

Gilbert P., *An A–Z of Childhood Health Problems*, Nelson Thornes, 1999

Keene A., *Child Health: Care of the Child in Health and Illness*, Nelson Thornes, 1999

Stoppard M., *Complete Baby and Childcare: Everything You Need to Know for the First Five Years*, Dorling Kindersley, 2008

11

Child protection

Learning objectives

Unit 1
- Promoting inclusion and anti-bias practice
- Promoting child protection in the home-based setting

Unit 2
- Promoting children's rights

Unit 3
- Understanding the need for inter-agency working and work with other professionals
- Promoting child protection

Unit 4
- Practising confidentiality, and understanding about data protection and the law

You have made your house and garden a safe place, prepared safety plans for when you take the children out of your house, and made sure that there are no avoidable health hazards due to poor hygiene. But there are other dangers in the environment. These days, there is a great deal in the media about abused and neglected children and, while we must be careful not to over-protect our children, we must always be alert to the dangers surrounding them. All home-based childcarers in Wales must have a child protection policy and many home-based childcarers in England will follow suit. This policy should be shown to parents at the first interview, and many home-based childcarers ask parents to read and sign the document.

The rights of children

In November 1959, the UN issued a document declaring the rights of the child. This was motivated by the parlous plight of some children due to wars and famine: children were left without parents, families and homes. The following rights are set out:

1. the right to equality, regardless of race, colour, religion, sex or nationality
2. the right to healthy mental and physical development
3. the right to a name and a nationality
4. the right to sufficient food, housing and medical care
5. the right to special care, if handicapped
6. the right to love, understanding and care
7. the right to free education, play and recreation
8. the right to medical aid in the event of disasters and emergencies
9. the right to protection from cruelty, neglect and exploitation
10. the right to protection from persecution and to an upbringing in the spirit of world-wide brotherhood and peace.

Thirty years later, in 1989, the Convention was adopted and further points were added. Applicable to child protection was the statement that it is:

- the right of every child to have a standard of living adequate for the child's physical, mental, spiritual, moral and social development.

The Convention contains more than 30 articles incorporating civil, economic, social and cultural rights. Article 3, 'The Welfare Principle' states that:

- in all actions concerning children, whether undertaken by public or private social welfare institutions, courts of law, administrative authorities or legislative bodies, the best interests of the child shall be a primary consideration.

Article 19 defines 'Protection from Abuse'. It aims:

- to protect the child from all forms of physical or mental violence, injury or abuse, neglect or negligent treatment, maltreatment or exploitation including sexual abuse while in the care of parent/s, legal guardian/s or any other person who has the care of the child.

Protective measures include:

- support for the child and identification, reporting, referral, investigation, treatment, and follow-up of instances of child maltreatment.

Article 34 concerns protecting the child from sexual abuse and sexual exploitation. This is defined as:

- inducement or coercion of a child to engage in any unlawful sexual activity
- exploitative use of children in prostitution or other unlawful sexual practices
- exploitative use of children in pornographic performances and materials.

It is clear that in many countries it would be impossible to grant all these rights, as even the basic needs for food and shelter cannot be met. It is an important document, however, in recognising the rights of children who have been abused. We need to understand the rights of children and respect them.

All children need and have the right to:

- physical care, ensuring safety, good health and nutrition
- emotional care, encompassing warm, caring, constant relationships
- intellectual stimulation, including education through play to develop language and cognitive skills to their full potential
- social relationships, developing friendships, mixing with other children and adults from many different backgrounds, and learning to value people for what they are.

Good practice in . . . CONTRIBUTING TO CHILDREN'S RIGHTS

1 Show sensitivity to and awareness of everyone's needs at all times.
2 Be aware of current welfare benefits and sources of help in the community.
3 Be aware of the financial pressures on some parents.
4 Have patience with those parents who place too much emphasis on one aspect of development, carefully explaining the all-round needs of the child, and the need to value children for what they are and not what you wish them to be.
5 Provide stimulating and varied play opportunities that cater for the learning needs of all the children.
6 Show by your example the importance of a healthy nutritious diet, the prevention of infection by scrupulous hygiene routines and an awareness of preventative health care.

The role of the home-based childcarer

The whole of society has an obligation to protect children. You, as a home-based childcarer, need to explain to the parents when making initial arrangements that you have a duty to report any suspicious incidents as well as accidents. You should emphasise that the welfare of the child is always your first responsibility. It is often difficult to be a 'whistle-blower' when you have a relationship with the parents. Common reasons given for not taking action are:

- disbelief
- fear of being seen as interfering
- fear of becoming involved in a difficult or distressing situation
- friendship and loyalty to parents
- fear that a family will be split up and the children taken away.

There is no doubt that you will feel conflict, as your professional approach to confidentiality will be at odds with the need to report your concerns so as to protect the child.

Very few children are removed from the family. Decisions are taken in the best interest of the child, and the usual policy of local authorities is to try to help and advise families in order to ensure the child's safety within the family. For home-based childcarers, there is also the fear of making a costly mistake, losing a child and income, and risking future livelihood by losing the trust of local parents.

As a home-based childcarer you have a professional responsibility to protect children and to help stop any abuse that you think may be taking place. Make sure that you:

- do not ignore possible signs of abuse; be sure to express your concerns
- listen to children if they state someone is upsetting or hurting them
- do not assume someone else will take action to help the child.

If you are concerned about a child, his parents may be the first people to talk to, as you may feel this is only fair and a continuation of your partnership arrangements. If there is a satisfactory explanation, it will avoid unnecessary investigations. On the other hand, before you do that, consider the possibility that you may be deceived by the parents, and only too ready to accept their explanation. You may be vulnerable if the parents accuse you to protect themselves or evidence may disappear as the parents are given time to prepare a plausible story.

If you feel a child is at risk you should contact the social services duty officer. You might also consider talking to NCMA, the NSPCC, or your local health visitor if you are unsure of the appropriate action to take. You are required to inform Ofsted of any concerns you have reported to social services.

Definitions of abuse and neglect

Child abuse is sometimes difficult to define, but a clear understanding is necessary so that you may act with confidence when working with children. There are some commonly accepted definitions of child abuse, but local authorities may differ in their definitions. The broad categories are neglect, physical abuse and injury, emotional abuse and sexual abuse, but all these categories overlap and interconnect.

Child abuse is a culturally defined phenomenon. Kempe commented on the rights of a child to be protected from parents unable to cope at a level assumed to be reasonable by the society in which they reside (Kempe, 1978). What is regarded as 'reasonable' changes within and between societies. In a country where a large proportion of the child population is afflicted by malnutrition, a parent's inability to provide the child with sufficient food would not be categorised as neglect on the parent's part. In more affluent countries there have been changes in the recognition of the potentially abusive nature of some behaviours, which were previously accepted as 'reasonable'.

Childhood abuse is not a concept that can be defined exactly. The point at which a child generates sufficient concern to be deemed in need of protection can be subjective. For example, when does smacking become hitting? When does demonstrative affection become a sexual assault?

Definitions

Abuse
A violation of an individual's human and civil rights by any other person or persons (*No Secrets*, DoH, 2000).

Physical abuse and injury

The intentional, non-accidental use of physical force and violence, which results in hurting, injuring or killing a child. It includes poisoning.

Physical neglect

The failure by the parents/carers to feed, shelter, keep safe, keep clean and provide medical care for a child.

Educational neglect

Failing to meet the child's need for stimulation by not providing any opportunities for play and education to encourage language and intellectual development.

Emotional neglect

Withdrawing or not providing love, affection and emotional consistency for the child, and not providing an environment of warmth, interest and care.

Sexual abuse

'The involvement of dependent, developmentally immature children and adolescents in sexual activities they do not fully comprehend, are unable to give informed consent to and that violate the sexual taboos of family roles' (Schecter and Roberge, 1976).

Emotional abuse

The exposure of children to constant criticism and hostility, always linked to emotional neglect.

Failure to thrive

The failure of a baby or child to achieve his expected weight or height with no obvious medical or physical cause. It is often associated with a negative relationship with the parent/carer.

Organised abuse

Sexual abuse, and perhaps physical injury, with a number of perpetrators and a number of children. There is an element of deliberate planning.

Factitious illness (previously Munchausen syndrome by proxy)

A psychological condition, where the parent/carer fabricates a child's illness, seeking different medical opinions and inducing symptoms in the child to deceive the doctors.

Statistics

NSPCC

According to the NSPCC, an estimated 150 to 200 children die each year in England and Wales following incidents of abuse or neglect. Thousands more suffer long-term emotional and psychological problems because of ill treatment by their parents or those looking after them.

A survey of the childhood experiences of a national UK sample of adults, aged 18–45 (Creighton and Russell, 1995), found that some 35 per cent said that they had been hit with an implement. Only 7 per cent felt that it was acceptable to do that to a child now. Parental behaviours towards children, that are deemed to be unacceptable, are continually evolving within societies.

The NSPCC website also shows that during the year 1 April 2002 to 31 March 2003 there were 4109 reported offences of 'cruelty to or neglect of children' and 1880 of 'gross indecency with a child under the age of 14' in England and Wales (Home Office, 2003). There were 30,200 children's names added to child protection registers during the year in England (DfES, 2004) and 2609 in Wales (National Assembly for Wales, 2003). There were 570,220 referrals concerning child maltreatment to social services departments in England during the year ending 31 March 2003 (DfES, 2004).

ChildLine

In the 2003 Annual Report produced by ChildLine, the figures show that 120,000 children were counselled, with thousands more receiving straightforward advice; 4000 children called every day of whom 1800 were put through to counsellors. During the year:

- 13,650 calls concerned physical abuse
- 8540 concerned sexual abuse showing that 58 per cent of the perpetrators were within the caller's family; 32 per cent of perpetrators were known but not in the family and 10 per cent were strangers
- 21,866 received advice concerning bullying
- 16,064 described family tensions
- 2000 children reported domestic violence
- 2541 children reported other abuse (risk/neglect/emotional)
- 3000 adults called to report children at risk.

Childhood Matters

The report, *Childhood Matters*, was a two-year evidence-gathering exercise, involving over 10,000 individuals and organisations. The researchers received over 1000 letters from survivors of child abuse. Of these, 80 per cent said they had been sexually abused. Only 32 per cent said they had told anyone, and 13 per cent had never revealed what had happened. The evidence showed that the abuse often began at pre-school age and continued well into adolescence. The annual cost of abuse was conservatively estimated at one billion pounds, but was impossible to assess accurately because of the long-term effects of abuse.

The Gulbenkian Foundation

The Gulbenkian Foundation published a report in 1995 on the incidence of violence to children (see page 212).

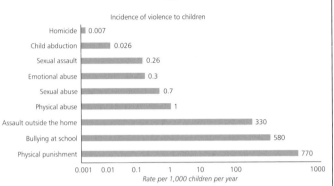

The extent of violence involving children

Children are far more often victims of violence than perpetrators of violence, and certain groups of children, including disabled children and some ethnic groups, are particularly at risk. One of the most disturbing social statistics is that the risk of homicide for babies under the age of one is almost four times as great as for any other age group. There is increasing knowledge of and sensitivity to violence to children – in particular to sexual abuse and to bullying and other violence in institutions; it is not possible to tell whether the incidence of these forms of violence has increased or become more visible. There are problems about building any accurate picture of violence to children within families, but the most recent UK research shows that a substantial minority of children suffer severe physical punishment; most children are hit by their parents, up to a third of younger children more than once a week.

Only a very small proportion of children – mostly male but with an increasing minority of young women – get involved in committing violent offences. Very roughly, 4 per 1,000 young people aged between 10 and 18 are cautioned or convicted for offences involving violence against the person.

In terms of trends it appears that children's involvement in some but not all crimes of violence in the UK has increased over the last decade. But in comparison with the USA, overall levels of interpersonal violence in the UK are very low, and there is recent evidence that in comparison with some European countries, levels of self-reported violence by children in the UK are also low.

A Gulbenkian Foundation report, 1995

Other statistics

Recent Home Office figures show that domestic violence claims 150 lives each year, accounts for a quarter of all violent crime and that on average there will be 35 assaults before a victim calls the police; domestic violence claims the lives of 2 women each week. It costs in excess of £5 million a year. It is estimated that 1 in 4 women may experience violence in their relationships with men.

A 1993 Hackney study, 'Links between Domestic Violence and Child Abuse', showed that half the women killed each year were killed by partners and that 100,000 women each year seek medical help for injuries caused by partners. A violent crime survey, conducted by the Home Office in 1989, showed that 25 per cent of all assaults recorded by the police were domestic violence offences and around 10 to 15 per cent of cases were of violence against the person.

In an NCH Action for Children study 'The Hidden Victims: Children and Domestic Violence' in 1994, a quarter of the mothers said that their violent partners had also physically assaulted their children. Several said that the children had been sexually abused. More than five in six of the mothers thought that the children had been affected by the violence in the longer term. Many of the children showed signs and behaviour indicators of emotional abuse.

In November 2004, a new law, the Domestic Violence Crime and Victims Act, came into being. It makes it easier for the Crown Prosecution Service (CPS) to prosecute the perpetrator and more difficult for the perpetrator to re-offend. Common assault is now an arrestable offence, allowing the police to remove the perpetrator from the scene more easily. Breaking a non-molestation order is a criminal offence with a penalty of up to five years in prison. Restraining orders may now be granted even after an acquittal if the court thinks it is necessary. The CPS is now able to take the decision to prosecute with or without the permission of the victim. A prosecution will not automatically be dropped if the victim withdraws his or her statement.

Recognition of abuse and neglect

As a person who cares for children in a professional manner, you need to be able to recognise the signs of abuse and neglect. Whatever sort of relationship you may have made with the family, your first duty is to the child. This is laid down in the Children Act 1989: 'the welfare of the child is paramount'. The following indicators should ring alarm bells:

- all bruises on the head or face of a small baby
- bruises on the cheeks of a toddler
- bald patches on the head
- cigarette burns
- two black eyes
- any neck injury
- fingertip bruising
- bruises on genitalia
- adult bite marks
- scratches
- scalds on the child's feet and legs, caused by 'dunking' in very hot water
- splash burns
- babies unable to move any limb
- bruises on soft tissue
- injury to ear lobes
- bruising of lips, gums or a torn frenulum (the piece of tissue that attaches the lips to the gums).

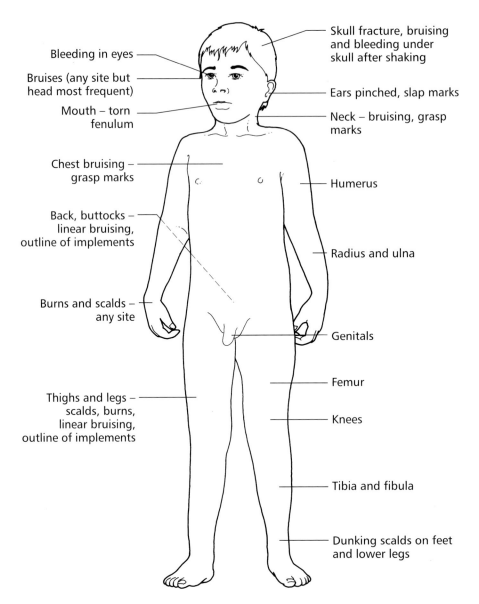

Bleeding in eyes

Bruises (any site but head most frequent)

Mouth – torn fenulum

Chest bruising – grasp marks

Back, buttocks – linear bruising, outline of implements

Burns and scalds – any site

Thighs and legs – scalds, burns, linear bruising, outline of implements

Skull fracture, bruising and bleeding under skull after shaking

Ears pinched, slap marks

Neck – bruising, grasp marks

Humerus

Radius and ulna

Genitals

Femur

Knees

Tibia and fibula

Dunking scalds on feet and lower legs

Principle sites of non-accidental injuries

Shaken impact syndrome

Shaken impact syndrome is a term used to describe injury caused by shaking. Babies under one year are the most vulnerable as their under-developed neck muscles are too weak to support their large and heavy heads. The brain and surrounding blood vessels are immature and fragile. Shaking causes the brain to move within the skull, causing the blood vessels to tear and blood to flood into the skull. The long-term effects can include:

- visual impairment
- hearing impairment
- seizures
- learning difficulties
- brain damage.

Shaking is usually triggered by a child's persistent crying.

In 2000, a Scottish study suggested that up to 170 babies may be injured each year in the UK by being shaken violently by their parents or carers. Some die, and nearly 80 per cent of the survivors are left with long-term learning difficulties, seizures and problems with movement.

In 2001, the neural damage in 53 children aged between 20 days and 8 years was studied by a group in Sheffield and London. They had died after non-accidental head injuries. The researchers were looking for a symptom known as diffuse axonal injury (DAI), thought to occur if severe force is applied to the brain by violent shaking or falls from heights. In the majority of cases the doctors did not find DAI. However, examination of the brains found signs of damage due to the brain stretching where it joined the spinal cord. This sort of injury could occur if the baby's head was allowed to flop backwards and forwards and could lead to serious breathing problems, resulting in oxygen starvation and eventual death. Contrary to previous thought, it was found that shaking need not be violent to cause fatal injury in a baby.

Signs to cause concern would be a baby arriving at your home, looking lethargic, with poor muscle tone, miserable, not interested in feeding and unable to settle. These signs may also indicate an onset of infection, but you should immediately discuss them with the parents and ask them to seek medical advice.

Activity

It can happen that child abuse is not deliberate cruelty but something that occurs when an adult loses control. Do you think that an adult who deliberately abuses children is more at fault than an adult who loses control? Discuss this with other home-based childcarers.

Most children will suffer accidental injuries. Deciding what is accidental and what has been inflicted upon a child can be a very difficult process, testing the skills of experienced paediatricians. See the diagram on page 214 for the principal sites of non-accidental injuries. Many signs that might lead you to think that abuse has taken place might be explained. For example, bald patches might occur if a child frequently pulls and twists his hair as a comfort habit. It is your responsibility to be alert to any unexplained or suspicious injury, making sure you record your concerns, and discussing it with your early years adviser or NCMA adviser.

Simone, a ten-month-old child of an African-Caribbean father and an English mother, was left with Jessie, a home-based childcarer. Jessie identified what she thought were bruises on Simone's buttocks. That evening, when she questioned the mother, she was reassured that the marks were Mongolian blue spot – an area of natural hyperpigmentation that occurs in many African, African-Caribbean and Asian babies at birth.

1 How would Jessie confirm this information?
2 Can you think of any other signs that might be open to the wrong interpretation?

Sexual abuse

Sexual abuse ranges from showing pornographic materials or inappropriate touching to penetration, rape and incest. It is found in all cultures, all classes and in all religious groups. It may involve very young babies. It often begins gradually and increases over a period of time. Children are trusting and dependent, wanting to please and gain love and approval.

The majority of abused children know the perpetrator who is often a member of the family, a close family friend or someone in a position of trust. The abuse rarely involves the use of physical force and there are usually no physical signs but, if you did see bruising in the genital area, bloodstains, torn underclothing or vaginal discharge, you would be immediately alerted and take steps to protect the child.

Changes in behaviour

Abuse and neglect may cause a change of behaviour that will vary a great deal according to the age of the child. You may see the child:

- withdraw from physical contact
- be wary of forming close relationships with adults and other children
- show apprehension when children cry
- appear to be frightened of the parent/carer
- display a lack of spontaneity and become wary of adult's reactions to him
- display self-destructive behaviour such as hair pulling and head banging
- display aggression
- begin to overeat or to refuse food.

Some areas of abuse are more difficult to recognise than physical abuse and neglect. For example, emotional abuse, such as shutting a child in a cupboard as punishment or constantly belittling and undermining the child in everything he does, can be almost as damaging as physical abuse. An indication that this is going on may appear in the behaviour of the child who may show:

- fear of new situations
- comfort-seeking behaviour, such as thumb-sucking, excessive masturbation and rocking to and fro
- speech disorders, such as stammering and stuttering
- delay in all-round development
- extremes of passivity and aggression
- low self-esteem and lack of confidence
- nightmares and changes in sleep patterns
- wetting and soiling after the child has become clean and dry
- temper tantrums that are not age-appropriate
- inability to concentrate for more than a few minutes.

Signs of sexual abuse

Many of the changes in behaviour would be similar to those described above, but in addition the child might:

- behave in a way sexually inappropriate to his age, particularly when involved in imaginary play
- produce drawings of sex organs and use sexual language
- display insecurity and cling to trusted adults
- act in a placatory or flirtatious way, or in an inappropriately mature manner.

Changes in behaviour are not necessarily due to abuse or neglect. Children go through many difficult stages in their normal development. It is only when there is a cluster of behavioural changes that you should begin to consider the possibility of abuse.

Signs of neglect

A child who is underweight, maybe small for his age, with poor muscle tone and a dry wrinkled skin, may be suffering from neglect. He may demand food immediately on arrival and display an enormous appetite during the day. If his personal hygiene needs are not being met, he may appear dirty and uncared for, smell of urine, have unbrushed hair and teeth, and wear inappropriate and dirty clothing.

The younger child may suffer from severe persistent nappy rash and/or cradle cap. He may appear constantly tired or lethargic, with frequent colds and coughs, stomach upsets and rashes; and the parents may appear reluctant to seek any medical help. You may find the child frequently arrives and is collected late. You may notice that the parents fail to express any affection or display warmth and interest in the child, and seem to have unrealistic expectations of his behaviour and capabilities.

List the ways in which you recognise distress in children.

Disclosure

If you find yourself in a position where the older child is disclosing abuse to you, you need to respond in a way that will not further harm the child. Listen carefully and patiently, without asking leading questions: that is, without putting words into the child's mouth, or making him give the response you want him to. You should:

- attempt to make the child feel secure and safe when disclosing to you
- reassure the child, stating that you are pleased to have been told and that you believe him
- never look shocked or disbelieving
- never express criticism of the perpetrator
- never promise to take an action, which you may not be able to carry out
- reassure the child that he is not to blame for the abuse
- explain that, in order to help him, you will have to tell other people what is happening
- keep calm
- resist pressing for information or questioning the child, as other agencies will have to interview him
- make an immediate timed, dated and signed record of the conversation.

Record keeping

As soon as you suspect that a child may have been abused, you need to be meticulous in your record keeping. Keeping the NCMA accident book, the existing injuries record (see www.ncma.org.uk) and filling in a record of concerns (see pages 219–20) may be helpful in any future investigation of suspected abuse.

Timing, dating and signing all noted incidents is essential as the record may be required at a child protection conference and may also protect you from allegations of abuse. All records should be factual and accurate, and you should be scrupulous in leaving out your own feelings and in being objective. These notes and records should be made within 24 hours of the incident or conversation if they are to be legally admissible. They should be kept in a secure, locked place where they are not accessible to anyone else. All records are highly confidential and should only be shown to and discussed with other relevant professionals with a responsibility towards the child.

RECORD OF CONCERNS

Name			Date of birth		Start date		
Date Time	Incident	Physical injury	Non attendance	Conversation	Behaviour causing concern	Action	Signature

11 chapter

RECORD OF CONCERNS (EXAMPLE)

Name	Gillian B		Date of birth	3.2.07	Start date	2.1.09	
Date Time	Incident	Physical injury	Non attendance	Conversation	Behaviour causing concern	Action	Signature
30.3.09		Bruises seen on both arms		G says she fell off bike		This chart started	CM
6.4.09 9.30am 12.15pm	G very hungry. Asked for food – 3 helpings at lunch					Noted	CM
11.4.09 21.4.09			Did not attend	Mother states child unwell. Did not see GP			CM
							CM
24.4.09				Avoided contact with me & other children all day	Quiet, withdrawn passive	Observe next week	CM
30.4.09	Mother collects child, smells of alcohol					Discuss with NCMA	CM
1.5.09		Small burn on leg?		No response from child	Found crying in sitting room	NCMA early years adviser	CM
6.5.09			Did not attend			To contact soc. services	CM

Referral and investigation

Once you have reported your concerns to social services, it becomes known as a referral and an investigation will be made in order to establish the truth of the allegation, to make a record of the allegation and to assess the current risk to the child. The diagram below shows the procedure for investigating a case. Social services will also decide whether protection procedures should be put in place. If you have not made the referral, but an investigation has been started on, say, the referral from a neighbour of the family, you will still be involved as the person outside the family who sees the most of the child.

Following the investigation, if there is no cause for concern, the person with parental responsibility for the child and the referrer are informed in writing. If there are grounds for concern, there will be a formal child protection conference. This conference is not called to apportion blame but to exchange information, decide on the level of risk and whether the child needs to be placed on the register. The conference will make some forward-thinking decisions

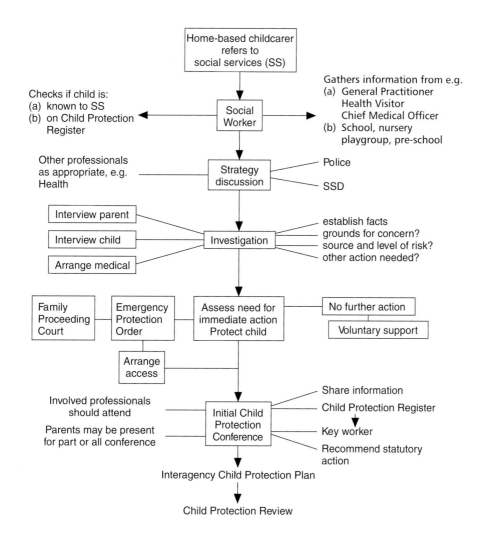

for the benefit of the family and the protection of the child. Conferences require a number of different agencies to be present before decisions can be made. Specialists may also be called to give advice.

As a home-based childcarer, you may be required to attend a child protection conference to present observations you have made of the child or an assessment of any recent changes in his behaviour. You will not be asked for opinions but only for objective evidence, and this is where your observations and record keeping will be most valuable. You should be sent an agenda in advance and a checklist of basic information about the conference. Parents and carers will be invited to attend the conference for at least part of the time and be given the opportunity to express their views. This can be a stressful experience, but you may find support from your early years adviser or from your local NCMA organiser. NCMA may be able to offer you support in preparing for and attending a child protection conference.

If the conference decides the child is suffering or is likely to suffer significant harm, the conference will register the child under one or several categories of abuse or neglect. It will appoint and name a key worker and recommend a core group of professionals to be involved in a child protection plan. A review date will be set.

In very serious cases the child protection conference may recommend that court proceedings are taken, and the courts will decide the future of the child. You may find yourself called as a witness. This is not a pleasant experience and you may feel anxious and worried about the event. You should be given support by social services and NCMA. You can obtain information from the court in advance about what should be expected of you as a witness. You may be able to visit the courtroom to familiarise yourself with the environment and the proceedings.

Activity

You have attended a child protection conference because a child you care for has been sexually abused by a family friend. As part of the child protection plan, you have been asked to monitor the child's behaviour and emotional development and keep detailed records.
1 How might you begin this task?
2 How might you seek the co-operation of the parents?
3 What additional support might you offer the parents?

Factors that contribute to abuse and neglect

There have been many theories put forward over the last 50 years as to why some children are abused or neglected. These include:

- separation of mother and baby at birth, preventing bonding
- maternal deprivation
- inequalities in society
- a patriarchal society
- scapegoating of some children within the family
- some abusers may have been abused when they were children.

Identify any theories you may have heard which try to explain poor parenting.

Current thought is that the reasons for child abuse must be looked at as a combination of social, psychological, economic and environmental factors. Abuse is found across a wider range of people than any one theory would have us believe. The table, 'What places children "at risk" of child abuse?' on page 225 shows some of the conditions and developmental stages of small children that may trigger abuse.

CASE STUDY

Sally is two and a half and has been looked after by you for six months. The family is affluent and lives in a large detached house. Sally's father is frequently away from home, and Sally is usually collected by her mother, Jane. It has been difficult to establish a relationship with Jane. She seems to have very little time for or patience with Sally, often describing her in a disparaging manner. Sally is becoming quieter and more withdrawn, and on one occasion said she had been shut in a cupboard for a long time. When Jane arrives to collect her that day, she looks tearful, upset and smells of drink. Sally runs and clings to Jane who pushes her away.

1 What factors might cause you concern?
2 How might her mother's rejection affect Sally's emotional development?
3 What are Sally's needs and what are the family's needs?
4 What might you do to help Sally and her family?

How to protect yourself from allegations of abuse

When working as a home-based childcarer you need to be aware that you are in a vulnerable situation. There have been some cases of home-based childcarers, or members of their family, being accused of abuse, so make sure your behaviour is professional at all times and open to scrutiny. There are steps you can take to prevent yourself or your family being unjustly accused of abuse. These include:

- making sure your record keeping is up to date; registers, observations, accident and incident report forms should be written up daily and kept in a safe place
- making a note of when another adult witnesses an accident to one of the children
- reporting your suspicions or concerns about a child to your early years adviser and keeping a written record
- joining NCMA and any local support group
- keeping the child's parents informed of any incidents, accidents or events concerning the child that have occurred during the day
- completing the existing injuries form to record any injury, however minor, sustained by a child when not in your care
- ensuring the children are well supervised at all times, and not leaving them in the care of unauthorised people, even a member of your family
- telling the child's parents if a child behaves in a sexually inappropriate manner towards you, recording the incident and making sure your early years adviser or an NCMA representative, knows about it
- encouraging independence in children, and not carrying out intimate tasks that they are quite capable of doing for themselves
- not asking children to keep secrets
- while managing children's challenging behaviour, never involving rough handling of a child
- never shaking, hitting or smacking a child in your care, even if the child's parents want to give their permission
- not shouting or using a sarcastic approach with children
- using appropriate language in front of children
- while responding to children's emotional needs, never forcing kisses and cuddles on children who do not wish it
- taking advantage of any child protection training courses.

You need to make sure that no one in your household behaves in a threatening or inappropriate manner towards the children in your care.

If a complaint is made against you or a member of your family, you must immediately contact Ofsted as it is now an offence not to tell Ofsted of any allegations of serious harm or abuse against a child, whatever the circumstances. This will make you feel distressed and most unhappy, but do not panic; all complaints have to be investigated. This is a legal requirement and everyone involved will be trying to reach an objective decision. Keep a record of all conversations you have, both face to face and on the telephone, concerning this matter. Include times, dates, places and participants. Keep copies of all correspondence. You should seek legal advice, either independently or through the NCMA.

WHAT PLACES CHILDREN 'AT RISK' OF CHILD ABUSE?

The 'seven deadly sins' – conditions and developmental stages that may trigger physical abuse of small children

Condition/trigger	Description	Age of most danger	Common abuse injuries associated	Advice for stopping/preventing abuse
Colic	All babies show some 'fussy' crying that is inconsolable. About one baby in ten will cry like this frequently and persistently in ways parents find impossible to stop, and for long periods.	1–3 months and then stops	Internal bruising in head, grab-mark bruises, broken arms, legs and ribs	1 Check for any medical causes and then reassure parents this is normal and will stop at about three months or before. 2 Help them to learn soothing techniques and give permission for them meeting *their* needs for sleep and time away from the baby.
Habitual night crying	Some babies develop a habit of waking in the night even after they no longer need a feed. They get to enjoy the extra attention or find it difficult to sleep without parental care.	4 months – 2 to 3 years	Injuries as above	1 Stop naps during the day, move cot to baby's own room and make bedtime calm. 2 Make 'check-up' visits short, boring and at long intervals. 3 Give more attention and stimulation during the day.
Clinginess and separation anxiety	At about six months a baby comes to depend upon his/her main caregiver(s) for security and will show clinginess and anxiety when separated. Some parents do not understand and see this as the child being spoiled.	6 months – 3 to 4 years	Spanking and slapping injuries. Emotional cruelty, e.g. locking up	1 Explain that this stage is normal and necessary for healthy development. 2 Help parents to make separation easier for child – by rehearsal, making it gradual etc. 3 Make sure child is always left with somebody they know, like and trust.
Curiosity and exploration	Children as they develop mentally and physically increasingly explore their surroundings as they become more mobile. Unchecked they can expose themselves to danger. Some parents expect them to follow adult rules and punish them for damaging property or making messes.	1–3 years old	Too little control – burns, poisonings, etc. Too much control – bruised from spanking and rough grabbing	1 Explain that exploration and curiosity are natural and necessary parts of growing up. 2 Safety-proof the home and draw up rules for protection, develop firm but non-abusive strategies for managing behaviour. 3 Provide an environment that allows plenty of opportunities to explore.
Disobedience and negativism	As children begin to develop a sense of independence, they often test this out by being disobedient and negative. Parents may feel feel very threatened by this disobedience.	1½–3 years	Slaps and punches to body and head. Cruel emotional punishment may include locking up, taunting, etc.	1 Explain the phase is normal however irritating. 2 Go for minimal rules and non-confrontation. 3 Offer child choices where possible but don't bargain where there is no choice.
Fussy eating	Because growth slows down, a child's appetite falls off somewhere between eighteen months and two years. Refusing to eat may become a child's way of self-assertion.	1½–3 years	Slap and pinch marks on face and injuries to mouth from force feeding. Children may choke or suffocate.	1 Explain that it is usual to eat less at this age and reassure that the child is fit and well. 2 Cut down on snacks and drinking too much milk. 3 Take the 'heat' out of mealtimes.
Wetting and soiling	Children gain control over their bladders and bowels only gradually. Parents may expect to toilet train too soon or see wetting and soiling as deliberate disobedience.	1–3 years	Bruises, burns and scalds around bottom and genital areas	1 Advise parents to wait until child is ready for toilet training. 2 Don't attempt to train child at times of stress. 3 Be sympathetic about 'accidents'. They are very seldom deliberate.

Helping children to protect themselves

Some of the children you care for will come from families who are demonstrative and show affection by frequent kissing and cuddling, while other families may be equally fond of their children but are not very outgoing with their emotions. You will need to build up a trusting relationship with each child and this will only happen with time. All children should feel they could come to you for help and protection. It is important to involve the parents in helping children to protect themselves, as the message must be consistent.

When children are mature enough, teach them:

- the difference between comfortable and uncomfortable touches
- that safety rules apply to all adults and not just strangers
- that secrets they feel uncomfortable about should be discussed with a trusted adult
- any cuddles and kisses given by an adult 'in secret' should always be disclosed
- to feel good about themselves and know they are loved and valued
- to trust, recognise and accept their own feelings
- that because their bodies belong to them, nobody has the right to touch or hurt them
- that they can say 'No' to requests that make them feel uncomfortable, even from a close relative or friend
- that they can rely on you to believe and protect them if they confide in you
- that they are not to blame if they are hurt
- that rules of good behaviour can be broken if they are in danger, and that it is perfectly all right to kick, bite, punch, scream and shout if they feel threatened
- that they must not speak to strangers, however kindly they may appear, or go off with someone they do not know.

An organisation called Kidscape was founded in 1984 to enable children to learn about personal safety and teach them strategies to keep themselves safe. Kidscape produces many useful leaflets and books. The NSPCC also produces a great deal of useful material.

Caring for children who have been abused

The vast majority of children that you will be working with in your career as a home-based childcarer will come from stable, happy homes, and you will work in partnership with the parents to meet the needs of the children and promote their all-round development. There are some children who are not so fortunate and, if you are caring for one of these children, you will play a key role in identifying abuse, observing the child and helping him to recover from the effects of abuse and neglect.

Persistent abuse discourages children from:

- learning through play and exploration of their environment
- making trusting relationships with adults and other children
- developing language skills.

Children who have been abused may experience many different overwhelming emotions. These feelings will depend on their age and their level of experience. These emotions include:

- fear
- a sense of isolation
- anger
- depression
- guilt
- sadness
- shame
- confusion.

Good practice in . . . HELPING ABUSED CHILDREN

1 Have a good understanding of child development, and how this can be affected by abuse and neglect.
2 Display empathy and understanding.
3 Encourage trusting relationships.
4 Respond to the child's wish to be held and cuddled.
5 Be professional and do not feel threatened or distressed by the child's expression of emotions.
6 Establish and maintain a professional relationship with the parents.
7 Give extra time to the child, whenever you can, on a one-to-one basis.
8 Provide activities every day to allow emotional expression and encourage communication.
9 Understand if the child's learning or behaviour regresses.
10 Applaud success, however small.
11 Accept challenging behaviour, showing disapproval of the action rather than the child. Set limits for the child to promote security.
12 Value the views and opinions of the child, involving him in decision-making and in becoming more assertive.
13 Show the child you care for him, but resist the temptation to over-protect.
14 Always touch the child gently and be aware of any movement that the child might see as threatening.
15 Continue to observe and assess the child's needs.
16 Take advantage of any training in child protection that might be offered by the local authority.

Maintaining relationships with the parents

It is part of the professional practice of home-based childcarers to work closely with parents, communicating effectively and regularly, respecting their greater knowledge of the child and involving them in all decision-making. The Children Act 1989 emphasises the need for partnership with parents and, where possible, enhancing and not undermining the parents' role.

The Children Act 2004 was introduced after child protection inquiries into the Victoria Climbié case, and it supports the outcomes of *Every Child Matters* (see page 43). It improves the way professionals should work together to support families, and sets out four key themes and five outcomes for chidren which providers must promote.

The Children Act 2004

Four key themes:
- Supporting parents and carers.
- Early intervention and effective protection.
- Accountability and integration (locally, regionally, nationally).
- Workforce reforms.

Five outcomes for children:
- Stay safe.
- Be healthy.
- Enjoy and achieve.
- Achieve economic well-being.
- Make a positive contribution.

If you have identified abuse, try not to jump to the conclusion that the parents are the perpetrators. It could be someone in whom the parents have placed their trust, such as a family member, a babysitter or a neighbour. Be available to support the parents, listen to them with sympathy, and respect and value their views and opinions.

You will be able to advise parents if they are going through stressful times by pointing out helplines, such as Parentline, and finding out if there are local support and information groups.

Worrying family behaviour that might cause concern

All families behave differently and some of the following factors might occur, from time to time, in families where there is no question of abuse. A number of these signs exhibited over a period of time should cause concern:

- frequent shouting and the smacking of babies and children, often for behaviour that is developmentally normal, such as a toddler wetting his pants
- expecting the child to be the parent, giving love and comfort to the adult
- parental indifference to the whereabouts and safety of their children
- barking orders at a child, without displaying patience or clear explanations of what is expected
- never giving praise or encouragement
- discouraging the child's natural curiosity, and not providing enough stimulation
- seeing the normal behaviour and actions of a child as a deliberate act to upset and annoy the parents
- knowledge of frequent rows and disagreements between the parents and other family members, perhaps leading to violence.

Kirsty looks after Joel, a two-year-old boy whose mother Faye constantly appears with bruises and cuts. Kirsty is unable to make a relationship with Faye who will not enter into a conversation, and avoids making eye contact. Kirsty is concerned about Joel's development, although there are no obvious injuries on the child. Faye arrives late one afternoon, with a fractured arm in plaster. She cries and begins to tell Kirsty about her partner's violence.

1 What immediate action should Kirsty take?
2 What action might be appropriate in the long term?
3 How might Kirsty help the child and the family?
4 What sources of help are available?

Working with parents who have abused

You may be caring for children where abuse and neglect has been diagnosed, or social services may have requested them to be placed with you as part of a child protection plan. You should not have to take on such an arrangement if you cannot cope with it, or if you feel that social services will not give you enough information or support. Whatever the type of abuse, try to build up a friendly relationship with the child's parents. Children can quickly sense bad feeling between adults, and it will help the child's recovery to know that the adults in his life are working together.

If you find yourself in the position of working with parents who have abused, you will attempt to:

- acknowledge your feelings, and seek support from your early years adviser, the NCMA or the child's social worker
- avoid colluding with the parents through fear of aggression
- be aware of the child protection plan for this family
- record in writing, conversations and decisions taken with the family
- acknowledge the stress of the family.

Remind yourself that you are helping to break the cycle of abuse. Try to assume a non-judgmental attitude, and refrain from questioning the parents about the abuse, or from challenging information they may give you, as this is the task of other people. Give them as much information as possible about the care of the child, listen to what they are saying and express appropriate concern and kindness, whilst remaining objective. Your behaviour towards their child will help them to realise that children respond well to love and firm consistent guidelines.

If one of your parents has been accused of abuse, and this has been shown to have no foundation, you may find yourself having to rebuild your relationship, and this may prove very difficult. If you both have the welfare of the child at heart, it is achievable.

Reflecting on Practice

You might think about:

- how to recognise types of abuse
- how you might record your concerns
- including a statement in your prospectus making clear that the welfare of the child is your priority
- to whom you might talk if you have concerns
- how you might protect yourself from any allegations of abuse
- how to maintain relationships with the families of abused children
- how you will teach children to protect themselves.

This chapter has contributed to the following learning outcomes:

Unit 1

- promoting anti-discriminatory, anti-bias practice in the home-based setting
- protecting children in the home-based setting

Unit 2

- demonstrating how the home-based practitioner can promote the rights of all children

Unit 3

- understanding the importance of inter-agency work and how the home-based practitioner can work effectively with other professionals
- understanding the main issues involved in the protection of all children

Unit 4

- communicating effectively with parents
- evaluating the role of the home-based practitioner when maintaining confidentiality

Want to Find Out More?

Websites

www.childline.org.uk

www.childrenareunbeatable.org.uk

www.childrenslegalcentre.com

www.cpag.org.uk

www.crb.gov.uk

www.csci.org.uk

www.kidscape.org.uk

www.ncb.org.uk

www.nspcc.org.uk

www.refuge.org.uk

www.relate.org.uk

Helplines

NSPCC at any time of day or night – Telephone: 0808 800 5000

NCMA office hours – Telephone: 0800 169 4486

Further reading

Department of Health, *Assessing Children in Need and their Families*, HMSO, 2000

Working Together to Safeguard Children, HMSO, 1999

Hobart C. and Frankel J., *Good Practice in Child Protection*, 2nd edition, Nelson Thornes, 2005

NCMA with the NSPCC, Safeguarding Children: A Guide for Childminders (booklet)

12 Communication skills

Learning objectives

All living organisms communicate with each other. Human beings are unique in that they communicate with words, with gestures and with body language. They listen to each other attentively, and record their thoughts and deeds in writing. These skills are passed on from generation to generation and affect all areas of achievement. Communication allows social and emotional relationships to flourish, allows the transmission of information and ideas and imparts the values and moral codes of society.

Lack of communication between you and the parents can lead to misunderstandings and this may affect the child you are looking after. Time needs to be set aside at the beginning and at the end of the day, to discuss any problems that may have occurred, achievements that may have been demonstrated and any changes to the daily routine.

Communication is a two-way process, and efforts will have to be made on both sides. You may be a person with an informal, easy manner, and there will be no problems for you, but some people find it harder to find just the right manner.

Communicating with young children

Children learn about the world around them through the senses: touch, sight, hearing, smell, and taste. The newborn baby will very quickly recognise her mother by using all her senses. Because of this, the way a stranger handles a baby immediately communicates to the baby either a feeling of security or of threat. People who wish to work with young children need to be responsive, warm and caring, and this will be shown in the way they hold and feed a baby, or bath and dress a toddler.

Good practice in . . . HANDLING YOUNG CHILDREN

1 Approach children calmly and quietly, using your voice to encourage co-operation.
2 Make eye contact with children before attempting to pick them up.
3 Sit on the floor with younger children; if you tower over them they might feel threatened.
4 Changing a baby's nappy, brushing a child's hair, and helping a child to use the lavatory are all intimate activities and, preferably, should only be carried out once a good relationship has been established. This is one reason why it is so important to have a settling-in period with the parent present, for as long as it takes to establish such a relationship.
5 A child's need to be cuddled should be met. A child will feel safe and secure if her needs are met swiftly and responsively. Refusing to pick up and cuddle a child who obviously wants you to is not only bad practice but can be harmful to the development of the child.
6 Be aware of the child's non-verbal communication such as smiling or snuggling up to you.
7 Understand how body language can vary from culture to culture. For example, some children may be brought up not to make eye contact with adults, as it is thought to be disrespectful.

Activity

Sit with a friend and brush the friend's hair, first roughly, not looking, as if your thoughts are elsewhere. Then repeat gently, talking softly to your friend. Change places with your friend and then discuss how you both felt.

Speech

You are obviously aware of the importance of spoken language, and the part it has to play in educational attainment. Children's ability to speak and understand book language is a key achievement in all areas of the school curriculum. The sooner children become fluent in speech and develop their understanding, the better they will get on in school and with their peer group.

From the very first week of life, and some people even believe from the womb, babies respond to the voice, learning to recognise the mother and close family very quickly. Most language is learnt in the family, and, as a home-based childcarer, you must understand the importance of talking and listening to the children in your care. You should be aware of what a child says, taking care to speak clearly, so as to extend her vocabulary and develop her language skills. Being given time to express herself fully, and to be listened to sympathetically, will promote her language development.

Children who use a different language at home from that of the home-based childcarer will have some initial difficulty in understanding all that goes on around them. To be fluent in two languages is a great advantage in later life, as it will lead to the easier learning of third and fourth languages. Children mixing with other children who speak English will find it natural to acquire English without any special provision for this, but the frequent use of rhymes and songs will make them feel secure and relaxed as they often learn these before they have the confidence to construct sentences. Young children do need an opportunity to use their home language. This should be encouraged if at all possible. Learning a few words and phrases in the child's first language will show that you value and respect that language. A child whose knowledge of English is only just emerging is very seldom delayed in other areas of development.

Developing language skills

At about nine months, children gain an understanding of what adults are saying, provided that they speak clearly and directly. Soon after this the first word might appear, and this is the time to start reading books and telling stories. Sitting down quietly with a child and reading a book together should now become a frequent event, promoting an interest in books for life. Emphasising important everyday words, such as 'drink' and 'bath', will enable a child to gain a large vocabulary from an early age.

A recent seven-year study was carried out, where one group of babies was talked to frequently, and the important words in the sentence were emphasised with inflection and gesture. Another group of babies from a similar background and likely inherited ability was not treated to the same input. When the children were seven, they were tested for reading ability and IQ. It was found that the first group was significantly in front in both attainment and intelligence. This shows how important it is to converse with babies in a meaningful way, even though you might think they do not understand.

At around two years, most children will be able to put two words together to make simple sentences. This is the time for quiet, relaxed conversations, always remembering to give the child time to answer. You should never correct or laugh at her grammatical errors, but it will help if you mirror her words, saying them correctly. For example, a child might say, 'Daddy buyed me this doll', and you could reply, 'It was Daddy who bought it for you, was it?' These mistakes are made because learnt rules of grammar are being applied. Too much correction might inhibit speech.

Try not to ask children 'closed' questions, when the answer is already known. (An example of a closed question might be, 'What colour are your shoes?' They will probably think it strange that you do not know your colours!) Questions that require only one-word answers, such as 'Yes' or 'No', do not allow children to extend their vocabulary. If they ask a question to which you do not know the answer, be honest enough to say so and discuss ways of discovering the answer together. Asking 'open-ended' questions, such as 'Why do you think some animals have fur?', will help the child to develop language skills more quickly.

If you ask a child to carry out a task, it must be explained simply and clearly. Asking children if they would like to help clear up might justify the answer 'No'. They are not necessarily being defiant, but will respond much better if told politely to do it. Never ask them to do several things at once.

Make sure the children are given time to work out what they want to say. Do not anticipate children's speech; let them find their own words. Four-year-olds are very excited by new words, and particularly by those to which they get a reaction. If a child swears, remember this is a normal stage and the best way to stop the habit is to ignore it. Children do not invent these words, so be aware that careless speech from adults is often copied. See Appendix B (page 298) for a comprehensive explanation of the sequence of language development.

Extending opportunities

You might read a favourite story to a child, recording your voice on a cassette. Later, she will enjoy turning the pages of the book and matching the pictures to the story she can hear on the tape. This helps develop listening skills and manipulation skills while encouraging early reading. You could make a simple puppet of the main character in a story that she enjoys. This will encourage her to look at the book on her own or with a friend, using the puppet to stimulate her imagination.

Some domestic activities, such as cooking and washing up together, usually generate discussion and lively conversation, which will help to extend vocabulary and understanding of mathematical and scientific terms. Shopping together will present opportunities for recognising familiar foods and becoming aware that the symbols on the cans and packages represent the names of the foods. All outings introduce children to the wider environment and stimulate language and the acquisition of vocabulary.

Communicating with adults

A professional home-based childcarer needs to develop skills in listening, speech and writing, and to be aware of her body language.

Listening skills

When communicating, it is as important to develop your listening skills as your speech. Being a 'good' listener does not come naturally to everyone. You need to listen carefully to others, concentrate, look interested, and not interrupt; never finish sentences for the speaker.

Remember that in some circumstances you may not be listening effectively. If you are worried or upset about something, your concentration may be diverted. Other noises or movements in the room may distract you. Your feelings about the person may distort what you hear.

Activity

Tape a conversation with a friend with average to good language skills. Note how much of the conversation is initiated by you, and how much by your friend.
1 How would you rate your listening skills?
2 Did you or your friend dominate the conversation?
3 What have you learnt by doing this?

Listening is a positive activity and, therefore, the good listener does not relax when listening but has to monitor and analyse what is being said in order to make an appropriate response. It may be necessary to indicate to the speaker that you are listening attentively by the use of sounds such as 'Uhuh' and 'Mmm', which display interest and understanding. Sometimes, summarising what the speaker has just said is helpful as it makes you listen carefully, lets the speaker know if the message was communicated correctly, and eliminates misunderstanding which might lead to conflict.

Spoken communication

You will be using speech in day-to-day conversations with the children, with your family, with parents and, perhaps, with other home-based childcarers. There is no better way of communicating than talking with people; it helps build relationships, which the use of memos, faxes and e-mail can never do. Always speak clearly, slowly and expressively, particularly when in formal situations, or when the information you have to convey is particularly important.

Try to present one idea at a time and make sure that it is understood before continuing. The drawback to using speech as a method of communication is that you have to make a quick response, which may be unconsidered and regretted later. Speech is generally not as precise as written language, and it is unlikely that you will keep a copy or record. Be aware of your listener's background, knowledge and feelings and what your ideas will mean to your listener. If you are speaking on the telephone in your professional role, speak very clearly, a little more slowly than usual and do not allow your voice to drop in tone at the end of the sentence, as this will distort the clarity of your speech.

Some people communicate better with speech than in writing but it may be the other way round. You will need both skills to be an effective home-based childcarer.

Writing skills

A professional person is presumed to be proficient in communicating information, ideas, directions and requests in writing, and this will take many different forms. When writing for your own information, such as a personal diary or a list of things to remember, you can record this information in whatever way is useful to you.

You may have to write items that need to be shared with other people, such as:

- observations of the children
- a diary to share with the family
- reports concerning accidents or incidents
- records of telephone messages.

Other correspondence may have to be written more formally. You may find yourself writing to parents, social services, schools, or NCMA.

Whatever you are writing, remember to:

- be clear about the purpose of your correspondence
- use short sentences that convey your exact meaning
- be as neat and legible as possible, checking the spelling and grammar (you may find using a word processor helpful)
- keep a copy (use a black pen as this will photocopy well)
- date all correspondence
- be professional, sticking to the facts and being objective
- avoid jargon and terms not necessarily understood by the recipient.

Data Protection Act 1998

This Act regulates the handling of information kept about an individual on a computer or in a manual filing system. The Act requires that personal information be:

- accurate and relevant
- kept secure
- obtained and processed fairly and lawfully
- processed for limited purposes and not in any manner incompatible with those purposes
- held for no longer than necessary
- only disclosed if specific conditions set out in the Act are satisfied.

Government guidance issued in May 2003 confirmed that disclosure of information should not be an obstacle if an individual has particular concerns about the welfare of a child, the information is disclosed to another professional, and disclosure is justified under the common law duty of confidence. See www.dataprotection.gov.uk for more detailed information.

Body language

Your body is sending out messages at the same time as you are talking and listening. To be effective, all messages should be the same, but sometimes communication is spoilt when body language differs from what is being said.

Think about:

- posture
- eye contact
- facial expression
- energy level
- position of your feet and legs when sitting
- personal space
- touching others.

For example, when you are engaged in conversation with a parent, positive body language would be maintaining eye contact, smiling, and leaning towards the parent, while speaking at a moderate rate and in an assuring tone. Negative body language would be yawning, looking or turning away, going off into a daydream and missing cues.

Activity

1 How would you communicate to parents your concerns about their child's behaviour?
2 How do you encourage parents to share their concerns about their child with you?
3 What communication difficulties have you had in the past with parents? How did you cope with these situations?

Communicating with other professionals

During your working life as a home-based childcarer, you may find yourself in occasional contact with other people from the educational, health and caring professions. You may be in regular contact with your Early Years Team adviser. A health visitor may visit you if you are working with young babies. You may be asked by the parents to take the children to the infant welfare clinic or health centre for developmental assessments or for immunisations. If the child needs specialist help, such as speech therapy or dental treatment, you may be asked to accompany her in place of the parent. You may be involved with staff at pre-school or school. To aid communication you need to be aware of the roles and functions of these professional colleagues, and of the extent of your own role.

Writing policies

Carol Banyard, Early Years Education Childminding Network Co-ordinator with Barnsley Choices (Barnsley EYDCP) and an experienced tutor, has provided the following information on writing policies, procedures plans and written permission.

- 'A policy should give detailed information about what a home-based childcarer will do.
- A procedure should explain how a home-based childcarer will do it.
- A plan is a practical list of actions which will be carried out.
- Written permission is used where proof of parental permission to undertake an activity is required for regulatory or insurance purposes.

All policies, procedures and plans should be drawn up with the following four points in mind: They should be:

- relevant
- owned
- practised
- reviewed.

Home-based childcarers should draw up their own policies, procedures and plans in order for them to be **relevant** to each individual home-based childcarers' circumstances, environment and service offered.

They should be **owned**. If a home-based childcarer does not take ownership of a policy, procedure or plan, to the point of having the understanding behind its origins, then it will be very difficult to put into **practice**.

Home-based childcarers should ensure that they can demonstrate their policies, procedures and plans in practice to parents and the regulatory bodies such as Ofsted and Network Co-ordinators (NCMA/EYDCP).

It is also important to **review** policies, procedures and plans on a regular basis in order to ensure that they are still relevant, owned and practised.

Signing and dating policies, procedures and plans will help to provide proof that they still continue to reflect the practice of care and education within the setting. Providing copies and sharing policies, procedures and plans with parents will help to support the relationship and the contractual obligations put in place with each child/family, offering peace of mind and continuity to the service provision.

When writing policies, procedures and plans it may also be useful to ask yourself the following questions:

- Why do I need it?
- Who is it for?
- What needs to be in it?
- When will it be used?
- How should it be worded?
- Where do I start?

The content not the length of the policy, procedure or plan is what is important. The language used should not be too jargonistic and you don't need to make it look like a legal document. Clear aims and objectives should be set.

Remember that these documents are unique to each home-based childcarer and should reflect the practice you wish to promote.'

Managing stress

Home-based childcarers sometimes find themselves in stressful situations. You need to recognise, understand and respond to the causes of stress so as to avoid harming your health or your ability to work in a positive way with children and their families.

Causes of stress

Working in a close relationship with parents who may themselves be experiencing stress can generate anxiety. Certain life events can generate a great deal of stress: for example, divorce, separation, bereavement, unemployment, moving house and even taking on new responsibilities as a home-based childcarer. In your professional role, stress might, among other factors, result from:

- taking on too heavy a work load
- not making as much money as you need
- minding a child with disruptive and aggressive behaviour
- dissatisfaction with your job
- feeling isolated
- spending too much time on work activities
- sickness
- difficult relationships with parents
- a child in your charge who has been abused
- taking on responsibilities which are not necessarily part of your job, but which you find difficult to refuse
- getting behind with the paperwork
- being unable to collect money from some parents
- parents who fail to keep to the contract
- pressure from your family, who may feel neglected.

Signs of stress

Signs of stress may include:

- variation in appetite
- insomnia
- tiredness or lethargy
- tearfulness
- tension headaches
- constipation or diarrhoea
- high blood pressure
- lack of concentration
- inability to decide priorities
- lack of interest in life

- feelings of inadequacy
- difficulty in making decisions
- feeling neglected, overworked, tense and anxious
- not keeping up with coursework
- suppressing anger
- low libido.

Employment patterns are changing and many people are expected to contribute more and more in the workplace while job security is decreasing. This may have a knock-on effect on you, as parents may have to work longer hours or collect their children at different times on different days. If one of your parents becomes unemployed or redundant, your services may no longer be required.

Someone who is stressed may find themselves often ill and having to take time off work. As so many people rely on your good health, your stress would affect many other people.

Coping with stress

First you have to admit and recognise that you are suffering from stress and discover how you got yourself into this situation. If it is the childminding itself that is the main cause, it may be difficult to extricate yourself because there are not many other jobs around and you have responsibilities and financial commitments. You must face up to the situation, be honest with yourself, look at alternative strategies such as working part-time, taking on an assistant, or even changing your career direction. If you cannot change the situation, look for further help. Think about the following:

- discussion with your early years adviser to help you change your pattern of work
- an appointment with your GP to discuss any symptoms you may have and to find out what sources of help are available
- personal counselling to help you reflect on your lifestyle and make possible changes
- courses on assertiveness, time management and relaxation techniques.

Coping strategies
- learn to say no
- learn how to express your opinions and feelings
- look for support from and offer support to other home-based childcarers
- try to relax on your days off and on holidays. Get your family to do the chores!
- manage your time more effectively, deciding what you want to achieve, and the priority, time and energy you are prepared to devote to each task
- look after yourself by eating a healthy diet and taking regular exercise
- do not rely on nicotine, alcohol, caffeine or other drugs to keep you going
- relax in a hot bath after work
- apply heat to the body using a heat pad or a hot-water-bottle; this may reduce muscular tension
- try massage, using aromatic oils
- explore techniques such as yoga or meditation to reduce the effects of stress; they may also boost your ability to avoid becoming stressed

- develop new interests and hobbies
- talk about your feelings to others and recognise your achievements
- be prepared to be flexible and do not live by rigid rules
- remember the good, positive things that have happened and do not focus on failures or difficulties.

CASE STUDY

Jasmin is caring for Sonia, aged two, as well as her own baby and her son Nicholas, who goes to school. Sonia's mother is a teacher in a failing school and has recently been promoted. During the last month she has been frequently late in collecting Sonia. As well as upsetting Sonia, it has meant that Jasmin has been unable to take Nicholas to chess club and karate after school.

1 Who is under stress in this situation?
2 What does Jasmin need to achieve?
3 How should she decide her list of priorities?
4 How can she manage her time more effectively?

Assertiveness

In response to any problem, people tend to react in one of four ways:

- aggressively, hurting and upsetting other people, perhaps making them feel inferior
- being indirectly aggressive, manipulating or humiliating someone, arousing feelings of guilt
- passively, avoiding conflict and refusing to make choices, allowing other people to take advantage of them
- assertively, with a confident approach, respecting their own opinions while not belittling the other person.

Each of the above will have a different effect on other people and on the way we feel about ourselves and how we have behaved.

Activity

Look again at the previous case study.
1 Why do you think Jasmin has allowed this situation to develop?
2 What action should she take?

It is particularly important for a professional person to be assertive, especially a home-based childcarer who has so many demands on her time. Learning to be assertive allows you to be open in expressing your feelings and needs, and encourages you to stand up for your rights and respect the rights of others. It has nothing to do with aggression, but is a technique that allows you to relate to others in an open and honest way, discussing problems and not personalities. Your assertive behaviour should encourage others to be assertive.

Being assertive will enable you to:

- handle conflict, dealing with difficult situations where people are angry or upset
- be more confident, decisive and comfortable in your role
- communicate better, feeling able to express your views, identify problems and work together with other people in finding solutions
- reduce levels of stress
- develop professionally and personally.

Once you are clear about your expectations, they become easier to state and therefore to achieve. Once you start to assert yourself, the approach is simple. You state your needs, rights and opinions in a clear way without qualification.

Good practice in . . . BEING ASSERTIVE

1 Be natural. When asking for things or giving instructions do not apologise or justify yourself. Ask politely and keep it short and to the point.
2 Do not attempt to flatter or manipulate other people.
3 Accept it when other people say no, and do not take it personally.
4 If you say no, give a reason and do not apologise. Be calm and warm to show you are not angry or unhappy.
5 If you are interrupted, stay calm, and continue to speak until you have finished.
6 Value yourself, and remember your feelings and opinions are as valid as other people's.
7 Challenge discrimination against yourself or other people.

Activity

You have decided to care for children on a part-time basis, so as to have enough time for your family and to fit in a course of further study. The mother of one of the children has been admitted to hospital for emergency surgery and is expected to take some time to recover. The father has been to see you, pressurising you to take his child full time for an unspecified period.
1 How do you respond?
2 How might you help the family, whilst meeting your own needs?

Managing conflict

If there are conflicts between you and one or both of the parents, the children you look after will sense the atmosphere and may become distressed. For example, you would expect the parents to pay your fees if they suddenly decided to go away on holiday, and they might feel hard done by. Whatever the reason, the only way to resolve a conflict is to communicate, and find out exactly what the problem is.

If a conflict exists, do not ignore it and hope that it will disappear on its own. Address the issue promptly but not impulsively, allowing yourself and the parent time to express views objectively and find a solution that suits both of you. You may both have to make compromises and show some flexibility. It is often useful to arrange a later date to look again at the problem, and see if your solution is working. Some tension within a relationship may be beneficial. In working together to sort out disagreements, people may begin to understand themselves and others better; the decisions made are likely to be thought through more and the process may be stimulating. If conflict exists, ignoring it and refusing to discuss it can be harmful and totally disrupt your childminding practice. Knowledge of assertiveness skills will help you put your view clearly and purposefully.

Sometimes, owing to a personality clash or inflexibly rigid ideas, it is impossible to come to an agreement and, for the sake of the children, it is better to terminate the contract. This rarely happens, if enough time and effort have been put into the original meeting and the drawing up of the contract.

Coping with violent behaviour from parents

This is an extremely rare occurrence but if you feel threatened you should discuss it with the adviser from your local authority Early Years Team, Ofsted or the NCMA. Do:

- remember your safety and that of the children comes first
- record all incidents and report them to your early years adviser and possibly social services
- express your concerns and fears and seek support if an incident occurs
- refuse to accept verbal abuse, it can be as harmful as physical assault.

As you become more experienced, you will become more aware of your communication skills. If you feel that you need a little help, this is readily available, as your local college will run courses in all areas of communication.

Reflecting on Practice

You might think about:

- how to improve your communication with parents
- where and how you record essential information
- how to make sure you present positive images
- your body language and understanding the body language of the parents and the children
- managing conflict
- how you might acknowledge and cope with your own stress
- writing clear policies and procedures.

This chapter has contributed to the following learning outcomes:

Unit 1

▧ promoting anti-discriminatory, anti-bias practice in the home-based setting

Unit 2

▧ providing for children's development and well-being from birth to 16 years

Unit 3

▧ showing an understanding of the skills and knowledge required to be an assertive practitioner and the importance of valuing the skills of the home-based childcare practitioner
▧ explaining the importance of inter-agency work and how the home-based practitioner can work effectively with other professionals
▧ identifying the main principles of developing and implementing policies

Unit 4

▧ communicating effectively with parents and knowing how to resolve conflicts
▧ showing an understanding of how to deal with complaints

Want to Find Out More?

Further reading

Bishop S., *Develop Your Assertiveness (Creating Success)*, 2nd Edition, Kogan Page, 2006

Griffin S., *Keeping and Writing Records*, National Early Years Network, 1994

Mukherji P. and O'Dea T., *Understanding Children's Language and Literacy*, Nelson Thornes, 2000

Ward S., *Baby Talk*, New Edition, Arrow Books, 2004

13 Observing and assessing children

This chapter includes:

- The value of observations
- How to record observations; some useful techniques
- Planning, evaluation and assessment

Learning objectives

Unit 1

- Providing play and other activities for children in the home-based setting
- Promoting inclusion and anti-bias practice

Unit 5

- Observing and assessing children's development in the home-based setting
- Meeting individual learning needs in the home-based setting

You are observing and assessing children in your care all the time, and have the advantage of working closely with the children you care for over a long period. In this way, you get to know them very well, but it is still of value to you and to the children to step back sometimes and watch in an objective way what the children are doing and how they are behaving.

Observing children in this manner, and recording what you observe, is an integral part of the role of any professional person who works with children.

Using a good dictionary, find out what is meant by the terms 'objective', 'subjective', 'hearsay', 'value judgements', 'assumptions' and 'perceptive'. You will find these terms used when observation of children is discussed, and you need to be familiar with them.

It is useful to observe children when they first come to you, and your initial snapshot observation (see page 249) should be completed by the end of the first week. In this way, you have a baseline with which to compare any future, more detailed observations and assessments.

Snapshot observation

Name: Date:

Date of birth: Starting date:

Age:

	Describe
Home language	
Other language	
Place in family	
Physical description	
Physical skills	
Advanced in areas of development	
Social skills	
Toilet trained	
Language skills	
Delays in areas of development	

This page may be photocopied. © Nelson Thornes Publishers Ltd

13 chapter

The value of observations

Observations are valuable because they help you to:

- understand the basic needs of children: for love, food, shelter and stimulation
- become sensitive and perceptive in meeting these needs, and sometimes in assisting the parents in doing so. By recording objective observations, you learn in a practical way to become aware of these needs, and how to meet them
- share information with parents. For example, your observation of a child who is often tired and reluctant to take part in any energetic activity, might lead you to discuss this with the child's parents. At another time, you might care for a child who does not want to go into the garden. Being aware of this might prompt you to discuss it with the parents, and find out the reason for his fears
- encourage the child's social development. By observing the way that the children play together, it is easy to see which children are particular friends, and which ones may need help in relating to others. Some children are more skilled at relating to adults, while others appear shy with strangers
- identify and understand changes in children's behaviour. Careful observations are useful in this case, as the change in behaviour might have a physical cause, such as the onset of illness, or it might be an emotional response to family problems or changes. You will grow to understand that all children are individuals and will

behave and react differently in similar situations. For example, taking a group of children to visit a farm will be an enjoyable experience for most children, but there may be one or two who cling to you, and appear nervous in the presence of large animals

- understand what might provoke a child to behave in a particular fashion. For example, a child who is particularly fractious just before mealtimes may not be eating enough at each meal and perhaps needs smaller more frequent meals
- understand normal development, so that if the pace of development of a child in your care were outside the normal range, either advanced or delayed, you would be able to plan a special programme for this child
- be aware of the possible hazards in your home. Linking this with your awareness of developmental stages will allow you to protect the children from danger
- be alert to signs of ill health. This could be obvious, such as a sudden skin rash, or a child who vomits, or lethargy in a child who is usually active and full of beans. It may be less obvious during the incubation period of an infectious disease, but a noted change in behaviour might cause you concern
- plan activities for the children that are age-appropriate and will extend and promote learning and development
- provide evidence in child protection conferences, on the rare occasion that you may be requested to do so.

You know a great deal about the children you care for, possibly almost as much as you know about your own children. This knowledge needs to be objective, not based on assumptions and value judgements. If a parent tells you something about one of the children, this is interesting but, in terms of objectively knowing the child, would be termed hearsay, as you have not observed the behaviour yourself, but heard about it from another person. For example, the parent may tell you that her three-year-old son can swim, but unless you see him do it, you have to take it on trust.

Being able to observe in an unbiased manner is not instinctive. If several people were to see a person being mugged, you would probably get many different versions of the incident, and many descriptions of the perpetrator. People's perceptions are coloured by their past experiences, expectations, desire to please, fears and anxieties and even last night's television viewing.

Activity

Sit down with a friend and watch a current affairs programme on the television.
1 Write down what you see as the six most important points made during the programme. Compare your lists.
2 Did you agree on the most important points?
3 Did your lists vary?
4 Why do you think this was?

Having preconceived ideas about the character or competence of individual children may influence your assessment. Expecting a child to succeed in a task may prevent you from acknowledging his failure. Knowing a child comes from an apparently happy and stable home might lead you to reject the thought that he might be at risk. You need to be honest when observing children, and not add anything that makes the observation easier to understand or more interesting.

Some of the children you care for will have been brought up differently from your own. In their families, there may be different expectations of children's behaviour. For example, some children may have been expected to take on some domestic tasks at an early age, while in other families the boys are allowed to be waited on. Some families may discourage their children from messy play, or dressing up in clothes of the opposite gender. The greater the understanding and knowledge you have of other cultures and various child-rearing practices, the less likely you are to make value judgements based on your own upbringing and background, and the more likely you are to view the children as individuals.

Activity

If you are part of a class, group or network, divide into groups of three, identify three different cultures and compare possible differences in family size, moral codes, diet and dress. Speculate how some of this knowledge might have an impact on your observations and evaluations.

If you have carried out an observation where you have found the behaviour of a child worrying, you will need to repeat it, as one observation will not give you the total picture.

Confidentiality

As you observe and record children's behaviour in your observations, you may well discover and identify information concerning the child or his family. Never record anything you would be unwilling to share with his parents. Because parents play the central role in their child's life, they should have the opportunity to provide information or correct any mistaken facts. If you have a concern about a child, such as biting or swearing, recording an event sample will show the parents in a professional way how their child is behaving. This can lead into a discussion that allows you both to develop a consistent approach and help deal with the problem. An observation that shows how well a child is reading will help both you and the parents extend the child's access to more challenging reading material.

You should never share information about the child with anyone, without first seeking the parents' permission, unless you feel the child to be at risk, in which case you would need to seek advice or contact the local social services department. This is discussed further in Chapters 1 and 11.

How to record observations: some useful techniques

The Children Act 1989 requires that all people looking after groups of children should observe children, assess their learning and development, report and record it. The Act acknowledges that it is not so easy in family daycare, but the Act refers to the importance of sharing information with parents, and of making notes rather than relying on memory. You may have kept a Baby Record Book for your own children and are pleased now, when you look at it, to see when they took their first steps and cut their first teeth. It is almost impossible to remember these important milestones without recording them, particularly if you have more than one child.

Formal or informal methods?

Many times, you will see or hear something that you wish to record quickly while it is still fresh in your mind. On other occasions you will plan to carry out a more formal observation, using an appropriate technique.

Informal methods

Always have a notebook and pen handy, to write down quickly some event that you find interesting. For example, you might observe a normally shy child joining in a group game happily for the first time. Taking photographs of the children, either individually or in groups, may demonstrate an aspect of behaviour or learning that you wish to record. You might have access to a camcorder, which can be used to show children at various stages of development. It might be fun, from time to time, to record children singing individually or in a group. All these informal records can be shared with the parents, who will enjoy seeing how their children spend their day. Also, by dating the record and naming the children, you will have a record of their development and progress that you can refer to. Records should be dated, and filed in a separate wallet for each child.

Formal methods

If a child in your care is causing concern to his parents and to you, you may be involved in liaising with social workers or medical practitioners. In these cases, careful objective observations of the child are very valuable. The most common technique used is the written record (see pages 254 and 255). If the concern is about the child's learning ability, you might wish to set up an activity in your house for all the children, and just closely observe the child about whom you are concerned. If at all possible, sit quietly in a corner and do not become involved with any of the children unless there is an emergency.

Your observation could record how the child you are observing manipulates the equipment you have provided, how much he talks about it, how he relates to the other children, how long he concentrates on the task, and anything else of interest. Several of these observations, carried out on a regular basis, will allow you, his parents and any other concerned adults to assess his progress.

Eleanor Smith   8 months   2.2.09

At childminder's home   Mother present

Ellie is placed sitting on the carpet by her mother. There are some
of her toys on the carpet. Ellie picks up a
rattle and shakes it. She looks around the room, lets out a squeal
and starts crawling. Ellie crawls under the table, a toy animal is on
the floor. She stretches her hand for it, but is unable to reach it. I
say "Go on Ellie, you can do it". Ellie squeals again, stretches out
and picks up the animal. She smiles and places the animal in her
mouth.

Concerns   Safety factors now Ellie is mobile –
                    barriers – need for me to be alert.

Next stage   Encourage Ellie in pulling to stand.

Written record observation

All observations need to have certain information recorded, such as:

- the name of the child
- the date of the observation
- the age of the child
- where the observation took place
- the ages, number, gender and initials of the other children involved
- the presence of any other adult.

If you have a child who is disruptive or aggressive, and you want to discuss this with the parents, using an event sample (see page 256) will show the parents a record of each time this behaviour occurs. The event sample should be completed over a period of time, perhaps a week. Noting down the time of day, the duration of the event, whether the child was provoked or not, and a comment on the severity of the behaviour will demonstrate in an objective way whether or not there is a problem. It is easy to imagine that one child is the cause of all disputes, and an event sample might show that this is not the case.

There may be a child in your care who is very shy, has difficulty in relating to other children and to adults, and seems isolated. Using a time sample (see page 257) is one way of trying to find out if this is really so and perhaps beginning to identify a cause. You need to observe the child closely for a short period of time over regular intervals (say, one minute every quarter of an hour), and write down exactly what the child is doing. You might discover that he relates well to one of the children, who is quiet and caring, and goes into his shell whenever a noisy child

Gross motor skill	Yes	No	Date	Comments.
Walks and runs on tip-toes				
Walks upstairs confidently				
Walks downstairs confidently				
Changes direction when running				
Enjoys climbing and sliding on apparatus				
Climbs and slides on apparatus confidently				
Kicks moving balls forward				
Can bounce and catch balls, and take aim				
Rides large wheeled toys using pedals and steering confidently				

Excerpt of a checklist observation on gross motor skills

Event sample

10.3.09
Gillian aged 3 years 2 months
C.M. and 3 children present

Concern:
Gillian frequently bites both adults and children. She is aggressive and demanding.

Day of week	No.	Duration	Provoked/Unprovoked	Comments on seriousness
Monday	1	2 secs.	U.P.	Gillian bit father as he left for work.
	2	1 min.	U.P.	Pushed Amit (1:9) over.
	3	2 secs.	U.P.	Bit Eric (2:3). Drew blood.
Tuesday	1	½ min.	U.P.	Hit Eric with a wooden brick. Raised a bump on Eric's head.
	2	2 secs.	P.	Bit Eric who pushed her over outside.
Wednesday	0			
Thursday	1	2 secs.	U.P.	Bit Amit. Not serious
Friday	1	10 mins.	P.	Gillian's father arrived ½ an hour late. Gillian had a tantrum – inconsolable. She threw furniture around and attempted to bite C.M.

Example of an event sample

13 chapter

Time sample

Concern: Home language:

Time	Setting	What was said	Number of other children present

13 chapter

arrives. You will need to do this sample for a whole day at least, and perhaps repeat it in a few weeks' time.

Checklists are often used for assessing a child on one particular day, but can be used over a longer period. They might be used for a child about whom you feel some concern, or regularly for all the children in your care to help you plan for each child's needs. They can be specific, looking at one area of development or one type of behaviour, or more general, covering all areas. You should have a good knowledge of the child before you attempt a checklist. Results may otherwise be distorted by the impact of an unfamiliar adult.

Checklists often highlight areas of a child's development that have previously gone unnoticed. For example, a child who appears physically competent sometimes has difficulty in controlling wheeled toys. Once you are aware of this, you will be able to provide practice and encouragement.

CASE STUDY

Melanie, an experienced home-based childcarer was really worried about Darren, aged two and a half, who was aggressive and disruptive. He was as much work as three children! Melanie seemed to be constantly saying, 'Stop it, Darren!' She spoke to his mother about his behaviour and was assured that he was an angel at home. So she decided to do an event sample, to show Darren's mother, in a professional way, how he behaved in her home.

After this record was kept for a week, it became obvious that many of the fights were not Darren's fault. Matthew, aged four, was found to be teasing him and calling him names. When Matthew started school the following month, Darren's behaviour improved beyond measure.

1 Why was doing the event sample good professional practice?
2 What should Melanie say to Darren's mother, without breaking the rule of confidentiality?
3 Should Melanie speak to Matthew's mother about his behaviour?
4 Why might Matthew be behaving in this way?

Planning, evaluation and assessment

Following on from observation are the essential steps of assessment and planning, reflecting on what you have observed and considering what you now know about the child, and how that fits in with what you might have expected of the child at that stage of development. Try not to make assumptions, using words like 'I think' and 'perhaps', but only comment on what you have actually seen. Beware of making judgements based on gender, class, disability or racial stereotypes. Do not be surprised if a girl enjoys rough energetic play, and a boy wishes to spend time quietly, reading on the sofa.

Remember to be objective, never repeating hearsay, or speculating and making unsupported value judgements, labelling children or being influenced by prior knowledge. Never personalise

Good Practice in Childminding

comments, for example making comparisons with your own children or the other children in your care.

Observations may reveal to you that a course of action or a medical referral is needed. Some actions you may be able to carry out on your own. For example, if you discover that a four-year-old about to start school is unable to use scissors in a practical way, you will be able to encourage him in learning this skill and give him plenty of practice. On the other hand, if you suspect that a child may have a hearing impairment, it is important that you bring this to the parents' attention, with the facts that you have collected from your observations, and encourage them to seek medical advice as quickly as possible.

Activity

1 How will you inform parents that you intend to record observations of their child?
2 How will you observe a child without influencing the child's behaviour?
3 What will you learn from observing children?
4 How do you use your observations to plan for the care and education of the child?

The assessment requirements of Ofsted

Childminders on the Early Years Register must meet Ofsted's assessment requirements. Within the EYFS, ongoing assessment is an integral part of the learning and development process. The Department for Children, Schools and Families tells us that assessment should be underpinned by the following principles.

- Assessment must have a purpose.
- Observation of children participating in everyday activities is the most reliable way to build up an accurate picture of what children know, feel, are interested in and can do.
- Observation should be planned. However, practitioners should also be ready to capture spontaneous but important moments.
- Judgement of children's development and learning should be based on skills, knowledge, understanding and behaviour that they demonstrate consistently and independently.
- An effective assessment will take into account all aspects of a child's development and learning.
- Accurate assessment will also take into account contributions from a range of perspectives.
- Parents and other primary carers should be actively engaged in the assessment process.
- Children should be fully involved in their own assessment.

Assessment at the end of the EYFS

The EYFS profile is an assessment document. All registered early years providers are required to complete an EYFS profile for each child at the end of the academic year in which they reach the age of five. This provides Year 1 teachers and parents with reliable information about each child's level of development as they reach the end of the EYFS. This enables the teacher to plan an appropriate curriculum that will meet all children's needs and support their continued development.

A practitioner will use their observations to make judgements and to record each child's development against the profile's 13 assessment scales. These are based on the early learning goals and divided between the six Areas of Learning and Development.

By following links on the National Assessment Agency website (naa.org.uk/eyfsp) you can view the EYFS profile, the EYFS profile handbook, the Assessment Scales Guidance sheet and other support materials.

Good practice in . . . RECORDING OBSERVATIONS AND MAKING ASSESSMENTS

1 Be ready to share observations and assessments with parents.
2 Respect confidentiality.
3 Keep records in a secure place.
4 Record observations on all children in your care.
5 Never jump to conclusions.
6 Do not label children.
7 Do not generalise from one observation.
8 Do not guess why children respond in a particular way.
9 Allow for environmental and cultural differences, while all the time guarding against racist and sexist attitudes.
10 While observing a child, do not involve yourself in his or her activity, or influence the child's behaviour by your manner or tone of voice.
11 Write up your notes as soon as you can.
12 Use your observations for the benefit of the children and to help you develop best practice.

Reflecting on Practice

You might think about:
- why observing children is important
- how you might record information about children
- how observation helps you plan play activities for individual children
- how being observant helps you recognise illness
- how recording observations helps you understand challenging behaviour and how to manage it
- sharing observations and involving parents in recording observations at home.

This chapter has contributed to the following learning outcomes:

Unit 1
- planning and providing appropriate play and other activities for children in the home-based setting
- promoting anti-discriminatory, anti-bias practice in the home-based setting

Unit 5
- using a range of methods of observation and assessment to support your work with children
- planning, providing and evaluating appropriate experiences and play
- explaining how you meet children's individual learning needs in the home-based setting

Want to Find Out More?

Websites
www.direct.gov.uk

naa.org.uk/eyfsp

www.ofsted.gov.uk

www.standards.dfes.gov.uk/eyfs

Further reading

Bee H. and Boyd D., *The Developing Child*, 11th Edition, Pearson Education, 2006

Drummond M., *Assessing Children's Learning*, David Fulton, 2003

Hobart C., Frankel J. and Walker M. (Series Editor), *A Practical Guide to Child Observation and Assessment*, 4th Edition, Nelson Thornes, 2009

Sheridan M., *From Birth to Five Years* (revised and updated by Frost M. and Sharma A.), Routledge, 1997

13 chapter

14

The business side of childminding

Learning objectives

Unit 1

- Promoting inclusion and anti-bias practice
- Starting a home-based childcare service

Unit 3

- Marketing and manage your home-based childcare service
- Meeting individual learning needs in the home-based setting

Unit 4

- Understanding contracts and how to deal with complaints

Becoming a home-based childcarer means that you are starting a business. You are a self-employed childcare and education provider, free to decide your own rate of fees and working conditions. If a business is to be successful, it needs to be well organised, with good systems of record keeping. You need to be sure that the parents are satisfied that you are doing a good job and that they understand and are happy with their contracts.

A wide range of business support resources for home-based childcarers is available free online at www.surestart.gov.uk. The materials are aimed at developing the business skills of all childcare providers.

Being a home-based childcarer can be a stressful job, and poorly organised business methods will add to the stress. If you are well organised, you are able to concentrate on your relationships with the children and their families, and on your professional practice.

NCMA Members' Handbook

One of the many advantages of joining NCMA is the quality of the support that it offers in its business documentation. *The Members' Handbook*, published annually, and available only to members of NCMA, will give you all the information you need concerning:

- fees
- expenses
- contracts and variations in arrangements
- public liability insurance
- home and car insurance
- legal advice
- legal expenses insurance
- social security benefits
- tax and National Insurance
- accounts
- milk refunds
- training.

Marketing

There are several ways of marketing your business: word of mouth, leaflets and business cards, posters and postcards, contact with local employers, contact with young parents, newspaper advertisements and articles, directories, websites, special services and the Children's Information Service (CIS).

Word of mouth

This is thought by many to be the most effective method of filling vacancies. Talk to family, friends, neighbours and the parents of children that you care for already. Get in touch with people who come into regular contact with parents and parents-to-be, such as midwives, health visitors, teachers, and people who run parenting and exercise classes for pregnant women and new mothers.

Leaflets and business cards

You might consider having a professionally printed business card with your details and qualifications. A well-designed leaflet will give you greater space to include more information, such as your working hours, fees and experience.

Posters and postcards

A well-designed poster or postcard attracts attention and can be placed on notice boards in schools and playgroups, health centres, GP surgeries, baby-changing rooms, church halls and community centres, sports and leisure centres, baby-clothing and equipment shops, libraries, supermarkets, and newsagents. You will need to ask permission and may have to make a small payment. NCMA sells a vacancy kit to help members promote their business.

Contact with local employers

Local employers may agree to give your details to staff looking for childcare or be willing to display your leaflets or posters.

Contact with young parents

There are schemes that help teenage parents and students with their childcare costs. You may reach these people through support staff at colleges, universities and the Connections Teen Support Centre in every local authority.

Newspaper advertisements and articles

Sometimes, it is worth spending some money on an advertisement in your local newspaper. This is often inexpensive, and you might be able to negotiate the rate. You might try writing an amusing article about your experiences or send information about your achievements. Don't forget to put your contact details.

Directories

As a small business, you can take out a free line ad in your local Yellow Pages, Thompson's directory and online at www.yell.com; however, you will have to publish a full address, and may not want to do this.

Websites

If you are technically minded, creating your own website can be very effective as you can add pictures and information, and update the site as often as you wish. Your own personal domain name costs around £10 a year and you will have to register your chosen name. There is some free software available from www.webs.com.

Special services

You might be able to offer some special services for local support agencies, such as:

- health visitors
- social services
- schools
- women's refuges
- police.

Chapter 7

Children's Information Service (CIS)

The CIS was set up in 2000 in every local authority, with the aim of helping local parents find the right childcare for their children. It holds lists of every registered childcare provider in the area. The CIS cannot recommend one type of childcare over another, but must provide information about a range of options based on each caller's needs. It is important that the CIS has complete and up-to-date information about you, and you must respond to its requests for information. It is best practice for you to contact the CIS every four to six weeks to check that its information about you is correct. Tell the CIS as much as you can about yourself, particularly anything that might set you apart from the competition.

> ## *Activity*
>
> Design a leaflet advertising your childcare provision. Remember to include anything unique or special you might have to offer, such as healthy home-cooked meals, readiness to walk children to school, or a large well-equipped garden. Your tutor might like to display the results of the group's efforts on a wall in the centre.

Any advertisement that you design should be proofread by several people to check that it is accurate and easy to follow, contains all the necessary information and has no spelling or grammatical errors. Do not include children's full names or your registration number, and be wary of including your address – your telephone number should suffice. NCMA offers advice. It is important to approach advertising in a professional manner as first impressions count.

The contract

The contract is important to both you and the family of the child. It is not a contract of employment. You are providing childcare for a negotiated fee under an agreed set of terms and conditions. The contract outlines clearly in writing what is expected from you and what is expected from the parents. Using the NCMA contract will put the partnership on a professional basis and provide evidence in the event of any disagreement. The NCMA contract includes guidance notes.

It is important that an opportunity is taken to sit down with the parents and complete the contract together, so that both sides are quite clear as to their commitment. It is also an opportunity to discuss your childcare practice and to discover if the parents have any strong preferences in the way you care for and educate their children.

Once all the details have been discussed and agreed, the contract should be signed and dated by all parties. It is then a legally binding document. There should be a separate contract for each child in the family. Make a note on your calendar when the contract is due for review, and give the parents adequate notice of this date. Explain that you will review your charges at this time.

NCMA contracts include a section for settling in a child. The home-based childcarer and the parent need to negotiate a time scale for this but an ideal period is usually four weeks, after which the full contract comes into force.

Disputes between parents and home-based childcarers are rare and always unpleasant. A calm professional approach will often resolve the matter. NCMA produces an online briefing sheet, called 'Contract Disputes', that may give you some guidance. If a parent complains to Ofsted about your practice, you should immediately contact NCMA for advice, and if you are member of NCMA you are entitled to free legal representation.

A copy of the NCMA contract is included in Appendix D.

CASE STUDY

Abimbola, who has just registered as a home-based childcarer, looks after her own two children and Sam, aged three. For the first two months, Sam's mother paid her fees regularly at the start of each week. For the past two weeks, she has given continual excuses for not paying: she hasn't got her chequebook with her; she forgot to draw out cash from the machine, and so on.

Abimbola feels very anxious the weekend before the third Monday, as she has not been paid for the last two weeks. Her partner has been nagging her, saying that childminding is not a charity, and she must be more businesslike. On Monday, Sam's mother says she has forgotten her chequebook and offers half a week's fee in cash.

1 What should Abimbola's immediate response be?
2 Suggest ways in which this might be resolved.
3 How can Abimbola prevent this happening again?

Fees

You are embarking on a highly skilled professional career and should be rewarded for your expertise. There are factors that you need to take into account. For example, if you live in an area of high unemployment, the demand for your services may be limited, and you might be in competition with a number of experienced registered home-based childcarers. If you live in an area where most of the families around are dual-income, professional families, you might find your services in great demand. It is also important to realise that your household expenditure will increase.

Your early years adviser or NCMA group may give you information about the 'going rate' in your area. Other factors that might influence what you charge would be:

- your experience with babies
- your knowledge and experience of children with disabilities
- any childcare training and qualifications
- your home environment, such as plenty of space and access to a garden.

Your fees for a full-time place may be assessed on an hourly, daily or weekly rate. Children aged four years who are attending school full time can now be counted in a home-based childcarer's school-age ratio instead of the under-fives ratio. Children who are attending school part time will probably have to pay full-time rates as, even though they are attending school for part of the time, they are taking up a full-time place with you. Some home-based childcarers offer a reduced rate to children from the same family, making it clear that the reduction is for the older child, so there is no confusion when he starts school. If a parent decides to keep the child at home for a half day, for whatever reason, you would still expect to be paid for that time.

After-school care is normally paid on an hourly rate for the hours that care is provided. It is sometimes paid at a higher rate in order to be cost effective. Holiday care is usually paid by the hour and is at the normal under-fives rate. You should consider the hidden costs of holiday care, such as outings, and these should be agreed with the parents in advance.

The contract should make clear what payment you expect for:

- absences of the child
- holidays (the parents' and yours)
- illness (the child's, the parents' and yours)
- older siblings
- playgroup, outings and other extras
- food, nappies, etc. (whether costed into charges or charged separately)
- part-time or unsocial hours
- retainers, including holiday retainers.

The contract should also make clear when and how you will be paid by the parents. In general, it is prudent to expect payment in advance. Never allow debts to mount up, and expect payment on the day agreed.

Expenses

It is easy to lose track of the costs of childminding in your normal housekeeping expenditure. There are some direct expenses such as:

- food and drink
- play materials
- equipment
- safety and First Aid equipment
- insurance
- transport, either petrol or fares
- NCMA membership and publications
- courses and conferences
- stationery
- toiletries
- nappies, if these are not provided by the parent
- outings, including cost of admission to various places of interest.

There are other expenses that are indirect, such as:

- heating and lighting
- rent

- telephone
- council tax and water rates
- wear and tear on household furnishings
- cleaning.

You need to be aware of the indirect expenses, as you can claim part of your household bills against your income tax. You will find this information in the NCMA members' handbook.

Activity

Calculate the cost of your provision against the above headings.
1 Does it cost you less per child if you take on more children?
2 Are there any other expenses unique to you, not covered by the above list?

Insurance

When you become a home-based childcarer, you will need to review all your insurance policies, and inform the companies of your new status.

Public liability insurance

Public liability insurance is a requirement of registration. It insures you against legal liability arising from:

- accidental injury or death to any person, including any looked-after children, in your care, caused by your action or negligence
- damage caused by the children in your care to other people's property.

NCMA members can obtain this insurance from the NCMA; you will then be issued with a certificate that you can show to the parents.

Home and car insurance

Because you now have a business, your household and car insurances will need to be updated. Failure to inform your insurers could invalidate any claim you might make. This is particularly important with your car insurance, if you are using the car to transport children as part of your childminding business. It has to be covered by your policy, as otherwise your car insurance may not be valid if you or the children are involved in an accident.

Some insurance companies regard childminding as a high-risk operation and have increased home insurance premiums. NCMA can put you in touch with a company with competitively priced insurance, designed for home-based childcarers and including many extras. NCMA also offers legal expenses insurance, for the defence of any prosecution arising from normal childminding duties.

Social security benefits

These benefits are increasingly complex and subject to change. If you have been receiving benefit, and you commence working as a home-based childcarer, you will need to seek specialist advice. NCMA provides up-to-date information on this to its members.

Tax and National Insurance

In April 1996, tax self-assessment was introduced in the UK, making it a legal requirement for all self-employed people to keep accurate business records, so it has become vital that you keep clear and precise records of your income and expenses. It is unlikely that you will be expected to pay tax, as after you have claimed expenses and allowances, your net profits may be too small to attract income tax. It is important to tell the local tax office that you are now a home-based childcarer, and you may have to demonstrate that you are keeping accurate records. The NCMA members' handbook clearly outlines the expenses you may claim and details of the agreements that NCMA has made with HM Revenue and Customs.

You will be liable to pay self-employed National Insurance contributions unless you claim exemption because of low earnings. You should consider carefully whether or not to make contributions, as non-payment deprives you of certain benefits, for example, sickness and maternity benefits, and retirement pension. The Contributions Agency has a pack called 'Working for Yourself'. National Insurance is a complex issue about which you might feel happier taking specialist advice.

Accounts

NCMA has designed a cash book and attendance register for home-based childcarers; it is acceptable to HM Revenue and Customs and the Department of Social Security as a method of recording income and expenses, and includes:

- details of the looked after children
- the weekly attendance and record of payment, countersigned by home-based childcarer and parent
- weekly expenditure and allowable expenses
- monthly accounts
- annual accounts
- annual statement of accounts that can be presented to the Tax Office.

Using this book and retaining all necessary receipts of expenditure should allow you to complete your own tax returns each year.

Milk refunds

Home-based childcarers are entitled to claim the cost of a third of a pint of milk per child under five per day (a day being anything more than two hours a day). For a baby under a year you may instead claim for dried baby milk made up to one third of a pint as instructed on the pack. This can add up to a substantial amount of money each year, and should be claimed, or it may cease to be available. You should keep receipts as proof of purchase, and keep accurate records of children's attendance. Claim forms can be obtained from Welfare Food Reimbursement Unit, PO Box 31048, London SW1V 2FD (telephone 08707 2030 63 or fax 0207 887 1258).

Record keeping

Home-based childcarers have a responsibility to know as much as possible about the children in their care. Much of this information is gathered during the first meeting with the parents. You will need to keep all the information you have about the child in a confidential file, secure from other people. The records on each child should include:

- name as shown on birth certificate
- name the child is known by
- date of birth
- address

- telephone number
- names of parents and where they can be contacted
- emergency contact's name, and where he or she can be contacted
- information about the child's health
- information about any allergies
- information about the child's immunisations
- doctor's name, address and telephone number
- name and address of any person allowed to collect the child, and information about anyone who may not
- written permission from parents to seek medical help in the event of an emergency.

You should also keep a record of the name and address of any person who assists you, and any person living on the premises, and be prepared to notify Ofsted in writing of any changes. When one of your own children reaches the age of 16, you will need to notify Ofsted for its records.

The other documents that you will always have to hand will include the following:

- your registration certificate
- public liability insurance certificate
- register of attendance, perhaps the most important document, which must always be kept up to date
- contracts between you and the parents
- forms signed by parents, giving permission for you to take the children on outings and to give medication
- your First Aid certificate
- your written policies
- an accident book, recording all the accidents occurring to the children and any First Aid given; entries need to be countersigned by the parents
- records of observations and assessments of the children.

Many parents will appreciate being informed of the weekly menus.

Activity

Where in your home is there a safe place to store your records, allowing easy access, while maintaining confidentiality?

In addition to the documentation you have to keep, some home-based childcarers like to keep a programme of activities carried out with the children, and have written a statement of how they implement equal opportunities. Parents should have access to all the above records concerning their child. Records required by registration are what will be checked at annual inspections.

You are required to notify Ofsted of any changes, such as:

- changes to your home
- changes to the hours during which you childmind
- change of name or address
- additional people living on your premises
- outbreak of any notifiable infectious disease
- any serious injury, illness or death on your premises
- any allegations of serious harm against or abuse of a child by any person looking after children or living, working or employed at the premises
- any serious matter, event or allegation, which is likely to affect the welfare of any child on the premises.

Although some of the documentation involved in running your business sounds daunting, it is necessary as it protects you and the children. It needs to be kept carefully and be fully up to date.

Reflecting on Practice

You might think about:

- whether your insurance policies are up to date and cover you for all eventualities
- the contract you have with parents
- admission and consent forms
- the fees you charge
- how you track expenses
- how conversant you are with tax and National Insurance matters
- keeping up-to-date records, to include activities with the children, accident and incident books, administering medicines
- preparing a folder or prospectus to hold your policy and procedure statements
- keeping your daily register of attendance.

This chapter has contributed to the following learning outcomes:

Unit 1

- promoting anti-discriminatory, anti-bias practice in the home-based setting
- identifying and evaluating key factors in setting up a home-based childcare service

Unit 3

- demonstrating how to market and manage your own home-based childcare service

Unit 4

- showing an understanding of contracts and how to deal with complaints

Want to Find Out More?

Websites

www.bitc.org.uk
www.businesslink.gov.uk
www.daycaretrust.org.uk
www.hmrc.gov.uk/childcare
www.nfea.com
www.nicma.org
www.startups.co.uk

Further reading

NCMA, *NCMA's Quality Standards: a Workbook for Registered Childminders*, NCMA, 2001

'Which?' Consumer Guides, *The 'Which?' Guide to Starting Your Own Business: How to Make a Success of Going it Alone*, Which? Books, 2003

15

A return to learning

Learning objectives

Unit 3

- Reflecting on your practice
- Continuing your professional development

Home-based childcarers have a central role in the government's childcare strategy. By seeking qualifications, you have recognised that you wish to improve the service you offer, extend your skills, and be ready to grasp new opportunities. You may already be familiar with adult education and training, or you may not have done any training for a long time. You have already taken one step by reading this book, and most of you have taken or are taking a preparation course before becoming home-based childcarers, so you have made a good start.

Training courses

The National Childminding Association (NCMA) worked with the Council for Awards in Children's Care and Education (CACHE) to develop the first national qualification for home-based childcarers, the CACHE Level 3 Certificate in Childminding Practice (CCP). CCP was made up of three units. From January 2006, the CACHE Level 3 Diploma in Home-based Childcare (DHC) replaced the CCP. To gain the Diploma, it is necessary to complete five units:

- Unit 1: Introduction to Childcare Practice (12 hours)
- Unit 2: Childcare and Child Development (0–16) in the Home-based setting (30 hours)
- Unit 3: The Childcare Practitioner in the Home-based setting (30 hours)
- Unit 4: Working in Partnership with Parents in the Home-based setting (30 hours)
- Unit 5: Meeting Children's Individual Learning Needs in the Home-based setting (30 hours).

Each individual unit can stand alone, is individually assessed and can be certificated. Unit 1, which must be taken first, is assessed by a multiple-choice question paper. Units 2–5 can be studied in any order, and each is assessed by an assignment.

The five units together provide the underpinning knowledge for NVQ Level 3 in Children's Care, Learning and Development. When undertaking any training, it is advisable to obtain written permission from the parents of children in your care to enable you to use their child as 'evidence' for your training.

chapter

15

National Vocational Qualifications (NVQs)

These are nationally recognised qualifications that state you are competent in your chosen area of work. NVQs can be gained at various levels. Each level consists of a number of compulsory units and a number of optional units. Children's Care, Learning and Development Level 3 is the appropriate NVQ for home-based childcarers, because you work independently without supervision. Level 2 might be more appropriate for assistants working under supervision.

An NVQ is not a course; it is an assessment of your competence. You must demonstrate your knowledge and understanding of why you work in a certain way.

Personal management

Before starting training, you will need to consider how to manage your personal and social life, so that you are able to meet the demands placed on you. Making plans to manage your more complicated life will enable you to succeed in gaining your qualification. It is important that you attempt to discover as much as possible about the course and its requirements, prior to making any commitment. It is a good idea to meet course members who are still on the course so that you can ask questions about any elements that may be worrying you.

Relationships

With family and friends
Many course members have found that it is easier to be successful when following an educational programme if they have the encouragement and support of their partners, the parents of the children they are looking after, their own children and friends. Having found out the requirements of the course, you should discuss them fully with all concerned. This way, you will be sure of help when you most need it. Other home-based childcarers can offer support and practical help. Tell them what you intend to study, and they may decide to join you.

Activity

Consider carefully who will be most affected by your new commitment and who will offer the most support.

Some course members will enjoy their studies so much that other people in their lives may feel excluded and left behind. It takes a great deal of tact to resolve this predicament. However, there will be help available, as tutors are familiar with this situation.

With your peer group
During the period of your course, you will be working closely with other home-based childcarers, engaged in learning together. You will all be expected to make positive contributions to discussions, and help maintain the security and confidence of the group. You may find

yourself with people from various backgrounds, ages, and varying abilities. It may take you some time to settle in your group, but you will soon relax and enjoy the company of most of the people. Communicating with everyone in the group will broaden your ideas and attitudes. You will be expected to display a professional attitude and enjoy the diversity of the group.

With tutors

Your tutor may be responsible for providing personal and group tutorial sessions. He or she will discuss your progress and personal self-development, help you to sort out any difficulties and prepare for your assessments.

All tutors will have a variety of approaches and teaching styles and you may find that you are more comfortable with some tutors than with others. Most tutors come from a childcare and education background, or have detailed knowledge of home-based childcare. They will have your interests at heart, and will be anxious for you to succeed.

Time management

The key to success lies in the way you manage your time.

The professional approach

Your timekeeping will be a crucial factor in assessing your professional competence. You will be expected to arrive punctually. You will need to have planned your journey, allowing plenty of time to ensure that you do not let anyone down by arriving late. Your attendance record will be monitored. If being late or absent is unavoidable, you must make contact as soon as possible, explaining your predicament, and make sure that you keep in touch at regular intervals until the crisis has passed.

Organising your time when studying

This is a key factor in ensuring success. You may be expected to spend some of your personal time in:

- organising handouts, portfolios and files
- further reading
- writing assignments
- writing up your observations of children
- preparing individual and group presentations
- using the library
- keeping a diary.

1 Obtain details of deadlines well in advance and plan to finish your assignments ahead of time.
2 Keep up to date with all aspects of your work.
3 File your work regularly.
4 Your work must be planned around your other responsibilities. Try to allow time for unexpected events or illnesses.
5 Note in your diary the dates of any course deadlines and avoid planning major social events at these times if possible. It may be useful to note a number of weeks ahead how much time you have left before reaching the deadline.

The home learning environment

There will be work and studying that you need to do at home, and you will have to consider whether:

- there is a room or a space where you can work and study without being interrupted
- there is a table or desk big enough for you to spread out your work undisturbed
- you have a comfortable chair
- your environment is quiet, warm, well lit and well ventilated
- you have somewhere to keep your books, files and completed work.

If it is not ideal for you to work at home, for whatever reason, investigate the possibility of studying at a friend's house or at your local library. Regular access to a computer would be helpful.

Stress management

In addition to the stress you may have experienced in your job as a home-based childcarer (see Chapter 12), you may find yourself under stress as a course member. The main causes may be:

- conflicting demands on your time – juggling family commitments with assignment deadlines
- difficulty with the course work and meeting professional standards
- lack of clarity about the expectations of tutors
- frequent absences from the course, leading to lack of information and inability to complete assignments
- tensions in your relationships with your peer group or tutors
- coping with constructive criticism
- personal problems unrelated to the course.

Managing stress when following a course of study

It is important to recognise and face up to the fact that you are stressed, and you need to attempt to identify the causes. Think about the following:

- arranging to see your tutor to discuss your problems
- arranging an appointment with your GP to discuss your symptoms and see what sources of help are available
- practising your assertiveness and relaxation techniques
- looking again at how you are managing your time
- looking at your diet and exercise regime.

It is perfectly normal to feel stress when you are studying. You are being constantly assessed and evaluated. The course requires a strong commitment and, as you know, working with children is very tiring.

Appeals and complaints

Grievances and complaints usually occur when there has been a breakdown in communication between the course member and the tutors. This occurs rarely, but, if it does, your tutors will be as anxious as you to resolve it as quickly as possible. Courses will have complaint procedures to follow, and tutors should bring them to your attention as you start the course. For DHC courses you have rights of appeal to the college or centre and, in the last resort, CACHE.

Learning techniques and working in a group

You know more than you think. You will already have achieved many things in your life, not all of them necessarily academic.

Activity

List your achievements and experiences to date.
1 What were the three easiest things you learnt to do? Why?
2 What were the three hardest things you learnt to do? Why?

To succeed on any training course, you will need to understand the variety of techniques used and the way in which different groups work. A good tutor will use a number of approaches in most course sessions, and you will need to be adaptable and flexible so as to maximise your learning.

Discussion in groups

Sometimes, your tutor will introduce a topic and then expect group members to spend some time contributing their own relevant ideas and experiences. Interactive learning can be one of the best ways of understanding and learning the core elements of the course.

It is not always easy at first to have the confidence to speak within a group setting. You might be afraid that your ideas are not valid, and that the rest of the group might reject or make fun of your remarks. To benefit from group discussion you should:

- listen to other people respectfully and without interrupting
- have pen and paper to jot down ideas as they occur to you
- indicate to the tutor that you wish to speak
- make sure your contribution is relevant to the discussion
- speak slowly and clearly
- try to avoid giving personal examples, particularly if it is going to cause you stress.

Remember that nearly everybody feels nervous at first when contributing to a classroom discussion. It becomes easier with practice. If you think that there might be an area of the course that you could find distressing, such as child protection or bereavement, be sure to mention this to your tutor in advance.

Functioning in different types of groups

Small groups
From time to time, your tutor may ask you to work in small groups of four or five to complete a particular task. You may be given pens and flip-chart paper, and one of you may be asked to record the ideas and findings of your group. Towards the end of the session, one of you may be asked to report back to the larger group.

Your course group
When starting the course, you may be placed in a group of approximately 10 to 20 people. This is the size of the group for most of your course sessions. As you spend time together, you will become familiar with the group relationships and behaviour. You will no doubt make some firm friendships.

Presentations

Rarely, you may be asked during the course to make a presentation of your work to the group, either on your own or with two or three other home-based childcarers. You will need to be clear about the purpose of the presentation, what you wish to communicate and how you are going to present the information. Remember to speak clearly, audibly and slowly enough so that the group has time to take in what you are saying. Face the group at all times, even if you are using visual aids. Remember to:

- be yourself, and find your own style
- be positive
- accept that you will be nervous beforehand and try some relaxation techniques
- concentrate on the task, remembering what you are trying to communicate
- monitor your vocal expression, thinking about volume, pitch and pace
- articulate your words more clearly for a larger audience
- avoid too many statistics; if necessary, put them in a handout and ask the tutor to photocopy it for the group

- check any visual aids, such as overhead projectors, beforehand
- never apologise for your presentation
- try to rehearse with friends before the actual presentation.

Role play

While on a course, you may be asked to take on the role of another person, so that you can begin to experience the feelings and emotions that someone might feel in a certain situation. This is unlikely to occur until the group has settled and the members know each other well.

Your tutor will brief you very clearly as to what is expected of you. Sometimes, role play will be between two people, with a third one observing what is happening. The observer will then report back to the other two. On occasion, for example if you were role playing a child protection conference, a larger group would be involved, and the rest of the course group would observe. It is always important to have feedback, and for the participants to have the opportunity to state how they felt. Taking on the role of others improves your ability to see other people's points of view. This ability is called 'empathy' and is different from feeling sympathetic, as it allows you to enter into the emotions of another person. To experience and think about how other people are feeling and to apply this to oneself is an important part of professional development.

Exploring together

On occasion, your tutor may ask you to explore a particular topic in a spontaneous and fast fashion. This will help enrich a subject with creative, lateral and original thinking. All ideas are accepted, however wild or extravagant they may seem at first.

Someone is generally elected (the scribe) to record the ideas on a large sheet of paper, or on a board, whilst another person acts as chairperson so as to keep some order in the proceedings. Everyone in the group is expected to participate in a positive fashion. The chairperson should prevent any negative attitudes, as these will inhibit creativity. The group may decide to set a time limit. The scribe will read back the list of ideas to the group on request and at the end of the initial session.

The group will now classify the entire list, combining and improving ideas. They may discover gaps in the topic and some areas may have been oversubscribed. The tutor may now intervene, and suggest unexplored concepts. A general discussion will follow and the ideas will be evaluated in a positive way. The value of the session is that:

- it helps you to reflect on what you already know about a particular topic before taking on fresh ideas
- it allows the whole group to contribute without inhibition
- it allows free expression and spontaneity
- negativity is ruled out
- some home-based childcarers explore thoughts and ideas that they would not consider on their own
- classifying and evaluating ideas is a useful exercise in organising one's own work
- working as a group on a topic demonstrates the value of teamwork.

Using worksheets with videos

As a home-based childcarer, you will need knowledge and understanding of many different children, from different backgrounds, with different needs, of different ages and in different settings. Your tutor may wish you to watch a number of videos to complement your experience. This is not a passive exercise, and you will be expected to join in discussion in a critical fashion. Always note the title, date and publisher of the video, as you may wish to include it in your bibliography.

When you first start to observe children, your tutor may ask you to watch a short extract from a video, record your observations, and report to the group what you have observed. To help you become more adept at close observation of video recordings, you might find it useful to watch a relevant television documentary at home and take notes.

Learning aids

You will find many useful resources in your local library that will help you succeed in any further training you may undertake. You will need to become familiar with the facilities and be prepared to ask questions; employ the skills of the professional staff if there is any area that is new to you.

Booklists

At the start of any course, you will be given a list of books that you will find helpful to read to complete the course successfully There may be competing demands on the library stock, and you will need to reserve them as soon as you can. If you are on a DHC course, discuss this with your tutor.

Handouts

Frequently, your tutors will distribute handouts about various areas of the work and will either refer to them in the course group, or expect you to study them on your own. You can highlight any particular points that you or your tutor thinks to be of vital interest, and this will help you later on when you might be writing an assignment. All handouts should be dated and filed with your course material.

Using books for research

As you know, all textbooks have a table of contents indicating the chapters and lists of charts and illustrations, and some will also have appendices, footnotes, bibliographies and an index. When selecting a book, look at:

- the introduction or preface, which may give you some idea what the book is about and at which level it is aimed
- the contents or chapter headings, which will indicate the main topics or areas covered
- the date of publication, which will tell you how up to date the work is

- the summary or conclusions, which may give you some overview of the book
- the index, which may help you find your topic if it is not mentioned in the contents list
- the bibliography; some books will suggest further reading, as well as resources, references or useful addresses
- the charts, diagrams, graphs and illustrations, which may be of help in your assignment.

You may not be able to find all you require on a particular topic in your local library. It is well worth enquiring if the librarians can order books for you from other libraries for a nominal fee. Consider buying books in partnership with other members of your group, and borrowing from people who have completed the course.

Using information technology

Although using a computer is not an essential part of the course, you will find one to be a very useful tool. If you can word-process, you will soon value the acquisition of this skill. If you do not have access to a computer at home, you may be able to book sessions in your local library or college learning resource centre.

Access to the Internet, either on your course or at home, will help you with your research, enabling you to access a wide range of up-to-date information. It will often give you a synopsis of books that you might want to read. Organisations such as the NSPCC and Kidscape have websites, and this is helpful in providing information quickly. Check what CD-ROMs are available at your library, as these can be invaluable in your understanding of certain topics.

Other resources

NCMA organises regular conferences at national, county, regional and borough level. These conferences are particularly valuable as they keep you up to date with all issues relating to childminding, offer programmes of workshops and seminars on current issues, and allow you to meet a number of home-based childcarers involved in working with young children.

The magazine *Nursery World* organises regular exhibitions of resources, books and equipment.

Organising your work

Filing work

One way of making sure that your course of study is a success is to have easy access to your material. All those notes that you so carefully wrote down, all those handouts given to you in class, and the records of those activities that you have planned and carried out in your placement: everything needs to be carefully sorted and filed. All written work that you complete should be dated, given a title and carry your name and CACHE pin number.

There are several methods of filing your course work. Most students prefer a different file for each subject. Within each subject, you may choose one or both of the following methods:

- date order (chronological): each piece of work is added to the file in date order, with the date in the top right-hand corner of the page
- topic headings: most subjects are broken down into topics. For example, in one file, you might put materials on pre-school provision and the National Curriculum, in another you might put notes on nutrition and physical growth and development, whilst a third might contain notes on the legal framework and on working with parents. This is a convenient method of filing but be careful not to view each topic in isolation.

Some home-based childcarers might find it useful to keep a list of contents at the front of the file for quick access. The use of dividers in different colours, with the name of each topic clearly depicted is another useful way of finding what you need quickly.

Assignment planning

You will be assessed on Units 2 to 5 by assignments that you will be expected to complete by a given date. These tasks require careful long-term planning, research and recording. Your tutors will make clear their expectations, and help you with the format. You will be given grading criteria for the assignment.

Having been set an assignment, clarify:

- what you are required to do
- what information you need to complete the assignment
- where you will find this information
- the date of submission of the work.

If the assignment requires you to undertake a piece of work or research in your home involving the children, you should discuss it with the parents before starting the project. Try to have a clear idea of how long it will take; allow yourself time to proofread the first draft and make any necessary amendments before submitting the finished assignment. It is important to follow instructions for the presentation of your work.

Writing assignments

When writing an assignment on any subject, you need to be clear that you are;

- responding clearly to the instructions in the title
- drawing on the relevant parts of the course
- showing a good understanding of the subject
- presenting a coherent argument
- using an objective style
- introducing appropriate evidence to support your argument
- attempting to present your work in a legible, easy-to-read style, with few spelling or grammatical errors
- presenting your work as attractively as possible, preferably typed or word-processed, using double spacing on A4 paper, and securely bound
- checking that you have covered all the grading criteria before handing in your work.

Referencing

You will obviously need to use and refer to other people's work when writing any type of assignment. Your tutor will advise you how to reference within the text. You must, however, be very careful to avoid the temptation to plagiarise. This means copying chunks of text and using it as your own work, without any acknowledgement. You will be expected to list, at the end of every assignment, details of any books or other resources to which you have referred. You might be asked to provide a list of the books and other resources that have helped you. This is known as a bibliography.

Multiple-choice questions (MCQs)

These are questions where one of four presented answers is the correct one. You will indicate the one you think is correct. Any MCQ paper will consist of a specific number of questions and you will be given a period of time to complete the paper. Generally, questions will test your knowledge or your practice. Your tutor will prepare you for this test, and will indicate how you are to record your response. If you do not know the answer to any question immediately, it is good sense to leave it, answer all the ones you do know and, in the time left, tackle the ones you are not sure about. Most tutors will ensure that you have plenty of practice with mock papers to develop and improve your technique. There are examples of MCQs on the CACHE website.

Distance learning

If you find it difficult to get to a college or other centres for courses, you may be able to study at home. The National Extension College offers a range of courses including units of the DHC. The course is also offered online.

Committing yourself to, and completing, a course of study is hard work, but well worthwhile. When you are qualified, you will feel immense satisfaction in your new professional status.

Keeping up to date

The longer you work as a home-based childcarer, the more you will realise how important it is that you remain in touch with recent research, publications and current best practice. Your confidence and skills will be developing and will be enriched by keeping up to date.

Being a member of NCMA will keep you in touch with current thinking and research in early years practice. NCMA publishes a regular magazine, *Who Minds?*, that contains a great deal of relevant information. Useful periodicals and newspapers are:

- *Nursery World*
- *Child Education*
- *Times Educational Supplement*
- newspapers, such as *The Independent*, *The Guardian*, *The Times* and *The Observer*.

Check radio and television coverage for interesting and relevant programmes.

If you are attending a course on home-based childcare, you may find the college or centre subscribes to:

- the National Children's Bureau
- Early Years Trainers Anti-Racist Network
- National Early Years Network
- Save the Children Equality Learning Centre.

These organisations all publish regular newsletters and up-to-date research and information. It is necessary to belong to a local library as that will help you gain access to new publications.

Twice a year, *Nursery World* publishes a supplement, *Training Today*. This is a good indicator of the vast number of courses on offer to people who work with children. It is advisable to keep a record of any courses you attend (see page 290). This not only reminds you of when you attended but can also be transferred to your curriculum vitae (CV), or used in your NVQ Portfolio.

Record of training and attendance at courses and conferences

Date	Length of course: Weeks Days Months	Funded by	Provider of training	Title	Course details	Certificate of attendance or qualification	Comments

You might think about:

- how to keep up to date with current issues in childcare and education
- how you will become a reflective practitioner
- how you might fit a training course into your busy schedule
- how you gain access to books and other information to keep up to date
- long-term plans for your professional development
- exploring your local library and its range of provision as a resource centre
- how studying might have an impact on your family
- how gaining a further qualification might offer new opportunities.

This chapter has contributed to the following learning outcomes:

Unit 3

- demonstrating the importance of reflective practice and how to become a reflective practitioner in the home-based setting
- explaining the importance of continuing professional development to the home-based practitioner

Want to Find Out More?

Websites
www.cache.org.uk
www.ofsted.gov.uk
www.qca.org.uk

Further reading

Cottrell S., *The Study Skills Handbook*, 3rd Edition, Palgrave Macmillan, 2008

Green S., *Research methods in Health, Social and Early Years Care*, Nelson Thornes, 2000

Hobart C. and Frankel J., *A–Z of Childcare*, Nelson Thornes, 1998

Walsh M., *Research Made Real*, Nelson Thornes, 2001

APPENDIX A
Developmental norms

0 to 1 year

	Physical development – gross motor	Physical development – fine motor	Social and emotional development	Intellectual and communication development
At birth	Reflexes: ■ Rooting, sucking and swallowing reflex ■ Grasp reflex ■ Walking reflex ■ Moro reflex If pulled to sit, head falls backwards If held in sitting position, head falls forward, and back is curved In supine (laying on back), limbs are bent In prone (laying on front), lies in fetal position with knees tucked up. Unable to raise head or stretch limbs	Reflexes: ■ Pupils reacting to light ■ Opens eyes when held upright ■ Blinks or opens eyes wide to sudden sound ■ Startle reaction to sudden sound ■ Closing eyes to sudden bright light	Bonding/attachment	Cries vigorously, with some variation in pitch and duration
1 month	In prone, lifts chin In supine, head moves to one side Arm and leg extended on face side Begins to flex upper and lower limbs	Hands fisted Eyes move to dangling objects	Watches mother's face with increasingly alert facial expression Fleeting smile – may be wind Stops crying when picked up	Cries become more differentiated to indicate needs Stops and attends to voice, rattle and bell
3 months	Held sitting, head straight back and neck firm. Lower back still weak When lying, pelvis is flat	Grasps an object when placed in hand Turns head right round to look at objects Eye contact firmly established	Reacts with pleasure to familiar situations/routines	Regards hands with interest Beginning to vocalise

0 to 1 year continued

	Physical development – gross motor	Physical development – fine motor	Social and emotional development	Intellectual and communication development
6 months	In supine, can lift head and shoulders In prone, can raise up on hands Sits with support Kicks strongly May roll over When held, enjoys standing and jumping	Has learned to grasp objects and passes toys from hand to hand Visual sense well established	Takes everything to mouth Responds to different emotional tones of chief caregiver	Finds feet interesting Vocalises tunefully Laughs in play Screams with annoyance Understands purpose of rattle
9 months	Sits unsupported Begins to crawl Pulls to stand, falls back with bump	Visually attentive Grasps with thumb and index finger Releases toy by dropping Looks for fallen objects Beginning to finger-feed Holds bottle or cup	Plays peek-a-boo – can start earlier Imitates hand-clapping Clings to familiar adults, reluctant to go to strangers – from about 7 months	Watches activities of others with interest Vocalises to attract attention Beginning to babble Finds partially hidden toy Shows an interest in picture books Knows own name
1 year	Walks holding one hand, may walk alone Bends down and picks up objects Pulls to stand and sits deliberately	Picks up small objects Fine pincer grip Points at objects Holds spoon	Cooperates in dressing Demonstrates affection Participates in nursery rhymes Waves bye-bye	Uses jargon Responds to simple instructions and understands several words Puts wooden cubes in and out of cup or box

1 to 3:11 years

	Physical development – gross motor	Physical development – fine motor	Social and emotional development	Intellectual and communication development
1 year	Walks holding one hand, may walk alone Bends down and picks up objects Pulls to stand and sits deliberately	Picks up small objects Fine pincer grip Points at objects Holds spoon	Co-operates in dressing Demonstrates affection Participates in nursery rhymes Waves bye-bye	Uses jargon Responds to simple instructions and understands several words Puts wooden cubes in and out of cup or box
15 months	Walking usually well established Can crawl up stairs frontwards and down stairs backwards Kneels unaided Balance poor, falls heavily	Holds crayon with palmar grasp Precise pincer grasp, both hands Builds tower of 2 cubes Can place objects precisely Uses spoon which sometimes rotates Turns pages of picture book	Indicates wet or soiled pants Helps with dressing Emotionally dependent on familiar adult	Jabbers loudly and freely, with 2–6 recognisable words, and can communicate needs Intensely curious Reproduces lines drawn by adult
18 months	Climbs up and down stairs with hand held Runs carefully Pushes, pulls and carries large toys Backs into small chair Can squat to pick up toys	Builds tower of 3 cubes Scribbles to and fro spontaneously Begins to show preference for one hand Drinks without spilling	Tries to sing Imitates domestic activities Bowel control sometimes attained Alternates between clinging and resistance Plays contentedly alone near familiar adult	Enjoys simple picture books, recognising some characters Jabbering established 6–20 recognisable words May use echolalia (repeating adult's last word, or last word of rhyme) Is able to show several parts of the body, when asked Explores environment energetically
2 years	Runs with confidence, avoiding obstacles Walks up and down stairs both feet to each step, holding wall Squats with ease. Rises without using hands Can climb up on furniture and get down again Steers tricycle pushing along with feet Throws small ball overarm, and kicks large ball	Turns picture book pages one at a time Builds tower of 6 cubes Holds pencil with first 2 fingers and thumb near to point	Competently spoon feeds and drinks from cup Is aware of physical needs Can put on shoes and hat Keenly interested in outside environment – unaware of dangers Demands chief caregiver's attention and often clings Parallel play Throws tantrums if frustrated	Identifies photographs of familiar adults Identifies small-world toys Recognises tiny details in pictures Uses own name to refer to self Speaks in 2- and 3-word sentences, and can sustain short conversations Asks for names and labels Talks to self continuously

1 to 3:11 years continued

	Physical development – gross motor	Physical development – fine motor	Social and emotional development	Intellectual and communication development
3 years	Competent locomotive skills Can jump off lower steps Still uses 2 feet to a step coming down stairs Pedals and steers tricycle	Cuts paper with scissors Builds a tower of 9 cubes and a bridge with 3 cubes Good pencil control Can thread 3 large beads on a string	Uses spoon and fork Increased independence in self-care Dry day and night Affectionate and co-operative Plays co-operatively, particularly domestic play Tries to please	Can copy a circle and some letters Can draw a person with a head and 2 other parts of the body May name colours and match 3 primary colours Speech and comprehension well established Some immature pronunciations and unconventional grammatical forms Asks questions constantly Can give full name, gender and age Relates present activities and past experiences Increasing interest in words and numbers
3:11 years	All motor muscles well controlled Can turn sharp corners when running Hops on favoured foot Balances for 3–5 seconds Increasing skill at ball games Sits with knees crossed	Builds a tower of 10 cubes Uses 6 cubes to build 3 steps, when shown	Boasts and is bossy Sense of humour developing Cheeky, answers back Wants to be independent Plans games co-operatively Argues with other children but learning to share	Draws person with head, legs and trunk Draws recognisable house Uses correct grammar most of the time Most pronunciations mature Asks meanings of words Enjoys verses and jokes, and may use swear words Counts up to 20 Imaginative play well developed

4 to 16 years

	Physical development – gross motor	Physical development – fine motor	Social and emotional development	Intellectual and communication development
4 years	All motor muscles well controlled Can turn sharp corners when running Hops on favoured foot Balances for 3–5 seconds Increasing skill at ball games Sits with knees crossed	Builds a tower of 10 cubes Uses 6 cubes to build 3 steps, when shown	Boasts and is bossy Sense of humour developing Cheeky, answers back Wants to be independent Plans games co-operatively Argues with other children but learning to share	Draws person with head, legs and trunk Draws recognisable house Uses correct grammar most of the time Most pronunciations mature Asks meanings of words Enjoys verses and jokes, and may use swear words Counts up to 20 Imaginative play well developed
5 years	Can touch toes keeping legs straight Hops on either foot Skips Runs on toes Ball skills developing well Can walk along a thin line	Threads needle and sews Builds steps with 3–4 cubes Colours pictures carefully Can copy adult writing	Copes well with daily personal needs Chooses own friends Well-balanced and sociable Sense of fair play and understanding of rules developing Shows caring attitudes towards others	Matches most colours Copies square, triangle and several letters, writing some unprompted Writes name Draws a detailed person Speaks correctly and fluently Knows home address Able and willing to complete projects Understands numbers using concrete objects Imaginary play now involves make-believe games

4 to 16 years continued

	Physical development – gross motor	Physical development – fine motor	Social and emotional development	Cognitive and language development
6 years	Jumps over rope 25 cm high Learning to skip with rope	Ties own shoe laces	Eager for fresh experiences More demanding and stubborn less sociable Joining a 'gang' may be important May be quarrelsome with friends Needs to succeed as failing too often leads to poor self-esteem	Reading skills developing well Drawings more precise and detailed Figure may be drawn in profile Can describe how one object differs from another Mathematical skills developing, may use symbols instead of concrete objects May write independently
7 years	Rides a 2-wheel bicycle Improves balance	Skills constantly improving More dexterity and precision in all areas	Special friend at school Peer approval becoming important Likes to spend some time alone Enjoys TV and books May attempt tasks too complex to complete	Moving towards abstract thought Able to read Can give opposite meanings Able to write paragraph
8–12	Movements well co-ordinated Physical skills improving Takes part in team games with enjoyment Swims	Skills constantly improving Drawings become more complex	Friendships become more important Independence increasing More understanding of self	Concentration improves Able to read fluently Can write a story May think scientifically Able to play complex games such as chess
12–16	Hormonal changes Puberty Skin changes Growth spurts Body hair develops Girl: menstruates breasts develop hips broaden Boy: facial hair develops voice deepens growth of penis and testes	Skills develop depending on interest and practice, for example playing guitar Nintendo games, model making	Mood swings May rebel against authority Interest in sex begins May experiment with different identities	Adolescents start to think about the future and if motivated will use all their intellectual ability to achieve their educational goals

APPENDIX B

Sequence of language development

Children's language develops through a series of identifiable stages. These stages are sequential, as outlined below. The level of children's development depends partly on their chronological age, but their experience of language from an early age is, however, just as important a factor. If children are exposed to a rich language environment this will be reflected in their language development. Children who have not had this opportunity will not have had the same chances for development. It is important to take this into account when assessing a child's stage of language development.

Children who are bilingual may develop their languages at a slightly slower rate than children who are monolingual. This is to be expected as they have much more to learn. Given an environment that promotes language development, bilingual children will become proficient in both languages.

Approximate age	Developmental level
Birth	Involuntary cry
2–3 weeks	Signs of intentional communication: eye contact
4 weeks onwards	Cries are becoming voluntary, indicating for example, unhappiness, tiredness, loneliness Children may respond by moving their eyes or head towards the speaker, kicking or stopping crying
6 weeks onwards	Children may smile when spoken to Cooing and gurgling begin in response to parent's or carer's presence and voice, also to show contentment
1–2 months	Children may move their eyes or head towards the direction of the sound
3 months	Children will raise their head when sounds attract their attention
4 months	Playful sounds appear: cooing, gurgling, laughing, chuckling, squealing; these are in response to the human voice and to show contentment Children respond to familiar sounds by turning their head, kicking or stopping crying Shouts to attract attention
6 months	The beginning of babbling: regular, repeated sounds, e.g. *gegegegeg*, *mamamam*, *dadada*; children play around with these sounds. This is important for practising sound-producing mechanisms necessary for later speech Cooing, laughing and gurgling become stronger Children begin to understand emotion in the parent or carer's voice Children begin to enjoy music and rhymes, particularly if accompanied by actions

Approximate age	Developmental level
9 months	Babbling continues and the repertoire increases Children begin to recognise their own name May understand simple, single words, e.g. *No*, *Bye-bye* Children continue to enjoy music and rhymes and will now attempt to join in with the actions, e.g. playing Pat-a-Cake
9–12 months	Babbling begins to reflect the intonation of speech Children may imitate simple words. This is usually an extension of babbling, e.g. *dada* Pointing begins. This is often accompanied by a sound or the beginnings of a word. This demonstrates an increasing awareness that words are associated with people and objects
12 months	Children's vocabulary starts to develop. First word(s) appear, usually names of people and objects that the child is familiar with. They are built around the child's babbling sound repertoire Children understand far more than they can say. This is called a passive vocabulary. They begin to be able to respond to simple instructions, e.g. 'Give me the ball', 'Come here', 'Clap your hands'
15 months	Active vocabulary development remains quite limited as children concentrate on achieving mobility Passive vocabulary increases rapidly Pointing accompanied by a single word is the basis of communication
18 months	Children's active vocabulary increases; this tends to be names of familiar things and people Children use their language to name belongings and point out named objects Generalisation of words is difficult, e.g. cat can only be their cat, not the one next door One word and intonation is used to indicate meaning, e.g. cup may mean, 'I want a drink', 'I have lost my cup', 'Where is my cup?'. The intonation (and possibly the situation) would indicate the meaning to people who are familiar with the child Children will repeat words and sentences
21 months	Both passive and active vocabularies rapidly increase; the passive vocabulary, however, remains larger than the active Children begin to name objects and people that are not there: this shows an awareness of what language is for Sentences begin. Initially as two word phrases, e.g. 'Mummy gone', 'Coat on' Gesture is still a fundamental part of communication Children begin asking questions, usually 'What?', 'Who?' and 'Where?'
2 years	Both active and passive vocabularies continue to increase Children can generalise words but this sometimes means that they over-generalise, e.g. all men are *daddy*, all furry animals with four legs are *dog* Personal pronouns (words used instead of actual names) are used, e.g. I, she, he, you, they. They are not always used correctly Sentences become longer although they tend to be in telegraphic speech,

Approximate age	Developmental level
	i.e. only the main sense-conveying words are used, e.g. 'Mummy gone work', 'Me go bike' Questions are asked frequently, 'What?' and 'Why?'
2 years 6 months	Vocabulary increases rapidly; there is less imbalance between passive and active vocabularies Word use is more specific so there are fewer over- and under-generalisations Sentences get longer and more precise, although they are still usually abbreviated versions of adult sentences Word order in sentences is sometimes incorrect Children can use language to protect their own rights and interests and to maintain their own comfort and pleasure, e.g. 'It's mine', 'Get off', 'I'm playing with that' Children can listen to stories and are interested in them
3 years	Vocabulary develops rapidly; new words are picked up quickly Sentences continue to become longer and more like adult speech Children talk to themselves during play: this is to plan and order their play, which is evidence of children using language to think Language can now be used to report on what is happening, to direct their own and others' actions, to express ideas and to initiate and maintain friendships Pronouns are usually used correctly Questions such as 'Why?', 'Who?' and 'What for?' are used frequently Rhymes and melody are attractive
3 years 6 months	Children have a wide vocabulary and word usage is usually correct; this continues to increase They are now able to use complete sentences although word order is sometimes incorrect Language can now be used to report on past experiences Incorrect word endings are sometimes used, e.g. *swimmed*, *runned*, *seed*
4 years	Children's vocabulary is now extensive; new words are added regularly Longer and more complex sentences are used; sentences may be joined with *because*, which demonstrates an awareness of causes and relationships Children are able to narrate long stories including the sequence of events Play involves running commentaries The boundaries between fact and fiction are blurred and this is reflected in children's speech Speech is fully intelligible with few, minor incorrect uses Questioning is at its peak. 'When?' is used alongside other questions. By this stage children can usually use language to share, take turns, collaborate, argue, predict what may happen, compare possible alternatives, anticipate, give explanations, justify behaviour, create situations in imaginative play, reflect upon their own feelings and begin to describe how other people feel

Approximate age	Developmental level
5 years	Children have a wide vocabulary and can use it appropriately Vocabulary can include colours, shapes, numbers and common opposites, e.g. big/small, hard/soft Sentences are usually correctly structured although incorrect grammar may still be used Pronunciation may still be childish Language continues to be used and developed as described in the section on 4-year-olds; this may now include phrases heard on the television and associated with children's toys. Questions and discussions are for enquiry and information; questions become more precise as children's cognitive skills develop Children will offer opinions in discussion

Source: Beaver M. et al., *Babies and Young Children, Book 1: Early Years Development*, 2nd Edition, Stanley Thornes, 1999

APPENDIX C

NCMA article: Prepare for self-assessment

1 Helping children be healthy

Things you could show the inspector:
- your sickness policy
- your first-aid certificate
- your first-aid kit
- any meal plans you've prepared
- the types of medical records you keep about each chiid, and records that you share with parents about medicines administered*
- equipment for sterilising babies' bottles and feeding utensils
- children's individual washcloths, towels, hairbrushes, etc
- certificates for any training you've done in nutrition, environmental health, food preparation, or anything else related to chidren's health
- any report or guidance you have been given by an environmental health officer.

Other things you could talk about:
- how you keep your setting clean and hygienic and minimise the spread of germs
- how you help children learn about personal hygiene
- the kinds of nutritious, well-balanced meals, snacks and drinks you provide
- how you ensure children always have access to drinking water
- how you help children to understand the benefits of exercise and ensure they keep phyically fit
- how you ensure that pets (if you have any) do not pose a health risk
- how you keep all rooms used for childminding at a comfortable temperature
- how you keep up to date with information on children's health.

2 Keeping children safe

Things you could show the inspector:
- safety equipment, such as stair gates, smoke alarms, fire blankets, highchair and pushchair harnesses, socket covers, carbon monoxide detectors
- your emergency escape plan and exits
- your child protection policy
- the types of records you keep, and share with parents, about accidents and incidents involving childminded children*
- paperwork and equipment that demonstrates your car (if you have one) is safe for transporting children (including vehicle insurance, driving licence, MoT certificate, car seats and harnesses)
- your clean, hygienic washing, toilet and nappy-changing facilities

- how you have made hazardous substances and equipment inaccessibe to children
- how you ensure the hygienic storage, preparation, cooking and serving of food
- how you keep your home (and garden) secure
- certificates for any training you have done in hygiene, food safety, child protection and anything else related to children's safety
- any report or guidance given to you by a fir safety officer
- gas and electrical installation and servicing certificates
- instructions and manuals for safety equipment, toys, etc.

Other things you could talk about:
- how you ensure that toys and equipment conform to safety standards, and are not used by children who are too young for them
- how you make sure toys and equipment are clean and in good condition
- how you ensure the children are within your sight or hearing at all times
- how you keep the children safe when you are out and about
- measures you have taken to keep your garden (if you have one) safe for children
- how you help children to understand how to keep themsleves safe
- how you might recognise possible signs and symptoms of abuse
- your knowledge of local child protection procedures and the government booklet *What To Do if You're Worried a Child is Being Abused*.

3 Helping children enjoy and achieve

Things you could show the inspector:
- children's artwork and craft projects
- photos (or video footage) of favourite outings and activities
- educational books, toys and other resources
- suitable toys and materials for indoor and outdoor play
- diaries, scrapbooks and/or observation forms in which you record children's development and achievements, and share this information with parents*
- equipment that helps children to become independent, such as booster steps, special toilet seats and child-friendly cutlery.

Other things you could talk about:
- how you plan activities and play opportunities
- the first-hand learning experiences you offer (cooking, gardening, visiting the shops, etc)
- how you help to develop children's language, mathematical thinking, imaginations and social relationships
- how you encourage all children to achieve, no matter what their age, gender, cultural background or level of ability
- how you praise and reward children's achievements and good behaviour
- how you use guidance such as the Early Years Foundation Stage (EYFS) (see pages 81-6) and the Code of Practice (2001) for Identification and Assessment of Special Educational Needs – to inspire activities and outings.

4 Helping children make a positive contribution

Things you could show the inspector:
- displays that show children's work and reflect their interests and backgrounds
- toys, books and display materials that reflect diversity and give the children positive role models of people like themselves and people different to themselves
- furniture, toys and materials that are accessible to children.

Other things you could talk about:
- how you involve children in decision-making when planning activities, outings, meals, etc
- how you involve children in household activities, such as preparing meals, sorting clean laundry and tidying up
- how you involve children in setting 'house rules'
- how you value children's individuality and help them to feel good about themselves
- how you help children appreciate and value each otheer's similarities and differences
- how you encourage children to use and value community resources, such as local libraries, parks, leisure centres, shops and visitor attractions
- how you find out about and acknowledge the customs and beliefs of each child's family
- how you communicate with the children's parents and seek their views (see page 8 for some ideas)
- steps you take (or would take) to promote the welfare and develoment of children in your care who have additional needs.

5 Organising your childcare effectively

Things you could show the inspector:
- proof of your identity (e.g. passport, driving licence, birth certificate)
- the kinds of contact details you keep for everyone who lives or works in your home*
- your childminding contracts*
- the kinds of records you keep about each child and parent*
- your attendance register
- your public liability insurance certificate
- paperwork relating to any assistant(s) you employ, including recruitment information, references, copies of training certificates, and employer's liability insurance*
- your behaviour management policy
- permission forms signed by parents for outings, transporting children, seeking emergency medical attention, etc
- any necessary planning permission documents, and paperwork relating to alterations to your home
- records of any complaints made against you
- your 'ground rules'
- any other relevant records, policies and procedures.

Other things you could talk about:
- how you keep families' personal details confidential

- how you meet reqquired adult–child ratios at all times
- how you source extra equipment and resources when you need them
- how you ensure that children with additional needs have privacy when intimate care is being provided
- arrangerments for any overnight care you provide
- how you support any assistant(s).

Please note

The information on these pages is not a comprehensive guide to everything you might be asked to show or talk about at your Ofsted inspection. It is very likely that your inspection will not cover everything mentioned on these pages, and will cover many things that are not mentioned. Please do not use these pages as a 'checklist', but simply for guidance and ideas.

* Remember your commitment to children's, parents' and employees' confidentiality when showing these sorts of materials to your Ofsted inspector.

Glossary of terms

Acquired immune deficiency syndrome (AIDS)
Caused by a virus and transmitted through body fluids. The body loses its ability to resist infection. The virus is very delicate and quickly dies outside the body.

Anti-discriminatory practice
Examining all areas of practice to ensure no discrimination occurs, that all resources project positive images and that the language used, including naming systems, is appropriate and correct, and that all prejudice and discrimination is challenged.

Aggressive behaviour
This describes behaviour that is disruptive, verbally and physically abusive and defiant, with the child resorting to tantrums and disobedience.

Allergies
An acute reaction of the body to something eaten, inhaled or touched, to which previous exposure has made the body sensitive.

Behaviour modification
To change unwanted behaviour successfully it is necessary for all the adults who care for the child to work together with consistent guidelines and boundaries, giving plenty of attention, and rewarding good behaviour while ignoring bad behaviour.

Bibliography
The listing of books read and used in an assignment or a piece of research.

Bonding
Becoming emotionally attached to one person. This usually describes the attachment of the mother to the newborn and of the newborn to the mother.

Bullying
Attacks on a child, which can be physical, emotional, verbal, racist and/or sexual; it is the main cause of school refusal. It can leave emotional scars that remain for life.

Challenging behaviour
Describes the child displaying behaviour that is inappropriate and attention seeking.

Child protection
Protecting children from abuse and neglect is the duty of the whole community. There are many statutory and voluntary agencies involved, such as the law, the police, social services, the health service, the NSPCC, ChildLine and education services.

Child-rearing practices
Children are brought up in many different ways with, for example, some families believing in firm discipline for even the mildest infringement of the rules, while other parents have far fewer rules and allow the children a great deal of freedom. A good understanding of such practices is necessary for any person working with children.

Comfort object
An object, often a blanket or a soft toy, which a child carries around as a comforter, and usually takes to bed with him or her. It may be used until it disintegrates.

Confidentiality
Entrusted with private information concerning a child or family that is not divulged to anyone unless it is the best interest of the child.

Congenital
Any condition existing from birth or perhaps resulting from the birth process itself.

Creativity
Bringing into existence something original.

Culture
The customs, values, civilisation and achievements of a particular group of people.

Curriculum
A course of study. The way that children learn as well as what they learn, encompassing their whole experience and influencing all areas of development.

Development
The acquisition of new skills, ideas, and attitudes that lead to progressive change.

Disability
The Disability Discrimination Act 1995 (DDA) defines a disability as 'a physical or mental impairment which has a substantial and long-term adverse effect on a person's ability to carry out normal day-to-day activities'. Long-term is usually taken to mean 12 months or more. This definition covers physical and sensory disability, mental health problems and learning disability, and a range of medical problems such as diabetes, epilepsy, and severe allergies.

Discrimination
Treating certain people or groups of people in an unfair manner based solely on prejudice.

Equal opportunities
Along with other professionals, home-based childcarers need to recognise that no member of society should be discriminated against because of his or her gender, race, disability, culture, religion, age, class or sexual orientation.

Evaluation
The term used by childcare practitioners to assess and appraise observations and activities, so as to plan for the future.

Exploration of the outside world
As young children venture outside their family home, they learn about different environments and different value systems. Most children adapt very quickly to outside stimulation and learn a great deal.

Growth
An increase in size that is measurable. Linear growth is the length of the baby or the height of the child. There should be consistent weight gain. Regular measurements of the head's circumference indicate the growth of the brain within the skull. Measurements are taken at birth and used as a baseline for future measurements. Figures should be plotted on a percentile chart.

Holistic approach
An approach to the care of the child where the total needs are recognised and met. A holistic education is one that educates the whole child in all the areas of child development, not just in basic cognitive skills.

Home-based care
This describes caring for a child either in her own home or in the home of the carer.

Inclusion
Inclusion means that children, young people and adults with disabilities or impairments are included in mainstream society. Childcare inclusion ensures that all children can attend and benefit from the same childcare provision.

Infant mortality
Deaths under one year of age.

Learning environment
When positive, this describes an environment that is stimulating and exciting, offering opportunities for learning new skills and for exploration.

Literacy
The ability to read and write. Literacy is attained in many ways, using reading schemes, (look and say, phonics, real books) and other techniques.

Medical model of disability
The medical model labels disabled people as ill and in need of treatment. It regards the disability as an illness, and the emphasis is on a medical cause, treatment or cure. The model disregards disabled people's own feelings and leaves them dependent on others.

Natural materials
Objects found in nature and used for activities with children, such as water play, sand play, mud, woodwork and clay.

Objectivity
Making judgements from collective data, not allowing one's own feelings to be of any consequence.

Parental rights and responsibilities
Parents should have responsibility for their children, rather than rights over them. Parental responsibility is defined as the rights, duties, powers, responsibilities and authority that, by law, a parent of a child has in relation to the child and to his or her property.

Partnership with parents
The Children Act 1989 laid down firmly that parents have rights and responsibilities, and all professionals are expected to work with them in partnership for the benefit of the child.

Peer group
People of the same age and stage of development.

Positive images
Developing a positive environment that reflects all the children in a positive way, for example showing women carrying out what traditionally have been thought of as men's roles. It is against stereotyping by race, gender and disability. It is reflected in books, posters, food, festivals and artefacts and in the involvement of all the parents.

Poverty
The lack of adequate resources to satisfy essential minimum human needs. It can be relative, being very poor in an affluent society, or absolute, being near to starvation.

Prejudice
The set of beliefs, generally fixed, that is learned and leads to bias for or against a particular group or idea.

Regressive behaviour
When a child is ill, or emotionally upset, he or she may behave in ways that are more suitable for someone younger. For example, a child, who can normally concentrate well, finds it impossible to do more than play with toys and equipment that would normally be considered too young. He or she might start wetting the bed again, having been completely dry for more than a year.

Safeguarding
Another term for child protection.

Scapegoating
Blaming a person unfairly for the shortcomings or problems of others.

Self-esteem
Confidence in oneself as a worthwhile person. Essential to learning and achievement. Abused children often suffer from low self-esteem.

Self-reliance
Independence. From a very young age, children strive to do things for themselves, such as dressing and washing. This can be helped by adult encouragement.

Social model of disability
The social model of disability acknowledges those with disabilities as people first. It emphasises the need for environmental and social change to allow disabled people to live in a society that is inclusive, accessible and supportive of personal rights. Impairments are a fact of life, but, if they are planned for and resources allocated well, they do not have to become a problem.

Special educational needs
The law states that children have special educational needs if they have a learning difficulty that requires special educational provision to be made for them.

Stereotypes
Generalisations about a particular group in society, for example believing that girls read earlier than boys.

Syndrome
A group of signs and symptoms which occur together and are characteristic of a disease or condition.

Theories
Attempts to organise information in order to explain why certain events occur. The goal of a theory is to integrate data or information, explain behaviour and predict behaviour.

Transitional object
An object, often a blanket or a soft toy, which a child carries around as a comforter and usually takes to bed with him or her. It may be used until it disintegrates. Sometimes called a 'comfort object'.

Values
The code of ethics (principles and beliefs) of a particular culture or of an individual that determines the way he or she lives her life.

Further reading

Axline V., *Dibs in Search of Self*, Ballantine Books, 1986

Ball M., *Consulting with Parents*, National Early Years Network, 1997

Beaver M. et al., *CACHE Child Care and Education Level 2 Candidate Handbook*, Nelson Thornes, 2008

Beaver M. et al., *CACHE Child Care and Education Level 3 Candidate Handbook*, Nelson Thornes, 2008

Bee H. and Boyd D., *The Developing Child*, 11th Edition, Pearson Education, 2006

Bishop S., *Develop Your Assertiveness (Creating Success)*, 2nd Edition, Krogan Page, 2006

Bonel P. et al., *Good Practice in Playwork*, 3rd Edition, Nelson Thornes, 2009

Bowlby J. and Fry M., *Child Care and the Growth of Love*, New Edition, Penguin, 1990

Brain C. and Mukherji P., *Understanding Child Psychology*, Nelson Thornes, 2005

Briffa J., *Natural Health for Kids: How to Give Your Child the Very Best Start in Life*, Penguin, 2007

British Red Cross, *First Aid for Babies and Children Fast*, Dorling Kindersley, 2006

Brown B., *Unlearning Discrimination in the Early Years*, Trentham Books, 1998

Bruce T., *Developing Learning in Early Childhood*, Paul Chapman, 2004
Learning Through Play, Hodder Arnold, 2001

Bruce T. and Meggitt C., *Child Care and Education*, 4th Edition, Hodder Arnold, 2006

Butler D., *Babies Need Books: Sharing the Joy of Books with Children from Birth to Six*, Revised Edition, Butterworth-Heinemann, 1998

CAPT, *Safety in Day Care and Play Settings*, CAPT, 2004

Cobbold S., *The Foundation Stage at Home*, Nelson Thornes, 2006

Coleman, A., *Creative Play for Ages 0–8*, Scholastic, 2003

Corbett P. and Emmerson S., *Dancing and Singing Games*, Kingfisher Books, 1992

Cottrell S., *The Study Skills Handbook*, 3rd Edition, Palgrave Macmillan, 2008

Dare A. et al., *A Practical Guide to Child Nutrition*, 3rd Edition, Nelson Thornes, 2009
A Practical Guide to Working with Babies, 4th Edition, Nelson Thornes, 2009
Good Practice in Safeguarding Children, 3rd Edition, Nelson Thornes, 2009
Good Practice in Caring for Children with Special Needs, 3rd Edition, Nelson Thornes, 2009

David P., *Young Children Learning*, Paul Chapman, 1999

Davy A., *Playwork – Play and Care of Children 5–15*, Thompson Learning, 2000

Deakin M., *Children on the Hill*, Quartet Books, 1973

Department of Health, *Assessing Children in Need and their Families*, HMSO, 2000
  Working Together to Safeguard Children, 2nd Edition, HMSO, 2006

Drummon M., *Assessing Children's Learning*, David Fulton, 2003

Elliott M., *Keeping Safe: A Practical Guide to Talking to Children*, Coronet, 1994

EYTARN, *Partnership with Parents: An Anti-Discriminatory Approach*, EYTARN, 1997

Geraghty P. and O'Hagan M., *Caring for Children* (3rd Edition), Baillière Tindall, 1997

Gilbert P., *An A–Z of Childhood Health Problems*, Nelson

Goldschmied E. and Jackson S., *People Under Three: Young Children in Day Care*, 2nd Edition, Routledge, 2003.

Green S., *Research Methods in Health, Social and Early Years Care*, Nelson Thornes, 2000

Griffin S., *Keeping and Writing Records*, National Early Years Network, 1994

Hall D. et al., *The Child Surveillance Handbook*, 3rd Edition, Radcliffe, 2009

Hobart C., Frankel J., and Walker M. (Series Editor), *A Practical Guide to Working with Parents*, 2nd Edition, Nelson Thornes, 2009
  A Practical Guide to Child Observation and Assessment, 4th Edition, Nelson Thornes, 2009
  Good Practice in Safeguarding Children, 3rd Edition, Nelson Thornes, 2009
  A Practical Guide to Activities for Young Children, 4th Edition, Nelson Thornes, 2009
  A-Z of Childcare, Nelson Thornes, 1998

Holtzman D.S., *The Safe Baby, Expanded and Revised*, Sentient Publications, 2009

Hyder T. et al., *On Equal Terms*, National Early Years Network/Save the Children, 1997

Hylton C., *Black Families Talking*, Exploring Parenthood, 1997

Jackson V., *Racism and Child Protection*, Cassell, 1996

Keene A., *Child Health: Care of the Child in Health and Illness*, Nelson Thornes, 1999

Kurtz Z. and Bahl V. (eds), *The Health and Health Care of Children and Young People from Minority Ethnic Groups in Britain*, NCB and DoH, 1997

Leach P., *Babyhood: Infant Development from Birth*, New Edition, Penguin, 1991
  Your Baby and Child, Dorling Kindersley, 2003

Lindon J., *Understanding Child Development Linking Theory and Practice*, Hodder & Stoughton, 2005
  Understanding Children's Play, Nelson Thornes, 2001

Lindon J., and L., *Caring for Young Children*, Macmillan Caring Series, Macmillan, 1994

Malik H. and Walker M. (Series Editor), *A Practical Guide to Equal Opportunities*, 3rd Edition, Nelson Thornes, 2009

Mathieson K., *Social Skills in the Early Years*, Paul Chapman, 2004

Millam R., *Anti-discriminatory Practice: Guide for Workers in Childcare and Education*, 2nd Edition, Continuum, 2002

Mortimer H., *Speech and Language Difficulties*, Scholastic, 2007
  Special Needs Handbook, New Edition, Scholastic, 2004

Mosley J. and Thorp G., *All Year Round: Exciting Ideas for Peaceful Playtimes*, LDA, 2002

Mukherji P., *Understanding Children's Challenging Behaviour*, Nelson Thornes, 2001

Mukherji P., and O'Dea T., *Understanding Children's Language and Literacy*, Nelson Thornes, 2000

NCMA, *Children's Learning: A Framework for Delivering Desirable Learning Outcomes*, NCMA, 1996
  The Member's Handbook, NCMA (available to members only)

Guide to Children's Safety, NCMA, 2005

Inclusive Childminding – Working with Disabled Children (CD-ROM for tutors)

NCMA's Quality Standards: A Workbook for Registered Childminders, NCMA, 2001

Children Learn Something New Every Day… What About You? (DHCL), NCMA, 2008

NCMA with the NSPCC, Safeguarding Children: A Guide for Childminders and Nannies (CP01), NCMA, 2008

Neaum S. and Tallack J., Good Practice in Implementing the Pre-school Curriculum (2nd Edition), Nelson Thornes, 2000

O'Hagan M. and Curtis A., Care and Education in Early Childhood, Routledge, 2008

Phinn G., Young Readers and Their Books, David Fulton, 2000

QCA, Curriculum Guidance for the Foundation Stage, QCA and DfES, 2000

QEd Publications, Trackers 0–5: Tracking Children's Progress Through the Early Years Foundation Stage, 2007

Raatma L., Safety at Home, Bridgestone Books, 1999

Rodd J., Understanding Young Children's Behaviour, Allen and Unwin, 1996

Sheridan M. et al., Play in Early Childhood, Routledge, 1999

Sheridan M., From Birth to Five Years (revised and updated by Frost M. and Sharma A.), Routledge, 1997

Silberg J., Games to Play with Babies, Brilliant Publications, 2004

Games to Play with Toddlers, Brilliant Publications, 2005

Games to Play with Two-year-olds, Brilliant Publications, 1999

Stoppard M., Complete Baby and Childcare: Everything You Need to Know for the First Five Years, Dorling Kindersley, 2008

Uppal H., Play Activities for the Early Years, Brilliant Publications, 2004

Valman B., ABC of One to Seven, 4th Edition, Wiley Blackwell, 1999

ABC of the First Year, 6th Edition, Wiley Blackwell, 2009

Walker M., A Practical Guide to Activities for Older Children, 2nd Edition, Nelson Thornes, 2009

Walsh M., Research Made Real, Nelson Thornes, 2001

Whalley M. and the Pen Green Centre Team, Involving Parents in Their Children's Learning, 2nd Edition, Paul Chapman, 2007

Working With Parents, Hodder and Stoughton, 1997

Ward S., Baby Talk, New Edition, Arrow Books, 2004

The 'Which?' Guide to Starting Your Own Business: How to Make a Success of Going it Alone, Which? Books 'Which?' Consumer Guides, 2003

Whiting M. and Lobstein T., The Nursery Food Book, 2nd Edition, Hodder Arnold, 1998

Wilkes A., Activities for All Year Round, Usborne Publishing, 2003

Winnicott D., The Child, the Family and the Outside World, New Edition, Penguin, 2000

Wolf C., On the Safe Side, Partners Publishing Group, 1999

Wolfe L., Safe and Sound: Complete Guide to First Aid and Emergency Treatment for Children and Young Adults, 2nd Edition, Health Education Authority, 1995

Wragg T., Key Stage 1 of the National Curriculum, Longman, 1996

Zealey C., 'The Importance of Names', in Equal Opportunities, the Co-ordinate Collection, National Early Years Network, November 1995

Index

Forms are in **bold**